WHAT OTHERS ARE SAYING ABOUT THIS BOOK...

"If you're a man, or a woman who cares about men, you need this book. You really do! We must have more good men in the world, and Stephen Johnson helps all of us to become the men we want and need to be for ourselves, our families, and our communities. At this critical time in human history, we require the power of spiritual warriors more than ever. If you buy one book this year, make it *The Sacred Path*. It may be the best decision of your life."

— JED DIAMOND, PH.D., author of *MenAlive: Stop Killer Stress and The Irritable Male Syndrome: Understanding and Managing the 4 Key Causes of Depression and Aggression*

"At long last, Dr. Stephen Johnson's *The Way of the Spiritual Warrior* provides us with a much needed spiritual-psychological map helping us navigate the rich territory of the self, assisting men to man up, stand up, and be guided with a fierce, compassionate, and mindful compass. This book is so needed for these difficult and trying times. It provides a light along the Sacred Path!"

— RONALD A. ALEXANDER. Ph.D., Executive Director of Open Mind Training Institute, Santa Monica. Author of *Wise Mind, Open Mind: Finding Purpose and Meaning in Times of Crisis, Loss, and Change*

"This is a wonderful book for women too, certainly for me it is, to understand men. I like it very much—kind, loving, understanding, organized well, really informative—not enough books like this for and about men."

— DOTTI ALBERTINE, Albertine Book Design

"Every decade a re-defining book emerges that energizes our thinking about a vital subject. Stephen Johnson eloquently, compassionately, and intimately reveals the essentials of how to embody wholeness, vulnerability, and spiritual awareness as a modern man. This should be required reading for every man, whatever his age."

— DAVID SURRENDA Ph.D., CEO, Kripalu Center for Yoga & Health, Author of *Retooling on the Run*

"Dr. Johnson not only outlines what the reader must go out and *do* to become a soulful man, he actually takes the reader there while reading his book. As the reader travels through the pages of *The Way of the Spiritual Warrior,* his brain clicks and heart swells because the importance of community and mentorship is experienced in real time. When finishing the book, one is not at the trailhead of becoming a mature man—he is already down the path to self."

— CANDACE DE PUY, Ph.D., Co-Author of *The Healing Choice*

"I love this book! You'll wish you had a dad like Stephen Johnson. In *The Way of the Spiritual Warrior*, like a wise elder at a ceremonial fire, he shares four decades of experience in helping men find the core of their manhood. Healing and uplifting, he takes us into the fire in our souls that burns rich with camaraderie, brotherhood, the father-son relationship, and all things male and brings us to see that the good life—no, the great life—lies in the direction of bettering that powerful man within us and the world around us.

We live in a world where many men are confused about what it means to be a man. Stephen Johnson isn't. He fully grasps the role of men in the world and in the lives of their families and children and lays out a logical path of improvement for all to follow. In this warm and immensely readable book, he opens his lifetime of wisdom, like a tribal father, pointing out commonsense principles and time-tested roads to betterment that will give any man a sound foundation for life that will fulfill his masculine destiny and make him proud. A must-read for all men and male youth."

— DAN STRADFORD, Author of *The Men's Code of Honor: 66 Principles That Make a Man*

"My husband has been involved with the Sacred Path Retreats for over twenty-two years, both as a participant and later as the associate director. It hasn't always been easy, but his time spent with this wonderful community of men, and the power of men's work under the guidance of Dr. Stephen Johnson, has been instrumental in helping him become the incredible man he is today. He is a loving husband and father, a forgiving and compassionate son to his elderly mother with Alzheimer's, a man with strong and deep male friendships, and a wise and respected elder within the Sacred Path Community. We are both very grateful."

— JAMIE and STEVE BRANKER

"Dr. Johnson's *The Sacred Path* is a book that I would strongly recommend for men of all ages. It provides an unbiased portrait of men to the core, a grounded view for readers to rely on as they go through their own struggles. In his mission to support men in their quest for fulfillment, Dr. Johnson has openly and fearlessly shared his own personal journey, going way beyond where most authors dare to go. I can also see women reading *The Sacred Path* and gaining a greater understanding of *their* men. I was especially impressed with Dr. Johnson's willingness to tackle the issue of dangerous relationships from the standpoint of both sexes. This fills a gap that no one else has had the courage to address."

— BRUCE DERMAN, Ph.D., Author of *We'd Have a Great Relationship if it Weren't for You*

"Dr. Johnson's personal journey and his clinical work with men in a changing world laid the groundwork for a very important book. We seem to have fewer healthy role models and guides to find our way through the adversity and joys of life. *The Sacred Path* appears to be a guide to the history of a changing world and provides information to men and their wives on how to normalize and negotiate the journey. I'm looking forward to using Dr. Johnson's book as a valuable resource for my male patients, as well as their partners. This book is the only one that I know of that is so focused on helping men through the developmental stages of relationships and aging. It can make a difference."

— JO CHRISTNER, Psy.D., Licensed Clinical Psychologist in private practice, Los Angeles, CA.

THE SACRED PATH

OTHER PUBLICATIONS by STEPHEN J. JOHNSON, PH.D.

The following articles are either written by Dr. Johnson (indicated with an asterisk) or contain quotes by him. They may be accessed at: www.DrStephenJohnson.com

A Circle of Men*
Anatomy of a Control Freak
Bash: In a P.C. World, Why are Men the Butt of Everybody's Jokes?
Bridges to Brotherhood: Taking Action with the Homeless *
Dealing with Ordeals: What's the Gift? *
Farewell to a Young Spiritual Warrior *
Four Words that Seduce any Man – Anytime
From Mind-filled-ness to Mindfulness *
Going Through the Change: Is There Such a Thing as Male Menopause?
Healing the Masculine Wound *
Helping Boys Become Men
How Do You Deal with a Difficult Boss? *
How Do You Deal with a Difficult Roommate? *
In the Trenches *
It's a Mad, Mad, Mad Men's World
Men in the Counseling Room*
Mindful Men *
Modern Rites of Passage: Reclaiming the Soul *
Natural Allies: In Search of a Mentor *
Rekindling a Loving Relationship *
She Says You Don't Communicate *
The Absent Father: Disconnected Dads, Confused Kids *
The Conscious Male
The Isolation Principle
The Quest for the Masculine Soul *
The Relationship Journey: A Map for a Bumpy Road *
What, Me Worry?
What Happened to the Men's Movement?*
What Your Marriage Needs to Survive *
What's the Best Way to Deal With a Bully? *
When Depression Turns to Anger *
Who Will Initiate Our Boys? *
Why Men Fall for Dangerous Relationships *

THE SACRED PATH

The WAY of the SPIRITUAL WARRIOR

Journey to Mindful Manhood

Stephen J. Johnson, Ph.D.

Sacred Path Press
Woodland Hills, CA

First Printing 2013

For information contact:
Sacred Path Press
21243 Ventura Blvd., Suite 214
Woodland Hills, CA 91364
www.SacredPathPress.com

Publisher's Cataloging-in-Publication
(Provided by Quality Books, Inc.)

Johnson, Stephen J.
The sacred path : the way of the spiritual warrior / Stephen J. Johnson.
p. cm.
LCCN 2012915884
ISBN 978-0-9849820-0-4 (pbk.)
ISBN 978-0-9849820-1-1 (ebook)

1. Men--United States. 2. Men--Psychology. 3. Men--Religious life. I. Title.

HQ1090.3.J64 2013 305.31'0973
QBI12-600191

Printed in United States of America

Cover image: ThinkstockPhotos/Hemera
Book Design: Dotti Albertine

Dedicated to the memory of my parents
Margie and Jerry Johnson

to my family
Fran, Derek, Ian, and Dana

and to my longtime brothers
Lance, Paul, Pat, Marty, Arnie, and Steve

CONTENTS

ACKNOWLEDGMENTS

I am indebted to some very creative and dedicated individuals who have assisted me with the birth of this book. It's effectively been at least a ten-year project. Sylvia Cary, my writing coach and editor, has been an inspiration and invaluable ally in the process of my sticking with the challenge of bringing the book to print. I am grateful for Dotti Albertine's design expertise and to Rich Manners, Pamela Guerrieri, and Kayleigh Gray for their proofreading skills.

My thanks go to Andrea Cagan, T. Jesse Goff, David Rudnitsky, and others not mentioned herewith but who assisted me in different ways with the process of eventually getting a book published. I am grateful to Sara Jane Freymann and David Groff, my New York agent and editor for their guidance and encouragement during the three years that I was endeavoring to publish the book through the traditional channels. I submitted a proposal two times and was turned down both times. I heard virtually the same thing from every publishing house: "Men don't read, and they particularly don't read self-help books about men."

I finally decided to just write the book and publish it myself. I created Sacred Path Press and became my own Indie publishing house. My belief that men *do* read or at least will listen to a book on CD and will also invest in a self-help book about mindful manhood has been the springboard for the evolution of this project along the way.

There are those who stepped onto the Sacred Path in the early phase of my work with men. Sam Sloneker was the first Spiritual Warrior to offer to assist me, and Paolo Mattioli, an accomplished percussionist, stepped forward to carry the beat; then down the road passed the drumsticks to Christo Pellani and Grant Mays. There were men like Jim Takacs and David Green who offered to cook the main meal, build the fire, or simply to make something happen or clean something up.

Robert Herstek, Dr. Alvin Ross, Founder and President of Ryokan College, and Mitchell Roth became the Board of Directors. Mitchell created the corporate structure of the 501c3 non-profit designation for the birth of The Men's Center Los Angeles. Robert's design creativity gave us the logo and the branding that provided needed recognition. In more recent years, Philip Dichter joined the Board of Directors, providing legal council, and Richard Bizzaro and Phil Gross offered business-related consultation.

Wonderful men like "BJ" Jakala, Steve Branker, Zoran Windrich, Dan Franklin, and Dan Stanton attended retreats and then broadened their participation through their involvement in taking on leadership positions within the Sacred Path Community. "BJ" was Associate Director of MCLA from 1992-1997 and then Steve and Dan became Associate Directors. They have been by my side for over twenty years. Steve has particular passion for the Call to Adventure program and has helped to keep the flame alive when it could have been extinguished or had simply gotten dim. His support over the years has been invaluable.

Timothy "Whispering Eagle" Aguilar became our resident shaman and along with Ray Bunch was up front with me taking the helm with the facilitation of each retreat. The three of us were ten years apart in age. Ray brought the grandfather energy, I carried the father energy, and Timothy conveyed the energy of the brother. Timothy, Conrad Burke, and Walter Atkinson have passed on but left a legacy that is indelibly etched into the evolutionary story of our 25-year history. Walter's son, Charlie, has taken the helm of Millennium Oaks Institute, handling the larger donations to our scholarship programs.

Zoran stepped forward to construct the container that provides the Sacred ambiance for our retreat community meetings and then passed the screw gun to David Green, who later passed it to Scott Edwards, who has been erecting the container ever since. Ed Munter became our minstrel followed by Tommy Holmes. David "Strongbear" Myers and Matthew Burke have been our poet/storytellers. Riccardo Morrison was my first dancer and movement expert who smoothed the way for Fred Sugerman to make it easy for men to move their bodies. Rich Manners and Grant Mays keep the communication vital so that we're all connected.

Master Albert Marrewa brought his Martial Arts teachings to the men. Tom Couper has been extraordinarily generous with his time and multifaceted support; he recently answered the call to watch over our Sacred Inipi Sweat Lodge materials. Over the years many Lakota Sioux Sun Dancers such as Michel Citrin, who put up our first lodge in the mid-1980s, Sam LaRoca, Walter Domingues, and Zack Terry, have poured water for our ceremonies. More recently Andrew Soliz and Thomas Alvarez facilitate our lodges and offer their medicine ways to our community.

I am very appreciative of the guidance from two Lakota elders, Soldier Bear and Standing Cloud, who have come from the Pine Ridge Reservation in South Dakota to bring the wisdom of our ancestors to us on retreat.

Over the years the Wisdom Council formed and expanded to approximately twenty-five men. The WC staff members meet once a month to support each other and to prepare for our bi-annual retreats. It has grown to include men who are still serving and those that are Emeritus. Among those not previously mentioned we have Alf Ackerman, Steve Aguilar, Jay Berger, Les Brown, Rob Bruce, Tim Cook, Bruce Dichter, Hector Escarcega, Bruce Figoten, Bob Fimiani, Phillip Jennings, John Mafrici, Clayton Norcross, Nick Rath, Steve Zelenka, and more recently, Jeffrey Young, Aubry Edwards, and Sterling Meredith.

Of course, there are many men who have graced the portals of our Sacred Path Community over the years. I have spoken of some of them in the following chapters. If I didn't single someone out it's not because the gift that was given or the mark that was made is less significant. I hold the image and memory of each of the men in my mind's eye, not only those in leadership staff positions, but also those who have attended just one retreat or those that have attended several.

I know that all of the men who participated carried away something from their experience on "the hill" that will forever guide them on their journey through life. I know that our hearts will always be connected. As long as we continue to traverse the Sacred Path, no matter how many miles separate us, we are never farther than a heartbeat away. To all the Spiritual Warriors in the world today, I celebrate you and your call to action.

FOREWORD

My first introduction to Stephen Johnson was at a party, a series of parties actually: the first Hollywood parties I ever attended, in a swanky section of Griffith Park called Fern Dell in Los Angeles, California, during the summer of 1976. I had just completed principal photography on ROOTS, the ABC Mini-series crafted from Alex Haley's best-selling Pulitzer-prize winning novel. The "swankienda" belonged to David Greene, the director of the first three hours of ROOTS, and his lovely wife Vanessa, who were committed to weekly salon gatherings at their home every Monday night that summer that included writers, musicians, and artists of every variety in pursuit of fine food, drink, and fellowship.

It was most probably over a game of eight-ball on the third floor pool table where we were first introduced by the actor Thalmus Rasulala, Stephen's best friend at the time, who played Omoro Kinte, the father of my character, Kunta, in my professional debut. I was a nineteen-year-old Bachelor of Fine Arts Major in Drama at the University of Southern California, and Stephen, age twenty-nine, had attained his three advanced degrees from USC and was an instructor in the graduate school department of Counseling Psychology. We had an immediate connection surrounding our zeal for everything SC. My life was about to be changed in the most unexpected and fundamental of ways, by a series of miraculous events.

As I look back on that transitional summer, two truths jump immediately into focus; my journey toward wholeness was indeed about to become a lot more complicated, and over pool and cocktails, I was meant to meet the man who would ultimately become my friend, brother, mentor, guide, family therapist, and all-around person of consequence in my life.

The points of intersection and interest that frame my relationship with Dr. J. are numerous and have most assuredly been explored over time. They include, but are in no way limited to, a passion for service, spirituality, and self-fulfillment in life, as well as a rabid interest in the vagaries of the football program at USC. As a therapist, he has seen me through existential crisis after existential crisis. As a friend and brother, he has been there for me through triumph and tragedy, career highs and lows, my marriage, and the birth of my two children.

He has introduced me to many of the modalities I continue to use in my daily life, in my never-ending attempt to achieve balance, the currency of the middle path: psychotherapy, re-birthing, Rolfing, and The Warrior's Way. Over the years, we have spent numerous hours in Sweat Lodge Ceremony, meditation, and once even collaborated on a ritual of manhood training for our adolescent boys, along with an African shaman, Malidoma Patrice Somé.

Although neither of us was reared in the Jewish faith or culture, when I think of Stephen, the appellate "Rabbi" comes immediately to mind. The essence of the word means "teacher," and he has certainly been that to me. However at the same time, he has stepped willingly and gracefully into a role in my life that is of much more significance; he is all the proof I need that God does indeed exist in this world, and His work is being carried out by good men like Dr. J.

Thank you, Stephen,

LeVar Burton

INTRODUCTION

Bring Good Men Together and Bring Out the Best in Them

You cannot stay on the summit forever.
You have to come down again…
One climbs and one sees; one descends and
One sees no longer, but one has seen,
There is an art of conducting oneself…
By the memory of what one saw higher up.
When one no longer sees, one can at least still know.
—RENE DAUMAL

I have practiced as a licensed psychotherapist since 1972. In the early days, most of my patients were women. There was a women's movement underway and women were certainly on the move. They were entering therapy in droves while men were heading for the jungles of Vietnam. Most of the ones who stayed behind, though supportive of the women's movement, were uninterested in exploring their own psyches.

The 1970s were all about freedom of expression and experimentation with drugs and love. It also fostered a generation gap between the parents and their children that would later be coined by broadcast journalist Tom Brokaw as "The Greatest Generation," described in his 1998 book by the same name.

A majority of youth from that period would come to distrust their parents, politicians, and those that supported the "war machine" which they felt was guilty of sending 56,000 boys to premature deaths in a far away country, fighting an immoral war that could not be won. It was a painful time marked by confusion and rampant mutual distrust and contempt that fathers and sons felt for each other.

This estrangement essentially set in motion the conditions that would be ripe for the birth of a men's movement in the mid-1980s to early 1990s as baby boomers moved into mid-life. The promised men's movement, however, did not materialize because the media had picked up on it and created parodies of men going into the woods, baring their chests, playing drums and crying about their woes and "psychologizing everything." This only served to send the majority of men, who had stuck their necks out, back into their typical modes of operation and away from the avenues that had been put in place for them to gather for the purpose of self-exploration and development.

The inner conflict and turmoil that most men felt, I felt as well. The polarization that many men felt with their fathers, I also experienced. Though the men's movement had collapsed, there remained some movement within some men who continued to pursue the quest for expanded consciousness. Those of us, who cared about what would soon become known as "*menswork,*" continued to pursue the task in spite of the fact that the momentum had dramatically fallen off.

I'm sure that all this contributed to my desire to do something specifically for men and for myself as well. I had been working with so many women and had co-led Heartswork retreats for men and women for four years. It was time for me to take a break from working with women and focus on men—but *how*?

The answer came to me one day while I was in my car driving across a bridge. I heard a soft, gentle voice say these words, "*The Sacred Path.*" The words were clear and distinct, as though uttered by an invisible passenger riding in the backseat. I even glanced in my rearview mirror to catch a glimpse of who might be whispering to me. The words came again, "*The Sacred Path.*" They hung suspended in midair.

For days afterwards, that refrain echoed throughout my whole body. It was a personal and discrete message that only I could hear. It randomly interrupted my concentration and became my new mantra. Seemingly out of nowhere my thoughts were punctuated with the refrain, "*The Sacred Path*... *The Sacred Path.*" Had I finally lost my mind? Was I experiencing some kind of flashback from the 60s and 70s? Too much therapy, I concluded.

The words continued to speak to me from a place far away while at the same time it seemed to resonate from a place deep within. It was a familiar place that I had visited before in my meditation practices. I had learned that through meditation I could experience clarity and insight that also seemed to bring with it an intuitive sense of personal mission or destiny.

I thought to myself, "*OK, God, now that you've gotten my attention what do you want*?" The answer came immediately from the same comforting voice, "*The way of the Spiritual Warrior.*" I repeated the phrase to myself a couple of times and then put both parts together, "*The Sacred Path: The way of the Spiritual Warrior,*" and with that I experienced a sense of inner knowing and peace. I intuitively knew what that meant. And yet I found myself asking out loud, "What am I to do with this?" God then shot back, *"Bring good men together and bring out the best in them."*

And that's what I did.

In 1987, I created the first Sacred Path: The Way of the Spiritual Warrior workshop for men. It was held high on a mountain overlooking the Pacific Ocean in Topanga Canyon. The venue was an aluminum covered geodesic dome house owned by a friend who had been gifted the plans for the complex by his mentor, environmentalist and futurist Buckminster Fuller. Forty-five men gathered for a day of self-exploration around what it meant to be a man. I was struck by how many men shared the common phenomena of not feeling close to their fathers, and being confused about what women wanted from them and what they should expect of themselves as men.

I continued to hold workshops for men on an every-other-month basis. As the format grew so did the length of the events and so did the number of participants. They expanded from daylong workshops to overnight retreats and from overnight to two night events and then eventually to the four-day format that has been in place for years. We have been holding Sacred Path Men's Retreats now for twenty-five years and have hosted over one hundred in attendance per event.

In 1988, I founded The Men's Center of Los Angeles that provides counseling and educational programs for men and those who share their lives. The Millennium Oaks Institute, a non-profit public benefit corporation, was formed in 1999 to support our rites of passage programs designed to provide initiation of youth into adulthood. Our Call to Adventure retreat for fathers and sons, boys and mentors, is constructed to bring men and boys together to introduce initiation into conscious manhood through a program of confrontive challenges. It is designed to teach boys the skills they need in order to attain a balanced masculinity and grow up to become good men. Over the years, we have brought thousands of good men together and have helped bring out the best in them and have helped to make them into the "spiritual warriors" they were born to be.

It has been a remarkable journey.

During the three years that I was endeavoring to publish this book through the traditional New York publishing arena, the title and content of the book proposal was changed on three separate occasions to make it more commercial. When I ended my attempt to get the book published I took a break for a few months and then sat down one afternoon to meditate.

I asked the question, "Okay, God, what am I to do now?" The answer came, "*I told you twenty-five years ago, The Sacred Path: The Way of the Spiritual Warrior. Bring good men together and bring out the best in them.*" Clear as a bell the words rung in my head and I had my marching orders and the true title of the book.

The Sacred Path: The Way of the Spiritual Warrior is intended to address the issues that I feel are the most relevant to men and those who care about men. In the nearly forty years that I have been practicing as a therapist and teaching in a variety of venues, I have come to understand these issues both personally and professionally and see how they not only impact the men's lives as individuals but also how they impact their relationships with other men, their mates, and their children. Each chapter in the book addresses one or more of these issues, sheds light on their roots and importance, and deals with the resolutions and solutions to the many challenges that men face today.

My hope is that men will find *The Sacred Path: The Way of the Spiritual Warrior* of value and that the women who love them will also benefit. I trust that the book will stimulate mindful contemplation and the thoughtful pursuit of improved communication between men, their partners, and their children. I would further hope that women, who so often carry the wounds delivered by men, will find some healing themselves through an expanded understanding of men and their issues and will, as a result, feel compassion and forgiveness.

My ultimate desire is that this book contributes to the cause of creating more safety for men to experience the vulnerability necessary to foster greater intimacy within their relationships. I trust that as a result, relationships can be restored, revitalized, and stabilized so that families can remain intact and children can grow up enjoying the kind of loving family closeness that they deserve.

Part I

THE SPIRITUAL WARRIOR'S JOURNEY

Chapter 1

When Your Life Begins to Go Adrift

He's not the finest character that ever lived. But he's a human being, and a terrible thing is happening to him. So attention must be paid.

— Arthur Miller, *Death of a Salesman*

I'D LONG KNOWN FROM my practice as a psychotherapist that men were hurting. They'd been coming into my office and telling me so for years. Since first putting out my therapist's shingle in 1972, I've seen thousands of men in individually scheduled appointments, in couple's sessions, as well as in groups, workshops, seminars, classes—or I have communicated with them by phone, letter, or email. Their presenting complaints (the reasons they give for entering therapy) are always the same: dealing with their marriages, anxiety and depression, their career challenges, the consequences of their affairs, or they are fighting any one of a number of addictions.

Most men are not in the habit of inspecting their psyches, so until they hit one of these crises points, they don't dwell on their pain and don't seek therapy. They resist anything that threatens to expand consciousness or asks them to improve their communications with those they love. They prefer their lives of quiet desperation. If they do end up in treatment, it's usually at the urging of a friend or family member or because of an ultimatum delivered by a hurt, worried, or angry spouse.

It is in my office that I get to see the results of what happens when men stuff their emotions instead of dealing with them. Hidden depression drives several of the problems we think of as typically male—self-medicating behaviors manifesting in alcoholism, drug abuse, sexual addiction, gambling, domestic violence, workaholism, antisocial behaviors, conduct disorders, and a deep suffering from a lack of meaning and self-worth. When men are in mid-life, they are even more vulnerable to depression and acting-out behaviors, cheating on their wives or loved ones, giving short shrift to their sons and daughters, fighting aging, despising their jobs or losing them, or becoming angrily attached to their jobs as measures of success and failure. They have no idea how to relate to other men outside the workplace because they haven't done it since they were sixteen or maybe twenty-two.

Male Estrangement

When I first began my group work with men, no matter what their background, I was stunned to realize that they were all making the same confession. They indicated that they felt a measure of discomfort and lack of trust and safety in the presence of other men. They sought mostly the company of women to meet their needs for companionship and intimacy. Each man had stories to tell as to how his own ill-at-ease feelings around men were generated. They shared how they didn't feel good about their relationships with their fathers and how the sibling rivalry with their brothers left them feeling estranged, bitter, and lonely. They spoke about not feeling competent athletically when they were growing up and would share details from past experiences on the playground or in phys-ed when they weren't picked for the team or would let the team down through lack of adequate performance. They often mentioned that they didn't have real male friends that they could count on, men who would be there for them in non-competitive ways. The common bond within each group of men that I worked with was the pain they all felt about their relationships with other men.

Men have also told me that they have become exasperated with their superficial contacts with other men but don't know how to improve the situation. There has been a build-up of toxicity resulting from too much exposure to the locker room or sports-bar mentality. They've grown tired of burning off steam or acting out in order to relieve their stress. As a result, they've turned away from other men and have gone inward, becoming withdrawn and isolative, even pulling back from their wives and children and disconnecting from social interaction. Many try coping with their anxious and depressed moods by turning to alcohol, drugs, porn, or some other diversion. Men with these symptoms often experience themselves as lone wolves, mavericks or misfits. Others turn to infidelity and clandestine affairs, symptomatic of an unspoken internal longing, confusion, and turmoil.

The statistics for men compared to women is pretty alarming—four times more likely to commit suicide; five times more likely to do so after age sixty-five; ten times more likely after a divorce; twenty-four times more likely to end up in prison; 90% more likely to become homeless; 43% more likely to end up in psychiatric hospitals; two-thirds more likely to become alcoholics; 50% more likely to become regular users of illicit drugs; 75% more likely to become a homicide victim; plus men are more likely to die sooner than women of all ten of the most lethal diseases. On average, men die seven years earlier.

When men suddenly (at least to them it seems sudden) find themselves in some kind of domestic, career, moral, or addiction turbulence, most are clueless about how they got themselves in such a sorry situation or what to do about it.

Psychological and Physical Disrepair

Many of the men who enter my office for the first time who are *older* are in a state of acute disrepair. Some have let themselves go physically to the point of chronic illness and emotional disease. They avoid going to doctors for such routine but vital concerns as prostate exams, and they pay the price that can sometimes be an earlier death. Many suffer from undiagnosed depression that takes a profound physical toll. They've never learned a truly important lesson—that embracing your wholeness begins with embracing your wellness.

It is no secret that men can experience difficulty with issues around aging—just look at the number of Grecian formula oldsters piloting two-seater sports cars, with a woman in the passenger seat young enough to be their daughter or even granddaughter. Men avoid growing old like the plague. I see my patients exhibit such dysfunctional behaviors as pushing themselves athletically to the point of debilitating injury, an obsession with appearance, and outright denial of physical warning signs about their health. Much of this behavior stems from their anger and fear about their declining youthfulness and approaching mortality. Other men succumb to issues related to work and success. Aggravating the problem in many cases is the man's ingrained belief that he is valued not for his innate worth but for his earning capacity. If women hate to be treated as sex objects, then men despise being treated as success objects, as Mr. Net Worth.

The Father Gap and the Missing Maiden

Central to the enduring trauma of most men I treat is the injury they suffer as young boys because of their unfulfilled, truncated, and intimidating relationships with their fathers, known as the "Father Gap." I go into this crucial topic in detail in the next chapter.

Because of men's unfulfilled father craving, they bring needs to their marriages that cannot be fulfilled there. Men seek in women the intimate connection they never had with their dads. But spouses and girlfriends cannot fill that essentially paternal role and shouldn't have to. This misapplied urge for intimacy ultimately leads men, and the women who love them, into caustic conflict.

Marriage is the main arena in which our misplaced cravings are played out. As stated above, couples enter wedlock with unrealistic expectations that cannot be met. Men, being mammals with a genetic imperative to procreate, seek to marry nubile maidens. Like bees gathering nectar, they are attracted to a woman's sweetness. And women, even those who have gained power in the world, still seek, through the men they love, a place of refuge where they feel safe enough to open the flowers of their hearts. When they find such a place in a man, they tend to shower him with the adoring attention he desires.

Each assumes going forward that the other will attend to them as a first priority. But then the ideal meets the real, the honeymoon is over, and the relationship typically plummets into power struggle. Men discover they have ended up being married not to their girlfriends but to the mother of their children. Their maidens have become matrons. Some women can become as engaged in their careers as their men are and distracted by attending to their children, which can leave men feeling neglected and estranged, valued only for their earning capacity and the duties they fulfill.

Ironically, men begin to glimpse that they are becoming more like their fathers, something they swore they would never be. "I don't enjoy my life," said Chad, a forty-five-year-old shipping executive. "I'm working exhausting hours with little satisfaction and don't look forward to coming home at night. I don't feel appreciated by my wife, and I feel taken for granted by my children. I feel like I come last." Another said, "I'm pissed. I'm just a human ATM machine for my family. I feel like my only real value is in what I can provide through working all the time. I keep the money coming in to meet everyone else's needs, but what about mine? When do my needs count?"

In the most intimate spheres of their lives, men seek slightly different things than women do, but both sexes have congruent needs. Men want to be appreciated and admired by their partners; women want to be nurtured and desired. Essentially, women want to be cherished and men want to be honored.

The Fall

When a man's life begins to drift off course, it often takes a meltdown or a crisis to get his attention to the point where he'll do something about it. Often this is called The Fall or, as Robert Bly, the best-selling author of *Iron John* (1990) calls it, "The Drop." This was the case with one man I know who had been hired as CEO to build many businesses into multi-million dollar corporate structures. But on a plane returning from a post-9/11 business trip to Japan, he drank himself into a stupor and caused a scene, which led to his being detained and to his getting fired. That's when he realized his life had to change.

Men experiencing The Fall dislike themselves for falling short of the mark and for not living up to their own expectations, let alone the expectations of others. They feel tremendous guilt. They tell me that they think that they are good men down deep, but somewhere along the way, often in their midlife years, they stumble and fall and lose their way. They don't know what happened, or where they went wrong, or where they stepped off the path. They don't like where they now find themselves. They want to save their marriages, enjoy their children and careers, and turn their lives around.

In a television interview with the 2012 Presidential candidate and former Speaker of the House, Newt Gingrich, about his own fall after his affair (and consequent resignation) with a U.S. Senate staffer, the Speaker said: "There was a part of me that was truly hollow, and the harder I worked and the more I did, the hollower I got."

No one is immune from a fall into crisis. In my late thirties I came face-to-face with my own shortcomings when I walked into the wall of a mid-life crisis that rocked my world. I was too smart for my own good and overlooked further elements of my unresolved issues that were looming and would trip me into an exploration of the dark night of the soul. Fortunately, my crisis resulted in some realizations that helped my wife and me, over time, rekindle and strengthen our relationship. But I had most surely been a man adrift, and I had to rise to the challenge of putting my life in order to clearly demonstrate my enduring devotion and commitment to my marriage.

The Four Crisis Points in a Man's Life

Most men will fall into a crisis at one point or another in their lives. For some, it's when they are quite young. With a high divorce rate and so many men out of the family, boys are growing up without their fathers (the "father gap") or without any other men to guide them into manhood. The consequences of this, as we'll see in Chapter 2, are severe. For other men, their crises will visit them at other points in their lives, anywhere between the ages of fifteen and eighty, and frequently more than once.

In fact, I believe there are actually *four* age-related crisis points in a man's life, each of which brings him to a crossroads and forces him to make discerning choices in order to rise up to the challenges that are presented to him.

1. The Identity Crisis

For most men, the *first* crisis hits between the ages of fifteen and twenty-five when they are trying to define their identities and individuate from their parental bond. This period is often characterized by confusion and uncertainty over such issues as autonomy, independence, career, and relationships. This is when the suicide rate in males surges. Men, looking to become princes, more often feel like frogs, awkward and troubled by a lack of awareness of how to handle themselves in the world of school, work, and women. It is especially trying for those without a father or mentor to help make their initiatory rite of passage from boyhood to manhood smoother. Men, left to their own devices, especially during hard economic times, have to ask themselves some penetrating questions: Now that I'm supposed to be a man, what does it really mean? Who am I, and what am I supposed to be doing with my life? What work am I cut out for?

Marco, seventeen, was hit with his identity crisis soon after he'd moved back home with his hardass Italian father, Anthony, fifty-six, and Anthony's new wife. Marco isolated himself in his room, smoked pot, played his punk music at high volume, and copped an attitude that announced to everyone, *I'll show you, and you can't make me.*

One day Anthony tried to discipline his son by removing the sound system from his room. Father and son ended up in an altercation leading Marco to punch his father in the face. Anthony refrained from hitting him back but gave Marco an ultimatum, as the result of which the boy left. Anthony felt hurt and angry over the fact that Marco had hit him but took solace in the fact that he hadn't struck back like his own father would have done. This ultimately led father and son into therapy where they confronted their bond and the legacy that was passed on by Anthony's father. Marco made significant strides in dealing with his identity issues, and later, when Anthony sustained a life-threatening head injury, Marco really stepped up to be there for his father. A new identity was crafted, and a new bond was forged.

2. The Mid-Life Crisis

The second crisis usually surfaces around the age of forty

when a man is clobbered by a myriad of issues that test his manhood. Because of his core issue, the Father Gap, a man realizes that he can no longer find in his romantic partner and mother of his children the remedy for the lifelong father craving that has plagued him from the gate. He seeks his solution in all the wrong places. He dyes his hair, spiffs up his wardrobe, buys a flashy sports car, and runs off with a young girl, thereby creating an earthquake that turns his life upside down.

When he comes to and finds himself in the midst of extreme chaos, he has to sort it out and make sense of it before he can successfully move into the second half of life. New questions arise: Where am I going with my life, and who is going with me? Why have I made such a mess of things? How can I fix them?

Lenny, thirty-eight, divorced and the father of two preteen sons, was clean and sober for twelve years when he finally came to the realization that he was still a practicing sex addict. Like so many men, he used "hot sex" as a substitute for his longing for real love and real communication. Our permissive culture only added fuel to the fire. He boasted about his conquests, each one a new notch in his belt. He was self-will-run-riot.

What Lenny really needed was to experience that he was loved, but it had to begin with self-care and self-love. His most recent relationship was epic, having crossed paths with a dangerous woman who took him to his knees. His helplessness, hopelessness, and despair caused him to miss work. There were days when he couldn't get out of bed and thoughts of suicide were increasing. If his concerned employer hadn't intervened, putting him on leave and getting him into therapy, he might not have made it.

3. The Existential Crisis

Round three hits at some point around the age of sixty when a man notices that instead of counting birthdays he's counting how many years he thinks he has left. While a forty-year-old man with the energy to get himself into trouble usually has the energy to get himself out of it, men closer to sixty who get into trouble may not have the same reservoir of energy to extricate themselves from the mess they're in.

A man of sixty starts noticing that he's not as young as he used to be. He's aware that physical movements are often accompanied by grunts and groans and that younger females either don't bother to look, or they give him a cursory glance that signals that he's the father to the man that they're most interested in pursuing. One man commented, "When I was younger, I was fairly handsome, and women would give me the eye. Now that I'm older, they just tend to keep their eye on me."

This period is marked by contemplative self-reflection, concerns over issues of health, aging, sexual potency, relationships, and, career disappointments. Men now face an existential crisis that can cause a world of anguish. (We've witnessed more than one prominent CEO or politician carted off to prison in his early sixties.) The man may find himself asking, what have I done with my life? What meaning and value do I give to my existence? Have I accomplished my dreams, and if not, will I be able to do so in the time remaining?

There are men that I have worked with that have been very successful during the peak earning years of their careers. When they were younger and were generating mega yearly incomes, when the economy was so robust, they lived life high-on-the-hog and didn't put enough aside for the future.

Like the squirrel that played and ate what he collected each day during the summer months rather than putting nuts aside for the winter, when the rains and cold weather arrived, he was not prepared. Now in their sixties and seventies, up against all of the changes that were unexpected, they dread not having enough time, a viable strategy, or the energy to execute a game plan to hedge against further disaster.

4. The Completion Crisis

The fourth test to manhood is encountered between the ages of seventy-five and eighty-five, at which point a man has to evaluate the life that he has lived and try to make peace with his mortality. He is on the downside of the mountain and approaching the last of the plateaus before the final stage of descent. He must evaluate his capacity for living the rest of his life to the fullest. He must determine how he wishes to wrap things up. He must also come to terms with what is incomplete in his life and how to approach the challenges of completion. The Completion Crisis can be fairly tricky because of one's natural resistance to endings and loss of control. The man must ask himself, how much time do I have left? What will I do with the time remaining? How has my life turned out? What is the legacy I will leave? What is it that I still need to complete?

Jack, seventy-five, had been an actor all his life. With a career that spanned from Broadway, to leading man parts on day-time television soaps, to character parts in major features, he was ill-prepared for the plunge he'd take when he realized that acting parts for old men are in short supply. He had never really considered that he wouldn't be able to make a good living in a business where he'd created such an impressive body of work. Men in many different kinds of careers bump into the same kind of ageism long before they are ready to call it quits. Jack battled back from bouts of depression and anxiety to recreate and accept himself as an "older actor" who still had the talent to offer to the craft he loved so much. This revised attitude made looking for work and accepting rejections easier.

Men's Secret Longing

What I've learned from all these years of working with men of all ages, as well as grappling with my own case, is that no matter what the man's initial presenting complaint is when he first walks into a therapist's office or shows up at a workshop, there is almost always something *else* at the root of his pain. There's a longing within him for something that is often unrecognizable and remains elusively out of reach, yet it is something his yearning impels him to attain.

What, then, are these men really longing for?

They are longing to be honorable men, respected and admired, men of integrity, men with a purpose. Ultimately, deep in their souls, men simply yearn to be good men; they yearn to be Spiritual Warriors.

Becoming a Spiritual Warrior is what this book is about. It's about learning how to meet the challenge of authentic manhood, embrace chivalry, practice the right use of power and truth, bring out the best in yourself, allow yourself to truly connect with your partner and your children, fulfill your long-suppressed father-craving, engage with a community of caring men, and perform worthy work in the world.

Becoming a Spiritual Warrior in your marriage means communicating with your partner as well as being responsible for your own needs. It means having the guts to cherish your mate actively and yet being reliable and strong enough so that, amid all the demands of work and family, she still feels safe and secure in your love, enabling her to soften and be sweeter—just like the woman you fell in love with.

With children, being a Spiritual Warrior means breaking the chain of dysfunction and estrangement. At work, it means being of service through your vocation and ensuring that your life is your career. In the world, it means being bold enough to explore your bonds with other men, to find mentors for yourself and to become a mentor to others.

Throughout *The Sacred Path*, I provide evidence of how men surmount the crises of manhood by integrating the Spiritual Warrior principles into their lives. To illustrate, I use stories of real men, many in dire straits—impending divorce, the throes of addiction, infidelities gone awry, or insidious discontent—which show readers where these men have come from and what they have been able to achieve.

Part I of *The Sacred Path* lays out the problems, followed by Parts II and III that are solution-oriented and lay out the prescriptive elements to affect change, the tools to help you become Spiritual Warriors so that you can access your innate goodness and enhance your capacity for true love.

In the pages of *The Sacred Path: The Way of the Spiritual Warrior*, I call upon men to break the chain of dysfunction that has dragged them down for generations—father absences, addictions, bad behaviors, infidelities, raging, irresponsibility, crime, sex and intimacy problems, immaturity, and a general confusion about what it even means to be a grown-up. Men can learn here how to transform their lives to become those good men and Spiritual Warriors they've always wanted to be.

It all starts when men connect with a *community of other men* who are also striving for the same goals and seeking, in their own ways, to be better men. This book can help you turn a humiliating fall from grace to a fall into grace.

CHAPTER 2

The Father Gap: The Hidden Wound that Just Won't Heal

What wound do we have that hurts so much we have to dip it in water?...Not seeing your father when you are small, never being with him, having a remote father, an absent father, a workaholic father, is an injury.

—Robert Bly (*Iron John*, 1990)

WHY ARE SO MANY men anxious and depressed, or rageful, without even realizing it? It springs from a painful longing for the unfulfilled relationship with the father, a core wound in a man's psyche known as the Father Gap. Many males, of all ages, carry this secret wound that was inflicted upon them by a father who was heavy handed and went over the top, crushing the boy's spirit, or by a father who was missing in action and goes down and out of his son's life. Males often bear unspoken shame and grief from having missed out on a loving and caring relationship with their fathers.

There is, in fact, a true crisis of fathering in this country. In general, one-third of our nation's kids will go to bed tonight without their biological father in the next room. Forty percent of children in fatherless households haven't even seen their fathers in at least a year.

These men have chosen to disconnect and drift from their families, leaving as many as fifteen million confused kids behind. In later life, many of these dismissed kids act out sexually or attempt suicide, the leading cause of death in the fifteen to twenty-four-year-old age group.

Crime, unwed teenage pregnancy, and suicide are huge problems. Studies show that the most reliable predictor of these manifestations is not income or race; it is *family structure*. Unwed pregnant girls and criminally oriented boys tend to come from fatherless families. Seventy percent of imprisoned minors have spent at least part of their lives without fathers. Gangs feed on fatherless boys. Without fathers and mentors around to teach successful ways of coping, adolescent boys are prone to create their own destructive rites of passage arising out of the rage they feel over being forgotten and abandoned. Random and serious violence can also be correlated to fatherless families. Wounded boys commonly grow up to be wounding men, inflicting on others the very distress that went unhealed within them.

The Father Gap in Black and White

The absence of fathers also goes a long way in explaining the continuing gulf between black and white America. It has been almost impossible to equalize opportunities between the races when a black child is three times more likely to live without a father than is a white child.

Underserved black children are among the most vulnerable people in the U.S. Of all African American fourth-graders, fifty-eight percent are functionally illiterate. It is my understanding that officials study the demographics of fourth graders to determine how many prisons will be required in the years ahead to incarcerate criminal adult males. In some cities, eighty percent of black males drop out before finishing high school. Every day, 1,000 black children are arrested, and one in every eight African American males ages twenty-five to twenty-nine is incarcerated. The top cause of death for black males is homicide.

Marquise, age nineteen, an inner city kid who attended our Call to Adventure Rites of Passage Retreat and was a youth volunteer at Helen Keller Park, was gunned down in the street when he went to pick up his father, an active gang member, from a party. Marquise had graduated from high school and was attending college when this incident tragically ended his life. Prior to his death, Marquise and his mother had attended the awarding of the "Certificates of Completion" event at Helen Keller Park. Marquise wore a suit and was proud to accept his certificate that he framed and hung on the wall of his garage. His mother was one of only a handful of relatives in attendance that day to celebrate the boy's achievement. That is not unusual. The fathers for the most part are missing in action, and the moms are stressed with the responsibilities of being single parents endeavoring to meet all the demands of keeping the family on track.

The Illusion of Wholeness

Men who haven't had adequate fathering grow up feeling incomplete and ill equipped to be men. They attempt to fill the gap with a number of substitutes, such as food, alcohol, drugs, work, and, as discussed previously, sex. They stuff as much of each into that empty space as they can. Such placebos provide a momentary illusion of wholeness, but it's a false front, artificially propped up by an inflated and grandiose sense of self. But the hole simply can't be filled from the outside. The hole has to be filled up from within with coats of what I call "soul-spackle", and then it's only a matter of time before a man feels compelled to search for something *real* to save him from his despair.

Boys, unable to get the kind of attention they crave from their fathers, often turn to their mothers or girlfriends or, later on, wives for the attention and nurturance they need. But often these are women who have their own deficit of fathering and are seeking to make up for it in their relationships with these men. Homosexually oriented men tend to seek father food from other father gap men. But as much as they can try to provide for their partners, men need something else to address their primal loneliness, something that can *only* be addressed and healed by being in the company of other men. A needy woman herself can only be healed by being in the company of a man who has *transformed his father hole into wholeness.* When a man accepts the challenge of becoming a better man, he realizes that that is exactly what his woman needs from him as well.

The Hole, by my friend and colleague, Bruce Derman, Ph.D. (Amazon, 2010), is a fable that takes you on a journey as you experience a man's struggles with his own emptiness. Bruce states, "Many men lose themselves by getting seduced into trying to fill the emptiness they experience in their life. They fail to appreciate that the emptiness that they dread is part of their basic nature. Instead, they chase after porn, drugs, alcohol, sex, money, women, status, destructive relationships, and possessions in an attempt to fill this hole, not realizing that it can never be filled from the outside or by anything external. This quest leads men to pursue a path of defending and proving, and moves them far away from what it means to be a true masculine man who can stand up for all that he is."

This endless trip to nowhere is beautifully laid out in *The Hole* as the fable follows a couple on a journey who are trying to get rid of a bottomless hole they discover in their living room floor. Each attempt to get rid of it only results in the hole getting bigger. Sound familiar?

Carl: "Cigarette Smoke Like the Fingers of God"

A TV producer, Carl, forty-three, a practicing alcoholic, entered my practice with his wife, who had forced him to come to couples counseling. The wife wanted him out of the house. When I questioned

Carl about his relationship with his father, he broke down sobbing. This took him back to his core trauma and opened up the opportunity for him to do his own therapeutic work.

During that first therapy session, Carl told me about a pivotal time in his life and how it set the stage for what was to follow: "When I was twelve my dad was my hero. And so were my uncles. Uncle Frank made Corvettes. Uncle Nick flew B-52s. Uncle Jimmy and Uncle Johnny worked in the steel mill. On Saturdays, they all got together at a bar near my home, and one day they let me be there. Sunlight streamed in through the front window and door, illuminating the cloud of cigarette smoke like the fingers of God. They drank and shot pool, and my dad let me take a shot with his pool cue. He showed me how to hold it, make a bridge, and stroke the cue. My heroes watched and cheered as I sank my first shot, two-ball in the corner pocket. At that moment I fell in love with bars. Everybody drank to get drunk; otherwise what's the point? As I staggered home, I thought; 'I am now a man. A man, like my dad.'"

But after that, when Carl was fourteen, his dad stopped coming to his high school sports events. "He came home late from work and stayed out as often as possible. When he was present he was never short of opinions about me. 'Why in the hell would *you* try out for football? You're a quitter. If you don't get that SAT score, you can forget it! Cut your hair, you look like a bum.' When I was sixteen and driving myself, I would pass the bar and see my father's truck parked outside, seven days a week. I could not verbalize this at the time, but my hero had fallen. He had abandoned me. I crashed three cars before I was nineteen, two for sure because of alcohol, the last one in a complete blackout. When I came to, I was upside down on the passenger side of the car. When the firemen arrived, one looked at me like he saw a ghost and blessed himself with the sign of the cross. The car looked like a handful of shredded tinfoil and shattered glass. I had hit two poles, yet I crawled out uninjured."

"In high school I always felt I was from the wrong side of the tracks, and actually, I was. The tracks were at the end of my street. Even when I was accepted by the kids from the right side of the tracks, the man they accepted was the nutty drunk guy."

"In college my drinking was my way of fitting in, and it worked. I never lacked the booze or the people who would drink with me. I went to school full time and worked a part-time job. This accomplished life style made it okay for me to drink away whole weekends or ten days of spring break, and, soon thereafter, every day of the week, kind of like my dad."

"I never imagined there was another way of living. I had good friends. I functioned. I had girlfriends. After two dates I would be in a relationship that would last two years, five times in a row. They picked me. Never did I choose them. I did meet a girl who stayed three years, so I married her. Over the next five years we had three kids, all boys. The more the responsibilities piled up, the more I drank and the more I stayed away from home. My car was parked at the bar, just like my dad. I was good at making everything her fault. I was just fine. My drinking was normal. *She* was the one teetering on insanity."

I interrupted him. "Your father has hurt you, hasn't he?"

Carl again cried like a little boy because that was it, that's what he was, a hurt little boy. From there, with therapy, Carl took over his own case. He found sobriety and self-respect. He learned that what he *thought* were acts of manliness were actually the many masks of false masculinity. He learned what it really means to be man.

Carl's story is not uncommon. I've heard it many times before. The details are different, but the theme is always the same. Men carry a tremendous amount of unexpressed grief, loneliness, shame, and resentment based in the Father Gap, and expressing this grief is the key to unlocking their suppressed emotions and resolving their anger-laden grievances. Until then, their pain smolders inside just waiting to ignite into a firestorm of rage. Substitutes such as addictive behaviors are just backfires set up to keep the firestorm from engulfing everything in its path. They ease the pain for a while, but then it all bursts forth into a crisis. Hopefully, the crisis is what finally gets the man's attention and gets him to take action.

Since crisis and opportunity coexist, when a man takes The Fall, he often lands in the seat of his unconscious genius or unrealized destiny—right into the mash pit of his core wound, his Father Gap. Unraveling the morass of symptoms and deciphering the clues hidden deep within are what allow one's brilliance to shine forth through the darkness of depression and despair and see the light at the end of the tunnel at last. For men to reconnect with themselves, with their romantic partners, with their children, friends, jobs, and purpose in life, they must heal the Father Gap. Only then can they return to being the good men they were meant to be.

When Men Don't Talk and What They're Not Telling You

Like so many men of my generation—baby boomers—the movie *Saving Private Ryan* was an eye-opener. Those brave men who landed on the beaches of France during World War II and survived (men so beautifully honored in Tom Brokaw's book, *The Greatest Generation*) didn't talk much about it when they returned home. Most, not being in the habit of dwelling on what they thought or felt, simply got on with their lives, married, had children, worked hard, attempted to live the American Dream—and basically kept their mouths shut.

As the son of one of these Greatest Generation men, I had little understanding of what my father had been through in the war until I went to see *Saving Private Ryan* with my own son, Derek, who at the time was eighteen. I remember sitting there in the movie theatre with tears streaming down my face.

When Derek noticed my reaction, he put his arm around me to

comfort me. Had I been watching this movie with my own father, I know it would have been painfully difficult for us both because we each would have held back, not wanting to cross some invisible threshold separating us. I wouldn't have wanted to invade my father's private world of feelings, and my father wouldn't have wanted to publicly display his emotions, especially tears: Crying was seen as weakness. But for Derek, reaching out to comfort me was second nature; and I was comfortable accepting his display of kindness.

Men like my father returned from overseas after World War II and didn't talk about what happened or what they saw, they just got on with their lives. These men suffered in silence and bottled up their emotions so that they could carry on with living the good life. They manned up as best they could yet found it difficult to communicate effectively about their innermost thoughts and feelings. It was easier to withdraw into the world of work and leave the childrearing to their wives. It gave the impression that they were missing in action or absentee fathers, and their sons tended to feel that their fathers were off limits concerning their own issues of manhood.

This illustrates the legacy that has been passed down through countless generations of men, that real men are the strong silent types and are independent mavericks that don't need anything or anyone because they are capable of going it alone and taking it like a man. I once heard someone quip that, "If men could speak this is what they might say." Well, it's time for men to turn up the volume so that they and others can hear what has been muted in the silence of their desperation to be known. What men mean is often not what they say. There *is,* however, a way to transcribe the hidden language of men, and that's through a better understanding of what they're really saying when they do say something.

In the movie *The Prince of Tides* there's a scene that sticks out in my memory. The adult son, played by the actor Nick Nolte, is standing on a pier with his aging, alcoholic father who is baiting a fishhook. "You know, I love you," Nolte says to his father. Without looking up, the father replies in a deliberate style after a brief pause, "The Padres beat the Dodgers last night. Did you know that?" He then furtively raises his eyes from the task of preparing the hook to glance at Nolte in a cryptic fashion. Women hearing that line might be inclined to say, "He's unable to communicate with his son." Men, on the other hand, see through the disguise. They know the father is communicating, "I love you, too."

This kind of communication typically serves to frustrate women. What men intrinsically seem to know is that when they are communicating they are also doing the best they can to express feelings. They just do it differently than women. In my psychotherapy practice with couples, I find myself constantly called on to help men and women comprehend and accept their different communication styles. Communication between men and women is a continual balancing act, juggling the conflicting needs for intimacy and independence. The language of intimacy expresses, *We are in this together, struggling for the same thing—closeness.*

The Masks of False Masculinity

Many men can look good on the outside but feel bad on the inside. Compartmentalization is a defense mechanism often used by men who are afraid to have the full story be known by all. The consequence of this defense is that it can leave the man safe from judgment but not really known by anyone at all—a lonely position for most people.

When men are in mid-life they are even more vulnerable to depression and acting-out behaviors. Research indicates that men go through psychological and physiological changes on a par with the menopause that women experience. The term "*manopause*" seems to capture this phase in a man's aging process. My friend and colleague, Dr. Jed Diamond, has written extensively about it in his trilogy of books called, *Male Menopause, The Irritable Male Syndrome and Mr. Mean.*

For some men, especially for those fortunate enough to have come of age during this time in history when communicating authentically and emotionally has been the thing to do, things have changed for the better. Many men have made great strides. They've tackled the communication gap they felt with their fathers, have endeavored to have closer relationships with their wives, sons, and daughters, are more comfortable about childcare, and more appreciative of women as power-holders in the workplace. But there's more to do.

There are still too many men that are walking around suffering from Father Gap wounds, and no one knows it, including themselves. They don masks of false masculinity to hide their pain. They tend to fall into one of these five categories:

1. The Sturdy Oak Man

Men who obey *The Sturdy Oak* dictate tend to follow the injunction that they should never show weakness and should endure difficulties without relying on others for help. They have difficulty in admitting the existence of a problem and unconsciously feel that they must conceal weakness, even from themselves. Men who fit into this category need to feel self-sufficient and can't tolerate feeling dependent on others. They have a hard time identifying and verbalizing vulnerable and caring emotions, known as *alexithymia.* Essentially, Sturdy Oak men have major challenges with emotional intimacy and have a tendency to sexualize close encounters with females and experience homophobic reactions in close encounters with males.

Sturdy Oak men don't seek out treatment. When we

think of men like John Wayne, the image we are most likely to conjure up is the Sturdy Oak kind of guy.

2. The Hyper-Masculine Man

He has no one to watch his back. He tends to push other men away with an overly aggressive, self-centered attitude. He may in fact prefer the company of women and shirk relationships with men altogether. He wears an impenetrable suit of armor from head to toe to fend off others because he doesn't feel safe enough to be vulnerable.

Hyper-masculine men tend to be overly concerned about their image, especially their body image and how they present themselves to others. They spend a lot of time in gyms and in front of the mirror, gazing at themselves with eyes of desire crafting their bodies to be bigger and increasingly more muscular. Compulsive body builders, they frequently use performance-enhancing drugs, and they will work out to the point of injury, exhaustion, and even collapse.

We might think of former California Governor, actor and bodybuilder, Arnold Schwarzenegger, as an example of this type of man. The roles he has played for the most part, such as *Terminator*, typify the epitome of a bigger than life untouchable. One woman is not enough for hyper-masculine men. They need to be surrounded by adoring dames and know that they can have their pick whenever the urge impels them.

3. The Cursed Man

The cursed man never got a blessing by his father or worse; he feels he received a curse. He projects his negative feelings about his father onto other men. Men who feel they've been cursed typically seek out the company of other cursed men. They may wind up in gangs, in prison, or homeless. The masks these men wear are constructed to be scary.

You may not directly encounter these types of men on a daily basis, but you probably see them even if it's just in passing. They have a particular walk and way of presenting themselves that expresses, *don't even think of fucking with me.* You avert your eyes so as not to engage them.

Mark's mother was very persuasive in requesting that I treat her son, an inveterate methamphetamine user, who was on probation for having beaten two unsuspecting male victims when he was out of his mind on speed. I don't typically work with hardcore drug users, and I tend to avoid those with pronounced personality disorders, but in this case I was open to give it a try.

Mark, who had been raised by his mother and taught to be a woman's champion, carried a father wound from a man he barely knew and rarely saw. At the time Mark was arrested, he was on the streets camping out with the homeless. He went to court and was given probation, required to reside in a sober living residence, attend mandatory Narcotics Anonymous meetings, be in therapy, and stay clean.

He was an intimidating looking character with a countenance that was designed to make one shudder. He sported a shaved head and unshaven appearance with dark penetrating eyes that averted contact unless he peered deeply into you. At our first meeting when I extended my hand to shake his, Mark slapped my hand away making a fist and giving me an aggressively strong knuckle bump. I avoided that ritual from that point forward.

During the interview he went on to tell me that he hated men and that I shouldn't expect to play the cliché card that it had anything to do with his estranged relationship with his father. I came to the realization that his father as well as other significant men had betrayed Mark over the years. His mother told me that he had been a wonderful little boy and that she raised him to care for females. His wound was deep and festering.

I found him to be exceedingly smart displaying a vast knowledge of literature and other impressive areas of learning, but there were also holes in his educational process that were revealed at times. He had attended an east coast Ivy League college and even Oxford for a while. There was something lurking inside of Mark as though he was possessed. I worked with him carefully and cautiously for about three months. As I got to know him, something about him touched my heart, and I wanted to save him from himself.

I hoped that we were making enough progress in mini-steps to keep him interested and engaged. But he didn't show up one day, and when I spoke with his mother she said that he had disappeared and had been spotted on skid row. She knew that he had once again relapsed and feared that he might not survive this latest bout with meth. I checked in again a week later, and his mother and other family members had not found him. She was afraid that he'd just disappear and wind up dead. I never heard anything further, and I suspect that his mother's greatest fears may have been realized.

4. The Lone Wolf

He tends to go it alone. In school, he was the last one picked for the games on the school playground, avoided proms and other social events that involved the opposite sex, and felt uncomfortable around other guys, especially if they were into sports and other ultra masculine areas. As an adult, he avoids dealing with other men and relies more on his wife or girlfriend, if he has one, to meet his needs. When he feels too unsafely vulnerable in the world, he heads for the hills or retreats to his cave to lick his wounds. The mask worn in this case is more sheepish than wolfish. These men lack the fierceness necessary to develop authentic masculinity, but they *can* grow and develop a more conscious masculinity.

Men often suffer their aloneness as "victims of loneliness" and need to learn to transform it into solitude through mastering their aloneness. When a man feels lonely it is because he cannot tolerate being alone with himself. When he resolves his internal issues he can befriend his aloneness and enjoy periods of solitude. Loneliness is often the symptom that arises from unrequited longing.

I have found that many men identify with being lone wolves. They were once strong, sensitive boys who lacked the attention of a loving father who recognized their innate gifts. They tell me that they are not "group" guys and that they felt like misfits when they were young, and now they just see themselves as mavericks that don't fit in or conform to the norm of society. Ironically, my retreats are filled with lone wolf men who describe themselves as not "group" guys.

I always ask them, when they disavow being group guys, what it would be like for them to meet other non-group guys. That question intrigues them and then I remind them that wolves travel in packs, mate for life, and are exceptionally loyal and protective. I love the lone wolves that comprise our men's community. Each is a uniquely sparkling facet of the diamond that reflects the men of *The Sacred Path.*

5. The Impinged Man

He's still tied to his mother who unwittingly interfered with his process of individuation as he was growing up by focusing her needs on him, causing him to undermine his autonomous self and binding him to her. Now he feels obligated to her, the result being that the addition of a wife or a girlfriend in his life is often experienced as an imposition. This mask displays the constricted smile that expresses, *I'm always Mr. Nice Guy, no matter what.*

These men grow up to be people pleasers. They're more concerned with what they need to do to please another than they are with attending to their own needs. It's not flattering to be thought of as a mama's boy tied to her apron strings. Sit-coms and commercials often depict such men as being soft, naïve, and at the beck and call of their women. The media has a field day promoting parodies of stupid males.

Impinged men lack spine and find it intensely difficult to be around assertive men and especially men that manifest characteristics and qualities of men's men. They find it hard to be autonomous and independent and frequently attach to another in order to create some forward movement of any duration and significance. In order for the impinged man to be liberated, the cord must be cut freeing him from his mother's spell so that he can get on with his journey into manhood.

The Mother Wound

This chapter has focused on the father gap and yet a mother wound can be just as problematic, if not more so. I have found that most men seem to need to put their attention on healing their father wound before they can even address the possibility that they may have been wounded by their mothers also. It's common for men that have absentee or over-the-top fathers to rely on their mothers for support, security, and even protection. Therefore it's inconceivable for many men that their mothers could have delivered a wound.

Many men have told me that their mothers were their allies and the only person that they could consistently count on during the formative years of their development. When you listen to athletes acknowledge a parent, especially black athletes, you hear the mother being acknowledged for always being there to make sure that he made it to the top, while fathers are often not even mentioned.

On the other hand, when the relationship with a mother is dysfunctional or interrupted due to a premature death or a mental, emotional, or physical health issue or some other cause, it can render a son incapacitated in more ways than one. Men have spoken about a mother that was chronically ill, and their feeling that *they* were the designated one to emotionally care for the mother because the father was too busy earning a living. A mother's impingement, when there is a symbiotic enmeshment, can cause a subtle wound, one that is more difficult to see but none-the-less one that can be as disabling as those that leave external scars.

Men have expressed dismay at having mothers who suffered from depressed or labile mood swings featuring random displays of irrational behavior or temperamental outbursts. I have been told of times when the men were young and felt like they were walking on egg shells around their moms, attempting not to detonate a mine as they traversed the perilous terrain of their households. One man said, "It was like being constantly on the front lines without a fox-hole." Several men have shared that they felt that their mothers were taking out their anger on them that should have been directed at the father. But if the father is MIA, the son can become the more available target.

At one of the men's retreats for fathers and sons, a man in his twenties confronted his fifty-year old father concerning the anger he felt about his parents' divorce. He said, "You know, Dad, when you left Mom because you thought she was crazy, I was just nine years old. Do you think she got any saner after you left? If so, you're dead wrong. She got crazier, crazed with anger and rage about being left, rejected, and abandoned by you. Because she couldn't get to you, she would unleash a torrent of rage on me every day and especially when I got home from school after she had started to drink herself into a stupor. I just hoped that she'd pass out before too long so that her insults would stop."

He went on, and his voice rose as he said, "I didn't know who to hate more, you or Mom. I guess both of you." His voice grew louder, and his eyes started to well up as he pointed his finger at his father and asked, "How could you do that? You went off and created a new life for yourself and left me to take care of Mom. Well, I couldn't do it. She wouldn't let me, and I just felt like a failure. I still do. I had to leave school and go into the army just to get away. You know what? I was so angry with you, and in fact, I hated you. I hated you and hated you and hated you." He was shouting at this point, just trying to get the words out that were being choked back by the enormous release of emotion. But then he paused, raised his head, looked his father squarely in the eyes and expressed, "I didn't want to hate you, because I loved you so much." At that point Kevin started sobbing and lowered his head. His father put his arms around him, holding him close as he apologized over and over. Both men cried out their pain and began to repair the bond that had been broken.

We had done so many healing-the-father-wound retreats over the years that at one point we decided to facilitate a retreat based on Michael Gurian's current book at the time, *Mothers, Sons and Lovers: How Your Relationship with Your Mother Determines Your Relationship with Other Women* (1993). We were ill-equipped, totally under-prepared for what was to result from the theme of that retreat. Mothers are hallowed ground for many of the men. It's the old adage that I can say anything I want about my mother, but don't you even dream of saying a negative thing about her. The difficulty was that those same men wouldn't even allow themselves to utter a negative word about their moms even though there was plenty that could be said. They were repressed, defensive, guarded, and oppressive.

This didn't play well with the guys that had real issues about their moms and wanted to vent their deepest feelings and clear out the backlog of suppressed hostility. During the ritual event on Saturday night, normally the culmination and pinnacle of the retreat, some of the men had created an "evil hag" out of sticks and straw to be burned in the fire. This "dark witch" effigy represented the shadow side of men's feelings about their mothers. As the men carried it down the hill toward the fire pit, a chant broke out, *burn the witch; burn the witch*. And then it turned to *burn the bitch, burn the bitch*

Conflict arose between what had become at least two factions of the community holding different emotions about their mothers and women in general. Some of the men were letting out their anger about the abuse they felt they had sustained at the hands of their moms and women, while others were outraged by the display and stormed off in disgust about the whole premise of the ritual. Some of the men even left the retreat grounds and drove down to the Dune Room, a local beachside bar, to drown their grievances and commiserate with each other about the outrageous and audacious behavior of some of the other men. Anxiety, if not abject terror, swept over me as I envisioned fifteen years of successful men's retreats coming to a crashing crescendo as word spread throughout the community that the Malibu men's retreat disparages women and mothers!

Fortunately, the last part of the ritual was set up to honor our mothers. The men spent the afternoon decorating one of the large rooms with sheer white cloth and a myriad of candles. They crafted an altar and adorned it with all of the pictures that the men had brought of their moms. The men that had stayed after the fire ceremony filed slowly into the room, one at a time in a procession, and approached the altar with great reverence.

I don't think that any of us were prepared for what was to follow.

The men broke down and cried from the depths of their hearts. Many forgave their mothers for issues that they had held onto for years. Others praised their moms for jobs well done and the sacrifices that were made on their behalf. And the most amazing thing was that the men who had stormed off returned to their rooms, including those that had left the camp. Something inside of them impelled them to come back and participate in the ceremony and experience the same depth of emotional release that the others experienced. The men held vigil all night in that room, sitting, standing, and kneeling by the altar. Some of the men didn't go to bed at all. It was quite a sight to behold.

My anxiety dissipated and when I retired I slept well. The next morning in our community room, man after man stood and shared how much he felt cleansed from the ritual process. There were men there who had barely spoken to their moms in years who now professed a new sense of commitment to resurrect their relationships. Other men pledged to improve their relationships with their wives and to rekindle their marriages or improve their dealings with former spouses. It was astounding to hear men in unison exclaim that that was the best retreat that they had ever experienced. It certainly is a retreat that I'll never forget. To date, after twenty-five years of retreats, I can only think of two retreats that carried such a punch—but I must admit that the Mother Retreat will remain as the one that took me from the depths of humility and despair to the towering regions of amazement, honor, and satisfaction.

CHAPTER 3

Why Men Fall for Dangerous Relationships

The life of a good man is a continual warfare with his passions.

—Samuel Richardson (1689 - 1761)
British novelist

I'LL NEVER FORGET BEING in a theatre, watching the hit movie of 1987, *Fatal Attraction*, about a married attorney (played by Michael Douglas) who has a fling with a work colleague (played by Glenn Close). When he later tries to pull away from the entanglement, the Glenn Close character becomes insanely obsessed with him and refuses to let go to the point where she goes to the man's house and tries to kill his wife (played by Anne Archer). I was riveted to my seat with a chill running through my body.

Somehow I knew this was more than a movie. It had a driving force behind it that seemed to connect men, without external acknowledgement, into a secret club to which no one wanted to admit membership. Without exchanging even a glance, men left the theatre having participated in an experience that portrayed a hidden ritual of manhood, of which most had firsthand knowledge. This movie sent a shockwave that moved deep within men's psyches. It touched the nerve endings of men's collective souls, unleashing a torrent of anxiety-bound confusion. He who succumbs to such a woman's manipulative ways may soon realize that something is terribly wrong, yet he doesn't know how to extricate himself from her snare, or better yet, how to avoid her from the gate.

At some point in the lifetime of every man a woman appears who can consciously or unconsciously collude with him to bring about his downfall. Unless the man knows how to spot her, how to deal with her or avoid her entirely, he may find himself an unsuspecting member of that secret club, exposed and disgraced along with such notables as former President Bill Clinton, presidential hopefuls Senator John Edwards and Senator Gary Hart, Governor Mark Stanford of South Carolina, Italy's Premier Silvio Berlusconi, talk show host David Letterman, Reverend Jim Baker, televangelist Jimmy Swaggart, Los Angeles Lakers basketball superstar Kobe Bryant, international golf pro Tiger Woods, Jesse James (husband of Oscar winner Sandra Bullock), and Arnold Schwarzenegger, with more men no doubt waiting in the wings for their turn.

In my forty years as a psychotherapist, I have worked first-hand with men whose dangerous relationship stories I have come to know intimately. I have been deeply touched by the toll such liaisons have taken on their lives. I've winced with each vivid realization of the wreckage inflicted on family members, friends, and even fans. It has felt increasingly uncomfortable to watch more and more men stumble blindly along the same perilous path that so many have traversed before.

What is a Dangerous Relationship?

Starting with that of Adam and Eve, a relationship qualifies as dangerous when the stakes are high and the consequences dire. ESPN baseball analyst Steve Phillips picked a twenty-two-year-old coworker to have an affair with, and when he tried to break it off, the woman scorned threatened Phillip's wife and children, just as in *Fatal Attraction* when the Glenn Close character tells the Michael Douglas character, *"I will not be ignored!"* It is a chilling moment as he realizes he's in big trouble. While not all such liaisons end in physical violence, many do end with the outing of the relationship, which may derail the man's career, destroy his family, and bring him to his knees in a painfully destructive way. Sometimes the man recovers; sometimes the consequences for him last a lifetime.

Look closely at those video clips of President Bill Clinton working the rope line one bright autumn day. There is a flirty girl in a beret that stands out from the crowd. She gazes at the President a little too adoringly, and the President gives her a hug that is just a bit too familiar. The potential for trouble is revealed in that picture, as the young woman we now know as Monica Lewinsky threatens to topple the venerable position held by the most powerful man in the world. It was ultimately Clinton's own brazenness that brought about the impeachment hearings. When asked later on why he had the dalliance with Monica Lewinsky, his reply was, "I've thought about it a lot, and unfortunately it was for the most morally indefensible reason—because I could."

The flirtatious exchange between Senator John Edwards and Rielle Hunter captured on camera long before their secret relationship was exposed telegraphed that danger was lurking. As we look back on the early days of a budding relationship we often glimpse that what will blossom will not necessarily reveal the most advantageous bloom.

The Forbidden Fruit

A run-in with such a woman happens to high-profile men, to ordinary men, and to men you know personally. You may have witnessed a good friend making a poor decision about the company he keeps, sometimes with unfortunate or even tragic consequences. Some of these men, thanks to their own dynamics, unwittingly conspire to bring about their own downfall.

We, the somewhat less powerful, the less influential, may envy the privileged pack that often gets away with being bad. While we may live vicariously through their exploits, they seem impervious to their own actions. However, should we slip away to consort with forbidden fruit, our wives would leave us, our kids would look at us in disgust, and our careers would falter. We would wind up living in a one-bedroom apartment, scraping by to keep our (former) families living in the style to which they had become accustomed.

There was an attorney in my practice who became involved in a dangerous relationship, careening from one eruptive episode to another. Each time he would attempt to extricate himself from his perilous partner she would become enraged, taking out her revenge in a variety of creative ways, including ordering a multitude of take-out food from various establishments to be delivered to his office all at the same time, throwing rocks through his windows, chasing him in her car and attempting to block him or smash into his car, putting a naked picture of him with his business card in prominent places throughout Beverly Hills, calling his elderly mother to inform her that he had been killed in an auto accident, and, much to my dismay, threatening to kill his therapist. Yes, the web of intrigue can ensnare other innocent parties within one's intimate circle. This woman, who clearly had mental and moral issues she failed to deal with, was eventually sentenced to prison.

How common are such relationships? More common than you might think, and one case in particular stands out as an example of a perilous relationship in which no one exited unscathed.

Real-Life Fatal Attractions

What follows is an example of a dangerous liaison that involved one of my patients, who we'll call Mike, and a woman who we'll refer to as Denise. They met in a bar one lonely night and struck up a conversation over many drinks. The alcohol made it ultra-easy for them to share far too much about each other in a first-chance meeting. Their instant passion turned volatile, and ultimately the relationship propelled itself to a tragic end. Mike had to face how his own neediness and narcissism blinded him to the allure of a borderline personality disorder suffered by his femme fatale. Mike recounts the story in his own words:

"I met Denise in a bar six weeks out of my marriage. She wasn't all that good-looking, yet I found myself strangely attracted to her. We struck up a conversation and talked until the restaurant threw us out at 1 a.m. I should have seen red flags in some of the things she told me, but didn't. For example, she told me she'd tried suicide; that she was out of work on disability for psychiatric disorders; that she was on Prozac; that she'd been in a relationship for fourteen years with a police officer who up and married somebody else after four years, but she still kept seeing him for another ten years. In addition, I could see for myself how much she drank. Still, I brushed all of this information aside and kept going.

"We went back to my house and proceeded to have the most fabulous sex I had ever experienced. She was unafraid and threw caution to the winds. I probably should have been suspicious about her ability to have this level of sexual connection and passion so early in the relationship. I invited her to go away with me for the weekend, mostly so I wouldn't have to be seen with her around town, where I was known, considering she wasn't cute enough for me. On that trip it became clear to me that she was a bore. On the way back, I was counting the minutes until we arrived home.

"Still, I kept seeing her about twice a week. It was always the same. We would have dinner, drinks, then go to my house and have sex. I kept reaffirming that nothing more could happen between us. She always agreed—but when she drank, her anger about my unavailability would manifest as rage. And if we were in a restaurant and anyone came up to me to say hello, she would get upset if I didn't introduce her as my girlfriend. I got the sense she wanted to tap into the energy I had with other people, but I didn't offer to take her there with me. I didn't want her to be part of my inner sanctum.

"Then the phone calls started coming. She left me one message ending with, '*Boy, I sure hope I'm not pregnant.*' We'd made plans to go away for another weekend at the beach. I didn't have the heart to break the date because she had worked so hard to arrange for the days off at work. What was one more weekend? One evening while we were away, she had too much to drink and became belligerent again. Finally, I said, 'I'm going to sleep. You do what you want.' She started pacing the room, chain smoking, and swigging vodka and wine from the bottle, all while looking at her reflection in the mirror, which was illuminated by the light of the burning fireplace. We were in Malibu on the beach, and the waves were roaring under our porch. It was just like a scene out of the old movie *Mildred Pierce*. All that was missing was a murder.

"I lay in bed pretending to sleep but all the while, watching her pace like a cat. I felt she was at least dangerous to herself, but for the first time I thought she might try to kill me. In that moment, my decision was made. I would break it off with her at the first occurrence of another outburst or when she got her period; whichever came first. Within a day or two, she had another raging moment in a restaurant. I told her I was through and to never call me again.

"From that point, she crumbled. She went back on disability, called me repeatedly, and basically refused to leave my world. One night, apparently upset when she couldn't reach me, she called the police and announced that she was going to commit suicide. They traced her number, went to her apartment, arrested her, and took her to the psychiatric ward of county hospital. She called me from there: 'Please bring me some cigarettes if you care about me at all.'

I didn't call and didn't go there. She called again with promises of good sex (that almost worked) and proclaimed a newfound stability. She kept leaving messages and even came over in the middle of the night banging on my door. Now I was really pissed. She was haunting me with her obsessive, stalking behavior, and I walked around constantly looking over my shoulder.

"I got home one night at eleven, and the phone was ringing. It was Denise, just calling to chat, she said, 'to chat.' My head felt like it was going to explode, and I unleashed all my pent up hostility toward her: I yelled at her to leave me alone, stop calling, stop all contact immediately or I'd call the police and charge her under the stalker law. Then I really dropped the big one. I said, 'You're such a loser that you can't even kill yourself successfully.' She hung up. I felt so liberated finally telling her off. At some point over the next thirteen hours, she wrote me a hostile letter, and a sweet card, and killed herself."

Mike, of course, was badly shaken by the tragic outcome of this perilous relationship. He roller-coasted from one emotion to another, from remorse, to guilt, and then to relief as he realized that she would never bother him again. This was his wake-up call. He told me during a session that he was going to take a break from dating and return to it only after he was convinced that he had figured out why he'd allowed himself to get caught up in this relationship and learned how to spot and heed the red flags, so it wouldn't happen again. Eventually, he went back to dating, married again, had two children, and today is appreciative of the fact that he leads a balanced, sane life.

Fall from Grace

When golf pro Tiger Woods toppled from his pedestal, you could hear the crash for miles around. The fallout from Tiger Woods' shocking collapse of character and popularity was considerable.

A *USA Today* Gallop Poll reported that Tiger sustained a drop in approval from eighty-seven percent in 2005 to thirty-three percent, with an unfavorable rating of fifty-seven percent.

We watched from the sidelines as Tiger attempted a comeback that some believed was too soon. We witnessed the physical and emotional strains on a champ attempting to climb back onto his pedestal. He sacrificed his number-one ranking in the world of golf, and many wondered if he'd have the mental capacity or even the willpower to do it again—if he has it in him to win as many majors on a yearly basis in order to surpass Jack Nicklaus' record, something that was undoubtedly attainable prior to The Fall. As of this writing, he seems to be on his way back up the ladder.

For the past twenty years I have worked with the Catholic Archdiocese counseling their priests who were in need of help for one reason or another. Among the priests were some who were having illicit affairs, relationships that were the result of loneliness or sexually compulsive or addictive behavior. Many of the priests had come to the realization, through treatment, that their personal falls were more *into* grace than *from* grace because they'd been forced to face their transgressions and learn things about themselves that actually improved their lives in the long run.

One married Episcopal priest who took The Fall was Father Tim, the priest of the church that my family and I were attending at the time. One Sunday while I was in church with my wife and our three children, we were stunned when an announcement was made that our pastor had just been relieved of his duties as rector of the church effective immediately, due to allegations that he had overstepped the bounds of propriety and had made sexual advances to a number of female parishioners. There were expressions of shock and disbelief on the faces of the congregation when they heard this.

Many wept while some looked blankly at one another, searching and hoping for some sign that might indicate that this was a mistake. How could this person who had been of such help to so many be accused of these indiscretions? He had been there during the births and the deaths, standing at the bedsides and the grave sites, baptizing the new little ones, giving counsel to those bereft, cheering on the school athletic teams. Everyone seemed to like and trust him so much. How could this have happened?

The thought immediately came into my mind—another fall from grace! There have been so many and now Father Tim. When it became clear that Father Tim was having an affair with one of the female parishioners and it was about to be exposed, the woman involved attempted to put the full blame on him, insinuating that he was acting out sexually with other women as well. But apparently no one else stepped forward to corroborate those insinuations. Father Tim subsequently left the priesthood and went through a divorce. His unwise choice brought him down hard.

Seven Types of Men Most Vulnerable to Dangerous Relationships

What kinds of men are most susceptible to the allure of dangerous women who entice them into liaisons and can turn treacherous when the men try to pull away or end it with them? Much has been written to help women spot and avoid dangerous men, but there's little out there to help men avoid similar disasters.

1. The Naïve Man

Known as Puer Aeternus or eternal boy, the naïve man is typically younger, softer, and more passive. He hasn't made transition from boyhood to manhood. Trapped in his boyish ways, he has poor boundaries, flies from commitments and difficult situations, minimizes ugly facts, transcends his own dark side, often sees the world through rose-colored glasses, and essentially resists growing up. He seems to feel a sense of satisfaction in being attacked by his woman and doesn't fight back. Instead, he retreats to his cave to brood. He may create a secret relationship with a woman he believes truly understands him and will treat his wounded inner child with kindness. He makes idealistic assumptions and doesn't examine the dark side of the woman he's with, setting himself up for betrayal by her in the end. Some women want a passive man so that they can control him as a result of acquiescing to or compensating for some familiar scenario in their own backgrounds. Perhaps they had a dominant mother and a passive father, or perhaps men had wounded them in the past.

Peter Pan is the epitome of this archetype. Peter flew away with the Lost boys and Tinker Bell in search of his shadow so that Wendy could sew it back on for him. Flying boys are inveterately naïve and disconnected from their shadows or dark sides. We gained much-needed insight into the life and persona of entertainer Michael Jackson when we understood that he flew away from his abusive father and wanted to inhabit the magical world of his idol, Peter Pan. He turned his ranch compound into an enchanted realm called *Neverland.* His obsession with altering his looks to resemble his idol, coupled with his fascination with young boys, reveal his penchant for remaining the eternal boy. It was ultimately all of his unresolved issues tucked away deep within his shadow that surfaced to create his downfall and untimely death just as he was positioning his comeback.

2. The Adrenaline Driven Man

This is the classic Type-A personality. His throttle is set for full speed ahead. He can't stand to be bored and avoids boring people. He loves challenges and risks. He won't settle for less than what he feels he deserves. He can't tolerate being stuck, held back, slowed down, or having to contend with the mundane. He participates in extreme sports and loves to stretch out of his comfort zone in everything he undertakes, from gambling and business ventures to women. He may volunteer to serve in the Special Forces division of the armed services or the bomb squad, where he overcomes his fears with a mixture of courage and adrenaline-driven bravado. The dangerous woman poses a challenge to him. She's wild and can't be tamed, and she would naturally be attracted to his style of living life on the edge. A dangerous woman will get his blood boiling and adrenaline flowing.

Adrenaline driven men tend to flare up, argue, fight, see red, and get into trouble. They tend to be arrogant, quarrelsome, bordering on antisocial behavior and run by anger. A girl may be attracted to his fiery spirit and may encourage him to fight because it turns her on.

An article titled "What Makes Them Stray?" ran in the *Los Angeles Times*. In it, the writer, Frank Farley, a psychologist and professor from Temple University, suggests that the very qualities that make for successful politicians may predispose them to sexual indiscretions. He posits the following: "There are many possible factors involved, a need to express power, a love of conquest, perhaps narcissism—all characteristics that may serve a politician well in other arenas. But the factor that is usually responsible for philandering by public officials is a predisposition for risk-taking, which also happens to be an essential quality for politicians. My label for it is the Type T personality, with the T standing for thrill."

He goes on to say in his article that "being a Type T personality doesn't need to be a problem or get one into trouble, and many Type Ts have done quite well for themselves and others without causing a problem. But Type T individuals may also be prone to negative types of risk-taking, including crime, drug use, or sexual encounters that end badly."

Dr. Farley suggests that risk-takers want to live exciting, interesting, challenging lives. They tend to believe they control their fates. They are often attracted to variety, novelty, intensity, and uncertainty. They are often creative, show independence of judgment, and tend to have strong sexual drives and high energy.

3. The Man in Mid-life

Question: It's almost a cliché, but what's a man looking for when he starts coloring his hair, purchases a new younger, hipper wardrobe, buys a convertible sports car, and equips it with a young blond? He's looking for trouble. Around age forty, this man may begin a quest for something better. He may begin parading around in peacock fashion, hoping that an attractive woman or women will notice. Inside, he is screaming to be seen, admired, adulated, and adored. When he no longer feels like a special person, he becomes vulnerable to anxiety and depression and may start abusing drugs and alcohol. He may also be facing looming financial, career, legal, or marital disasters.

Coming off a period of adrenaline driven loftiness these men are prone to a sudden descent from the high they were on to a new low. The ancient Greeks referred to this as *katabasis*, Great Fall, the same phenomenon that Robert Bly refers to as "The Drop."

The Man in Mid-Life may seek relief from his despair by encouraging an out-of-bounds relationship with a woman who tells him he's special, although he lacks the clarity to make a wise love choice. At first, he's just relieved to have finally found the one until it sours.

4. ***The Man Filled with Longing***

Typically, women marry men and want to improve them. They want them to change. Typically, men marry women and want them to stay the way they are. They don't want them to change. Men, as pointed out earlier, love maidens. When a woman ages and moves from the enchantment of Maidenhood into the mundane world of Matronhood (after the children are born) and then later to the Crone stage after menopause, men are prone to lose interest. Often a man longs for something other than what he's got. He fantasizes about his younger years and starts eying women half his age. It's not uncommon for men who are in their mid to late fifties, who have been married for twenty or more years, to experience their relationships as dull and devoid of romance and passion. He knows he's beyond midlife and feels an urgency to recapture his youth before it's too late. In the movie *Moonstruck* the question is asked: Why does an older man have an affair with a younger woman? The character played by the actress Olympia Dukakis responds, "Because he's afraid to die."

A man like this fears aging, so when his wife matures and he's no longer interested, he turns to maidens who are succulent and carry the nectar of eternal youth. He may rush into a divorce or drive his wife into dumping him. As a therapist, I know that aging men and women can do the work to help weatherproof their relationship and protect it from the transgressions of a dangerous woman, but the work is painful, and many couples aren't willing to do it.

There is a growing trend today among aging baby boomers labeled, "gray divorce." Boomers, always proprietary about their autonomy and freedom, are choosing at a higher than normal divorce rate to end marriages while they still have a chance to regroup and move on with their lives. They are choosing not to remain in a loveless marriage as they enter their elder years. Women are taking the lead on dumping their marriages. They just don't want to have to care for an aging husband headed for the sick bay. They want out, leaving many men adrift without a port in the storm.

5. The Narcissist

Narcissus was a beautiful man who was promised a lavish life so long as he heeded his mother's warning to never gaze upon his own features. Ignoring her pleas, Narcissus saw his reflection in the waters of a spring and fell in love with himself, gazing at the mirror of water until he starved to death. According to Greek legend, a flower named for him sprang up in the spot where he died. The moral of this story warns of the perils of self-absorption.

The Narcissist is doomed by his own shallowness and dominated by his needs. He fears mediocrity and wants to be seen as special. Charming, intelligent, and talented, he may rise to prominence, but inside he feels empty, fears intimacy, and seeks approval and admiration. He fears aging and losing control. Desperate to restore his feeling of youth and vitality, he seeks out the company of beautiful women. He's a magnet for young maidens who will adore him—at least temporarily. When the luster fades, and he loses control, he starts to resort to less than charming behaviors. Narcissistic males fall along the continuum from being fairly benign to being pathologically malignant—overly controlling, deceitful, manipulative, threatening, and even psychopathically dangerous.

A male manifesting a more severe form of narcissism may have suffered an attachment disorder arising from an early break within a primary bond typically existing between him and his mother. This can cause a deeper split in his psyche creating the development of a borderline personality disorder. A man with this disorder can appear to be quite charming and together; however, his persona has been crafted to hide a dark shadow side to his personality. Narcissists are often ingenuous and duplicitous. Men like that lead double lives and are the prototype of the wolf in sheep's clothing; the personifications of the modern day false prophet.

As with borderline women, men with this disorder don't maintain proper limits or respect appropriate boundaries, exhibiting a lack of impulse control. At first, a woman will believe that she has met Mr. Wonderful only to later realize that her dream-guy has become Mr. Nightmare. If he seems to be too good to be true, she'll undoubtedly discover that her initial suspicions were correct. The Jekyll-Hyde split in his demeanor will betray that he is no doubt a borderline-disordered male and that things will typically begin to go from bad to worse before the relationship explodes or implodes.

A man with this disorder is love-avoidant. It's not that he doesn't crave love; it's just that he doesn't trust it or understand it in its fullest expression. A borderline male tends to pull women toward him and then push them away when they get too close. He starts off adoring the objects of his attraction and then winds up devaluing and rejecting them. Seducing women feeds his narcissistic longing for attention. It holds the hope of filling his core emptiness and quelling his addiction. The problem is that he can't live with them, and he can't live without them. Therein lies the rub.

Since a borderline can't form healthy attachments and sustain solid viable relationships, he takes hostages. He will typically choose women that are needy and that he can control. This is a way of avoiding the more together and powerful woman that would trigger his fear of rejection and abandonment. If he should happen to choose a solid and healthy partner he will have to weaken her by reducing her through derision to self-doubt and lowered-self-esteem. This way he can maintain his artificial sense of control and stave off his dreaded fear of being alone with himself.

6. The Man Who Would be King

He's the ultimate success object. He's successful, ambitious, with a ravenous appetite for power and possessions. He may unwittingly be willing to sacrifice hearth and home for something that he feels he must have—more money, prestige, fame or adulation. Charismatic and intelligent, he commands attention and displays his wealth and power in the company of others. He has a sense of entitlement and surrounds himself with admirers who do his bidding. But he's perpetually dissatisfied and must continue to pursue new conquests. He is an easy mark for a dangerous woman looking for a man-on-the-rise, a woman who believes that only she has something to offer him that he needs in order to fulfill his quest. She opens the door to heightened passion and ardor so enchanting that he cannot resist her. She imbues him with intoxicating nectar, setting him on fire.

The man who would be king feels privileged to reach out for whatever he desires and longs for and has an unconscious drive to own all the best women in the land. We might think of former presidents John Kennedy or Bill Clinton as being the prototype for this kind of man. Clinton, similar to his hero, John Kennedy, felt a sense of inflated entitlement manifesting in the belief that he deserved to satisfy his desire for whatever he wanted, whenever he wanted it, including women. In fact, Kennedy evidenced that he felt he deserved to have his pick of the best women in the land, and he chose perhaps the epitome of the most widely desired vixen of the moment, Marilyn Monroe.

7. The Sexually Addicted Man

Lust has been around since the dawn of time. The theories on why people self-destruct using sex and love run the gamut. One man acts out his addiction by having multiple sex partners and another man obsesses over a woman who is emotionally unavailable to him. Others derail their lives by compulsively masturbating (sometimes as much as five to twenty times a day), having inappropriate fantasies or extramarital affairs, continually logging onto pornographic web sites on the Internet, or hurting themselves sexually with a variety of objects or self-destructive behaviors.

Anthony Weiner, former U.S. Representative who served New York's 9th congressional district from January 1999 until June 2011 and who potentially could have been the next governor of New York, had to resign from his congressional seat because he was caught sending explicit pictures of himself through the Internet to women he had never met. The new technology has been the downfall of many a man recently. It just takes one "tweet" to topple a lifelong career. An impulsive decision made in one second can end years of hard work.

Sometimes children of broken families, who live in environments that feature molestation or affairs, may grow into adults who can't distinguish between what's acceptable and what's not. The problem can be made worse by the many sexual images portrayed in the media. And, of course, alcohol and drugs never make a potentially bad situation better.

It's important to understand that sexual addictions don't happen overnight. They take time to develop. But when they're full-blown, a man won't be able to resist the repeated urge to enter into a potentially dangerous love relationship with a sexual object or experience that gives him pleasure and the illusion of intimacy. This last sentence is what defines an addict: He's hooked and can't say no.

Not everyone who struggles with sexual compulsions is an addict. Some men abuse their sexuality for a period of time and then grow out of it. Another man with a regrettable sexual experience in the past puts it behind him and moves on. But not everyone is so fortunate. Some men block emotional pain with sexual pleasure. Over time they have to try increasingly risky forms of sexual behavior in order to deaden the pain. Eventually their world revolves around sex and dangerous relationships. Their obsession has taken over their life. Male and female sex addicts are magnets for each other.

Newsweek's December 5, 2011 issue featured an article titled "The Sex Addiction Epidemic" by Chris Lee. It states that, "Reliable figures for the number of diagnosed sex addicts are difficult to come by, but the Society for the Advancement of Sexual Health, an education and sex-addiction treatment organization, estimates that between three and five percent of the U.S. population—or more than nine million people—could meet the criteria for sex addiction.

It Takes Two to Tangle

Dangerous relationships don't take place in a vacuum. Most often, neither the man nor the woman has a clue about why they are involved in relationships that could hurt them both. And often, even when they know they're stepping into big trouble, they do it anyway. Knowing this on an intellectual level doesn't help. A man can say, "I always pick women who destroy me," but if he does it repeatedly, what use is the insight? Seeing the truth has to happen at a deeper, gut level.

For example, the kind of woman who is drawn to The Man Who Would Be King type desires to profit from the man's position on the ladder of success whether he's the CEO of a company where she works or the President of the United States. The woman feels she will benefit from being associated with his fame and fortune, however immense or meager it may be. She feels the relationship gives her greater security, immunity, self worth, and status. Her sense of self is bolstered by her ability to entice him, as she perceives that she has landed a great catch.

Seven Types of Women Who Collude in a Man's Downfall

In many ways, the seven types of women most likely to conspire to bring a man down parallel the seven types of men who are most vulnerable to them. They are a good fit. Men and women in some ways are hardwired to play out genetic predispositions to assume roles. Men are natural protectors, and women tend to seek safety and protection. In our society, money and status translate as safety and protection. The bottom line is the need for survival, and when one's survival is on the line it can bring out very primal instincts in how one conducts oneself. As with the men, the seven types of women run the gamut from benign to malignant. Not all the players fit neatly into one type. Sometimes a woman will display traits from one or more of the following types:

1. The Damsel in Distress

This is the woman who is looking for the white knight to rescue her. Some damsels are truly dependent and need a man to save them from one crisis to another, and some men are total suckers for this type of woman. They feel better about themselves when they can rescue her from a dragon or some other potential tragedy in the making. The downside of this type is that sometimes the woman's helplessness masks defects in character or pathology that get revealed later on. Like the Naïve Man, the Damsel in Distress doesn't want to grow up. She does not want to mature because to do so would mean to accept and embrace the process of being an adult. This is an intimidating prospect and is to be avoided at all costs.

2. The Drama Queen

This woman needs to be the center of attention. Often lively and dramatic, she may initially charm new acquaintances by her enthusiasm, apparent openness, or flirtatiousness. These qualities wear thin, however, as she continually demands to be in the spotlight. She is theatrical; she exaggerates expressions of emotion. She often embarrasses friends and acquaintances by excessive public displays of emotion. She has problems with intimacy in romantic or sexual relationships.

Flights into romantic fantasy are common. Without being aware of it, these women often act out a role such as queen or victim in their relationships with others. When a man who would be king partners with a woman who is acting the role of queen while disguising her inveterate princess tendencies, he will eventually become disenchanted. Drama Queens typically remain unrequited princesses incapable of ascending to the queen's throne.

3. The Seductress

She seeks control of her partner through emotional manipulation or seductiveness on one level, while displaying a marked dependency on him. She comports herself as the archetype of the vixen, siren, or fury. She requires the attention of all the men in the room and gets it by dressing provocatively and displaying a variety of sexually suggestive behaviors. She tends to have impaired relationships with same sex friends because of her sexually provocative interpersonal style. She craves novelty, stimulation, and excitement and has a tendency to become bored with the usual routine. If not the center of attention, she may become depressed.

One of my clients told me about a meal with a woman he had invited out in which she ate a hot dog in a most sensually erotic fashion. It might have been enticing if the performance had not been graphically acted out in front of his parents and his minor age children. He felt like crawling under the table but was afraid that she might follow him. I've had patients involved with such women tell me that even though the relationship with the psycho babe was a roller coaster ride from hell, "It was the best sex I've ever had," or, "Nothing like a little psycho-sex to work the kinks out."

4. The Power Seeker

She's only interested in men who have personal power, men who can advance her lifestyle in some generous fashion.

These women are social climbers who use relationships to elevate themselves on the ladder of success, even though it is leaning against his wall, not hers. Getting to the top and taking advantage of the prizes along the way is the primary focus. Some women like this are derogatorily referred to as "star-fuckers." They can leave a man in the rubble of his indiscretion while they rise out of the ashes of his destruction like a phoenix. They may launch an acting career, start their own clothing line, or become newsworthy in some other manner. The man's stars fall while the woman's continue to twinkle.

Obviously, not every woman who dates or marries a powerful man fits this type. However, where a pattern is established in which men are traded and discarded as one more powerful takes the place of the preceding one, it may be evidence that the power seeker is at work. Often, these women have no personal power of their own and tend to cash in on the man's station in life. Some time ago in Los Angeles there was a support group made up of the ex-wives of famous men. Many shared their desire to get themselves another famous man to marry, unsatisfied with marrying just anybody.

5. The Desperate Woman

She sets up a man to marry her or impregnate her simply to have a baby. The primary agenda is the baby, even under adverse conditions. Sometimes a woman gets pregnant to trap the man into staying with her. Desperate, she feels that she will be fulfilled only if she can have a child. She also wants to have the financial support so that she can put her attention into mothering rather than employment. Many paternity suits are filed each year to determine the father of origin of a baby.

I have worked with men in therapy who have told me stories about being in brief relationships in which the woman gets pregnant, has no intention of terminating the pregnancy, and is not interested in whether or not he sticks around. She does want to make sure that the check arrives on a monthly basis until the child turns eighteen. Often, these men want to have access to the child as father and the woman blocks this in some way, including moving out of state.

A former client had met a woman in a bar and had foreplay with her in the bathroom after she lured him in and locked the door. On their next date they had sex on his boat. He had used protection. When he withdrew after coitus, he was shocked to see that the condom was not where it should have been. He remembered her hand working its way down toward his penis during intercourse. He realized that she had rolled the condom off during the act. Surprise: she wound up pregnant, and after she won the paternity suit and full custody of the child, he wound up with a ruling to pay a lump sum per month each year until the child was no longer of minor age. Some women go after married men specifically because they believe that they will get the kid and the money without being exposed. Most of these married men will not want to reveal the scenario, running the risk of losing everything.

In the article "Blackmailed into Fatherhood: Borderline Women and the Men who Love Them," author Shari Schreiber, M.A., states, "It's disheartening to think that women intentionally entrap men by getting pregnant, and in this woman's opinion it's a form of blackmail, and there ought to be laws prohibiting it. Women with agendas to have children give men no say in the matter and for the most part, are looking for a free ride in terms of financial support and/

or emotional security. They carry significant abandonment issues from childhood, so having a man's baby will insure he cannot sever all ties with her and leave."

6. The Borderline

Characterized by extreme feats of attention seeking, manipulative behavior, and rapidly shifting emotions, this woman is also distinguished by self-destructiveness, angry disruptions in close relationships, chronic feelings of emptiness, and identity disturbance including hostile and even violent acting-out forms of conduct disorder. She may appear normal until a stress incident sends her regressing into a more primitive psychotic state.

Typically, borderlines suffer from an acute form of traumatic wounding marked by abandonment and perceived rejection, typically by the mother at a very early age. She exhibits an attachment disorder and has learned to distrust that people will be there for her. She is hypersensitive to abandonment (real or imagined) yet is terrified of closeness and attachment. If a man gets too close, she pushes him away; if he steps back, she will try to lure him back with everything she's got—or she'll lash out with a vengeance if he doesn't respond. Because she feels so empty, she'll seek out relationships where she can get involved quickly to fill up that emptiness.

While the male narcissistically wounded personality thrives on being mirrored as special, the female Borderline Personality is driven by an intense, often debilitating fear of loss and longs for connection. Having suffered the real physical and/or emotional abandonment of a primary caregiver during early childhood, borderlines grow to idealize potential caregivers. The borderline will tend to initially mirror her attractor in an idealized fashion, only to later knock him off his pedestal when she discovers that he's just like all the other men that have betrayed, abused, and abandoned her. Her one-time prince becomes the prick that he obviously was all along.

Male and female borderlines tend to become entwined as their connection devolves into a symbiotic enmeshment. A major power struggle over issues of control ensues as the push-pull, approach-avoidance dance spirals into chaos. Like an insect on flypaper, the more one struggles to get free the more entrapped one becomes. Disentangling a relationship between two borderlines can seem a lot like herding cats.

The kind of woman who tends to snare a man into a dangerous relationship typically is one who seems to have no limits and who respects no boundaries. She doesn't care if the man is married or single. It only matters that she wants him, and she will stop at nothing to have him. She will seduce him, manipulate him, and threaten him—all because of a craving for control. She is terrified to be alone, and eventually the object of her desire begins to feel that, instead of being in relationship with her, he has become her emotional hostage.

Such a woman doesn't engage in a relationship, she takes a prisoner. As things unravel, she can be treacherous. She may stalk him, scream at him, slash his tires, threaten suicide, write letters to his wife—or worse. It has been said that, "Hell hath no fury like a woman scorned," and the reality of this can become all too apparent to a man who has fallen under her spell.

7. The Sex Addict

A fine line exists between what may be considered by most people acceptable sexual behavior and what is sexually addictive or compulsive. This is especially true for women in a society such as ours where sex is often treated as a commodity. Our culture at one time had discouraged women from being assertive and direct in the expression of their sexual needs, thereby encouraging a less direct and potentially seductive or manipulative style. Since the women's movement of the 60s we have witnessed a progressively more overt style of sexual expression among women. Some women, however, go beyond these culturally sanctioned behaviors and use sex compulsively as a means of gaining power, control, and love.

The idea of being sexually alluring may be preferred by sexually addicted women because it fits the romantic, nurturer model of woman, whereas the term "sex addict" connotes a pejorative image of a "nymphomaniac," "slut," or "whore." The "love" that these women describe is often an addiction to the yearning or euphoria of romance, but has little to do with love.

The elements of sex addiction (any addiction for that matter) are compulsion, continuation despite adverse consequences, and preoccupation or obsession. These are the same in women as in men. Most sexually addicted women haven't had parental role modeling for how to have emotional intimacy in nonsexual ways. Research has shown that there is often a combination of rigidity and lack of emotional support in the sex addict's family of origin. Up to 78% of female sex addicts, says one study, were sexually abused in childhood.

The Relationship Minefield

Sometimes relationships between men and women can seem like minefields strewn with carefully concealed IEDs. Relationships are constantly being blown apart, leaving survivors maimed and traumatized. I recommend that you tread cautiously when entering new relationships, utilizing discerning mindfulness all along the way. Take heed. Keep the faith. Stay the course. Chapter 13, "Finding and Renewing Your True Love," will provide a roadmap for traversing the bumpy relationship ride. It will show you ways to avoid or deal with the perilous twists and turns that tend to arise on your journey to being a mindful and loving man.

Chapter 4

Shoulder to Shoulder

Our dads weren't there for us, so we were all raised by women, and we can't learn about manhood from women, so we have to learn about manhood from each other.

—Robert Bly (*New Age Magazine,* May 1982)

WHEN I FIRST BEGAN my group work with men I was stunned to hear so many of them make the same confession—that they felt discomfort, distrust, and threat around other men. Suffering from the ingrained effects of the Father Gap, they sought out the company of women to meet their needs for companionship and intimacy. Most had only superficial relationships with other men—back slapping pals—but lacked close male friends they could count on and trust. Around other men, what most of them felt was pain.

As men grow up and enter the world, they have diminishing opportunities to heal their pain through healthy, positive male-male bonds. With marriage and fatherhood, less free time, and the pressure of other responsibilities, men tend to let go of their friends (more than women do), or else, once their friends also marry and become husbands, they socialize only as couples. There's no more going fishing, no more pick-up basketball, no hunting, no washing a car together or painting a fence. There are fewer opportunities for men to focus on some mutual activity while telling each other what's going on for them, which is how men communicate best. Women relate eyeball to eyeball, and men relate shoulder to shoulder.

The Blessing

However, something special happens when men are in the presence of other men and women aren't around. They benefit from interacting with others who share their wiring. They start to shake loose from their numbness, reconnect with their non-aggressive fierceness, feel again, and recognize what isn't working in their lives. They begin to talk, listen, and learn from each other. And they gain from the insights and attentions from the older men in the group.

In this kind of a setting, a man is able to receive something from another man that he was never able to receive from his own father—a blessing—an acknowledgment that he is man enough. I encourage men to seek such blessings. I have observed how positively younger men respond when they can drink deeply from the well of admiring attention that older men can bestow upon them. Men have a need to be seen and the admiring gaze from someone who is interested and demonstrates sincere concern and caring can make a positive difference.

Typically, men who begin to question their lives prior to their mid-thirties are the exception rather than the rule. Younger men tend to be more interested in their careers and external relationships than they are in exploring the hidden realms of their psyches or souls. As men move closer to mid-life however, they sense an inner churning and longing for something more than the material trappings of the world. There is a spiritual questing, often arising from a personal crisis that prompts men to inspect their lives, ask penetrating questions, and seek meaningful answers.

Getting the Words Out

The power of older men in the lives of younger men can make a world of difference. During the retreats that one of our elders, Conrad Burke, would attend with his son Matthew, he would seize the opportunity to take the talking stick. Our talking stick is a five-foot staff carved at the top to reveal the head of a polar bear. It was presented to our community by one of our men, Dan Stanton, who acquired it from an American Indian carver in Colorado. Over the years thousands of hands have held it while the men speak from their hearts during community council.

Conrad would walk to the center of the circle and call Matthew up to stand before him. Placing his hands on Matt's shoulders, Conrad would speak to his son in a straightforward, loving, and blessing manner. It was a highlight for the men to witness. Here, at last, was an example for men of how to get the words out, a model for how to deliver a blessing. Through the years I have witnessed many men do this for other men who had never received that all-important blessing from their fathers.

The good news is that even men who have stumbled or fallen can get up again and turn things around. Midlife is when most tend to hit a wall, but midlife is also a good age to learn how to fix things. That's why, when a man around the age of forty comes into my office and tells me he has just made a mess of something in his life, I say, "Good!" Usually, he's taken aback by my response and asks me why I'd say such a thing—why good? I tell him it's good because if a man his age has the energy to get himself into that much trouble, then it usually means he's got the energy to get himself out of it.

Those of us who are interested in men's issues have observed that a meaningful shared passage into manhood for men is sadly lacking today, as it has been for several generations. Historically, men as hunter-gatherers and farmers knew who they were as men. Their sons spent many hours every day with their fathers and grandfathers, learning through the process of being together what manhood was about. The elders would informally and formally induct the young men into the community of men. But as technology evolved, our great-grandfathers went from the rural farming culture to the urban industrial culture. Men moved from the farms to the cities and into less meaningful and/or unfulfilling work. This was a profoundly significant shift because our work is such an important part of our identity.

Involuntary Abandonment

The involuntary abandonment by fathers established that, for several generations, boys in our culture have been raised almost entirely by women. Women, simply because they are women, cannot teach boys about manhood. Without men, there is no possibility of any rite of passage into manhood. Therefore, men have been losing the sense of what mythologist Michael Meade calls "gender ground."

For centuries, men in indigenous cultures had gathered to seek counsel and perform ceremonies and rituals to initiate boys into manhood and to receive guidance and blessings from elders and to mutually support the community of men. Secret societal groups like the Masons, the Elks, Moose, Knights of Columbus, and others served as opportunities for men to come together.

During the 1960s, driven by the Vietnam War, older men and younger men became suspicious of each other, causing distrust, polarization, and estrangement, eventuating in a rift in the community of men that would last for more than twenty years.

The women's movement only served to further confuse men, causing men to question and doubt themselves. Men tended to perceive themselves through eyes that often held them with contempt to the point where many men distrusted each other and avoided identifying with traditional masculine values. In the 1970s the divorce rate began to rise, families split apart, and individuals went their separate ways setting the stage for the birth of the age of narcissism. The advent of the "me generation" came into full bloom during the 1980s.

It was in the mid-80s that, through the help of men such as Robert Bly, James Hillman, Michael Meade, and Sam Keen, younger men began to seek the mentoring guidance of older males who understood what was going on with them. The identification with the concept of "father hunger" swept through the community of men like wildfire. Unfortunately, at the crest of the Men's Movement, the media did not approach what was happening in men with respect or reverence. TV sit-coms poked fun at men depicting them in foppish and feminized fashion baring their chests, dancing around an outdoor fire, having hug-fests, and crying on each other's shoulders. Men's need for fellowship was viewed as unmanly, weak, and silly. Men reacted to the parodies of their inner longing to gather with other men with shame and dropped their pursuit and retreated to their customary practices.

But slowly, over time, men cautiously reached out to other men again—men who were exploring what had come to be called men's soul work. Leaderless men's groups were spawned from the Mythopoetic retreats that were conducted by Bly, Hillman, and Meade as well as from Justin Sterling's retreats, the Promise Keepers Christian Men's events, and the New Warrior's Network (aka: The Mankind Project). These men's groups, also referred to as teams, determined the frequency and location of their meetings.

Leader led therapeutic support groups are typically facilitated by trained counselors and psychotherapists that may also specialize in treating male clients. Psychotherapists bring their clinical expertise to the exploration of the underlying psychodynamic during the process of men supporting each other to be their personal best. Therapeutic men's groups typically are comprised of eight members and meet in the therapist's office once a week.

Men's support groups emerged out of the energy of the women's movement and its "consciousness-raising" groups designed to liberate women from what they experienced as a male-dominated culture and were also influenced by the many established twelve-step groups created to deal with specific problems such as gambling, over-eating, or addiction which have a recovery oriented coping-better-with-the-problem focus. Essentially, men's groups were created and have continued to act as sacred containers for participants to explore their wounds, to bond, and to support the evolution of men's mental, emotional and spiritual development. In some cases, what happens as a result is often quite amazing.

The Purpose of Men's Groups

Traditional forms of talk therapy are ultimately not the best ways to reach men. Individual counseling sessions may be a suitable way to introduce the therapeutic process, establish rapport, and identify the issues. But in the long run a better way to deliver counseling services to men is through a group setting that utilizes a cognitive-behavioral approach. This allows men to tap their innate masculine power and energy, focusing it in ways that feel more natural to men dealing with their own healing process. Men, in the company of other men, discover that they're not alone or the only ones to experience what they're going through. They learn from each other.

Men like to explore and discover ways to fix problems. They serve as accountability partners within a therapeutic support group setting. They sit on each other's Boards of Directors and hold each other's feet to the fire. I have facilitated mixed gender groups in the past but have found that men and women are more honest when solely in the presence of their own gender. Just the presence of one woman in a group can alter the candor and authenticity of the men's sharing.

Utilizing a gender-sensitive approach makes it possible to reframe behaviors traditionally perceived as problematic in male clients: resistance to expressing feelings, being overly task-oriented, and withdrawing from intimacy. A gender-sensitive leadership style can provide male clients with a fuller understanding of how gender role expectations and their socialization have influenced their lives. Even more important, the group can help them discover a greater sense of freedom and expression.

The purpose of a men's group is to lend support and help for one another in learning new ways to be in relation to each other. Groups need to be a safe place to try out new behaviors such as being more assertive, relaxed, and confident. Groups should allow members the freedom to talk about unusually sensitive topics related to issues of relationship, sexuality, health, career, and other intimate concerns. The mission is to develop a process by which a group of men, who are reasonably compatible and who come together with a mutuality of intention, will learn to resolve conflict, earn trust, and care for each other.

The essential ingredient in men's groups is a willingness to stay with your group and learn through being together. This requires commitment. Without commitment the group doesn't work. Commitment ensures the longevity necessary to build the trust and safety essential to open up, risk, and share more of who we are. I always encourage a new member to consider being in the group for a minimum of a year and probably longer. Most men don't really comprehend what can be gained from a therapeutic support group until they have participated for at least a year. The real gains typically come in the years that follow, and many of the men I work with have been in their groups for several years. They have experienced the benefits first hand of that level of commitment to the work of deep self-examination.

What is generally missing for us in our society is the safe space that supports our telling the truth at deeper levels. The group provides that opportunity. It is imperative that the group welcomes conflict and supports the sacred trust that empowers the members to learn and transform. One definition of conflict is simply: "You want one thing, and I want another." So defined, conflict is a natural and important part of any relationship. The successful resolution of conflict will involve you and me in telling the often hidden truth about why we want whatever it is we happen to want. In this open sharing we come to know new aspects of each other.

As M. Scott Peck states in his book, *The Different Drum*, "The essential dynamic of pseudo-community is conflict-avoidance. True community is conflict-resolving." The group must support a commitment to intimacy. Intimacy is sharing those most private thoughts, feelings, and secret parts of ourselves over a long period of time. It is something we all need and crave though few men have known the comfort or experienced the joy of true intimacy, especially with other men.

Meeting the challenge of opening ourselves to others and finding acceptance is a vital step toward becoming able to know our own power. This is not the old dominating "power over" but the personal "power to" create our own lives, as we want them to be. Inherent in the ability to be intimate is the power to trust and love who you are at this moment.

A Circle of Men

One-day workshops and longer retreats can be life-changing experiences for men providing a new source of self-expression and engagement with others. They provide opportunities for individuals as well as for a team of men already bonded. A four-day retreat can further energize, deepen, and empower a men's group. When the group attends the retreat it has an opportunity to gain something to bring back to the team meetings that can be very invigorating.

However, Father Gap healing doesn't happen only in men's group therapy or men's retreats. Everyday life offers men all kinds of opportunities to informally address these issues with solid, therapeutic results.

For example, a computer programmer who lost his father to divorce when he was two—and was then moved by his mother to another country—has never been in therapy but has nonetheless managed to become a good man thanks to his connections with other men that arose through a series of job situations that put him in constant contact with men.

He came to the United States as a professional soccer player. On the road a lot, he was in constant shoulder-to-shoulder relationships with other men, both literally and psychologically. Later he was on the road again as a bass player with a band. When he finally settled down in his early forties to a desk job as a computer programmer, he connected with a group of like-minded computer geeks, and the group has now been meeting together on a regular basis for over twenty years to discuss computers and talk about their lives.

A Great Team

I recommend to men that they take up golf or tennis, join a bowling league, a weekly poker game, a softball league, or some other form of friendly activity. Via conscious effort, a different attitude within men as compatriots, not competitors, is fostered as they join forces in a choice of activities that are shoulder-to-shoulder.

One man has made an effort not to allow marriage and a new baby to keep him from his weekly basketball or beach volleyball games with the same guys he's been playing with for years. (Yes, he got some grief for this, but he prevailed.) Once a year these guys would take a week off and go to some exotic spot on the globe for scuba diving. However, this annual trip finally fell apart when some of the wives insisted on going along.

In another case, the owner of a sporting goods business, who has a learning-disabled daughter, has been in charge of an annual walkathon fundraiser for special needs kids for years. This puts him in contact with other men who have things in common with him (many have special needs kids themselves), and they get to work shoulder-to-shoulder on a worthy project.

Men can manage to create amazing communities for themselves in all sorts of settings, even without the conscious recognition of its therapeutic value. Men have been doing this intuitively since the dawn of time—from hunting parties to classic men's organizations like the Kiwanis or Elks. Men can become a band of brothers, no matter what their age or situation or where they live. The positive results that can come from the simple action of connecting shoulder-to-shoulder with other men can be inspiring.

As men learn to man up in the presence of other men, they tend to age gracefully while maintaining their youthfulness in appropriate and wise ways. A former patient, Jack, was only in his late forties, but presented himself with all the debility of a seventy-year-old ruin. Morbidly obese, he needed to lose over a hundred pounds. Jack's weekly support group helped him engineer a program to rehabilitate him and achieve something that he never thought possible, a muscular physique, improved body image, endurance, stamina, increased energy, and a sense of vitality.

It's important for us, as we age, to sustain our cardio, strength training, balance, and flexibility. Also essential are the benefits of yoga that I have practiced and espoused for over thirty years and the physical and spiritual sustenance of prayer and meditation. The men in Jack's group held his feet to the fire so that he maintained the motivation to create the results that he had never been able to enact in his life before then.

Women benefit too because a man's commitment to a woman can be fostered by the depth and power of his relationship with other conscientious men. In the company of good men, men also learn to deal with women and come to terms with their issues around intimacy, either working to maintain their marriages or, if they're single, preparing themselves to be better romantic partners.

Course Corrections

No matter how old a man is when he falters, he can use it as an opportunity to make a course correction and get back on track. Every problem we face brings with it an opportunity to learn something important about ourselves. In other words, facing adversity does tend to make us stronger and helps us to expand our awareness. For a man past middle age, a course correction might be for him to discontinue being led by the values of his youth—pursuing money, prestige, fame, or position—and begin to reinvest his energies in a different facet of life, such as the spiritual path, or complete the unfinished business he has with people in his life. This pursuit can catapult him into a whole new dimension of his life purpose or destiny.

I Sought My Soul

I sought my soul,
But my soul I could not see.
I sought my God,
But my God eluded me.
I sought my brother,
And I found all three.

—Anonymous

CHAPTER 5

Being the Father You Always Wanted

The degree to which fatherhood is valued by our culture depends fundamentally on the stories men tell each other about fathering, and on the stories we tell our children.

—Richard Louv, author of *Father Love*

MANY MEN, LACKING IN adequate fathering when they were boys, continue to deprive themselves from the fathering they secretly long for by estranging themselves from other men and treating themselves in unloving, if not self-loathing ways. More and more fathers—feeling betrayed by women who have left them, confused by unspoken expectations of them as men, incapacitated by court-mandated agreements, and feeling like failures as fathers and men—are physically, emotionally, and spiritually abandoning their children.

When a man feels that he has failed, he is likely to cut himself off from his past and start again. Many men, instead of cultivating their age-appropriate grandfather energies, resurrect their father energies instead, take on a younger wife, and create a whole new family. Too often the old family is left far behind. One profound difference from our ancestors' societies is that now, if a man leaves his children, there are not usually other men from his family or community to stand in his place.

How can a man move from the process of healing his own Father Gap to becoming a good father to his children? Spiritual Warriors in the role of fathers can specifically provide the needed support for their son's journey into manhood and their daughter's journey into womanhood. Princes and princesses can be prepared and blessed as they mature into becoming kings and queens in their own right.

Trading in one's victim shroud for the mantle of personal accountability, as one chooses to be the father-to-the-man, can be quite liberating. As well, a mentor who can help to close the Father Gap can become the ally that the man was seeking from his own father. Men can mutually mentor each other and therefore create an alliance that allows and supports the growth and development of the internal father archetype, a prominent cornerstone in the foundation of a man's life structure.

When a man becomes aware of his own core wound—his Father Gap—he obviously can't ask for a do-over of his childhood. But what he can do is seek to heal the wound by reaching out to other men, thereby indirectly "re-parenting" himself and satisfying some of those lacks in his own life. This not only provides him with some of the self-fathering he craves, but it is also a significant step toward becoming a Spiritual Warrior who gracefully accepts the challenge of attaining conscious masculinity. In turn, he will be better at parenting his children and being the parent his children deserve, and he will be so much better at being able to mentor others.

A Tumultuous Time

My often strained relationship with my own father came to a head back in the 60s during the Vietnam era, a time when men in general were less interested in exploring their psyches and more interested in saving their asses. In 1965, after graduating high school,

I moved out on my own. I met Lauranne, a Licensed Vocational Nurse, while I was working as an orderly in a hospital. We started dating, wound up living together for two years, and married in 1967. I was only twenty-one years old.

The war in Vietnam was heating up, and I was hanging around with a bunch of people who had come to distrust their parents, politicians, and those who supported the War Machine. Most of my peers were opposed to the war. Many were dissidents and conscientious objectors, and a few were even draft dodgers who left for Canada.

My father had been in the service during World War II. He carried a strong sense of pride for what could be accomplished by those serving their country, especially during critical times. Needless to say, my father and I were at odds about the anti-war movement. He was opposed to demonstrations and protests, and I was an avid anti-war activist. I marched in the streets and attended peace rallies.

It was a painful time, marked by confusion and rampant mutual distrust and contempt that many fathers and sons felt for each other. This exacerbated the estrangement that had probably been fomenting for years and essentially set in motion the conditions that would be ripe for the birth of a men's movement in the mid-80s as we baby boomers moved into mid-life. My father and I found it best to avoid discussing the topic of the Vietnam War at all in order to avert a clash of our disparate ideologies.

The closest we came to any agreement was when we both admitted that under other circumstances it would have been a positive experience for me to be involved in the service. My father felt that the fellowship, camaraderie, and esprit de corps provided character-building opportunities for turning boys into men. I understood what he meant and could sense that I was missing something that he held as sacred, the ability to serve one's country as a patriot. I also knew he saw it as an initiatory right of passage into manhood.

The Vietnam war aside, my father wasn't an easy man to deal with—a complex individual who could be loving and kind one minute; stern, angry, and demanding the next. I found it difficult to live up to his perfectionist standards. I was never quite sure how to please him, which left me feeling unsettled and anxious whenever I was around him. The intimidation I felt carried forward into my relationships with other authority figures.

It became apparent to me that my self-esteem was at low ebb. I was accustomed to manifesting an assortment of neurotic symptoms since childhood, such as anxious and depressed mood swings, nervousness, irritability, and angry outbursts including explosively judgmental and hypercritical reactions directed toward Lauranne (Laurie). Essentially, I was an obsessive/compulsive perfectionist prone to displaying the classic characteristics of a control freak. I suppose it was not at all surprising that, under stress, I was resorting to the same behaviors that I experienced from my father. As they say, the apple doesn't far fall from the tree, and I was no exception.

In 1967, I transferred from Pierce College as a mid-year sophomore into the University of Southern California (USC) in Los Angeles. I was a full-time student with a student deferment. However, due to the Tet Offensive in 1968, I knew that the draft boards were discontinuing these deferments and beginning to call up students as well. A draft lottery was instituted and would determine whether or not I was draft eligible. When my lottery number turned out to be in the high range, I knew I would not be called. I continued to attend peace rallies and actively participated in the protest at the University following the Kent State shootings. I facilitated teach-ins or intense rap groups designed to help students deal with their feelings of confusion and despair concerning the direction of our country.

By the mid-70s the war was coming to an end. Laurie and I finished school in 1974, giving birth to our degrees. She earned her

B.A. and R.N. and I had earned my B.A., M.S., and Ph.D. degrees as well as a couple of counseling credentials and a license as a Marriage and Family Therapist granted in 1972. I had set myself up in private practice as a licensed psychotherapist.

A Working Therapist

Many couples that got married in the mid to late 60s were divorcing in the mid 70s, a time marked by individuality of expression and freedom from traditional and conventional ways. My seven-year relationship with Laurie also ended. We separated and divorced a year later. Looking back on it, I don't believe I would have had the discipline to work as hard on my studies had I been single through my undergraduate and graduate school years.

But by the mid-1980s, married again and the father of three young children, I was in the midst of a full blown mid-life crisis. Even though I felt that I had been going through a journey into the dark abyss, I also felt that I was finding my way to a deeper connection with my soul. I had come to realize, through my own therapy, that I had always longed for a closer relationship with my father and had turned to my mother for what my father found difficult to provide.

My mother was much easier to relate to, outgoing, and positive. I generalized the feeling of loving companionship that I had with my mother to other women. I think, like many men, I tended to turn to women for nurturance and support during trying times. This established the pattern of needing to have plenty of women around. Women were a convenient source of comfort as well as an escape from the harsh realities of life. I was beginning to understand this dynamic and to dismantle the neurotic pattern. It further served me in rising to the challenge to be a more involved father to my own children. I haven't always measured up to the standard that I set for myself, but my relationship with my own three children has grown and developed over the years. It was helped through my realizing that I needed to re-parent myself, become the loving father to the inner son, and allow that to enhance my relationship with my own children.

It is enlightening to experience, from the perspective of a father, the other side of the conflict that entangles fathers and sons during certain periods of their lives. This is a common dynamic. It is said that one will gain a greater appreciation for one's own father after becoming a father. Men frequently do not reach out to their own fathers until they are in their late thirties or forties, and their fathers are in their late sixties or seventies. Older fathers have mellowed some by then, and the experience of being a father for the younger men softens the resentments and creates a bridge of understanding that is paved with compassion for each other.

Fathers and sons know that they only have a limited number of years remaining before the father makes way for the son to ascend to the role of elder. This unspoken awareness creates the rapprochement that serves to heal the relationship and establish the intimate bond between the father and son, typically a bond that is painfully severed at the occasion of the father's passing.

When men gather in the company of other men who have discovered what really matters and who have healed their own father gap, something important begins to happen to the newer men. It's like watering wilting plants; you can clearly see them begin to revive. In the company of men who have resolved their father wounds, the new men find a home, a place to speak about their concerns—their personal pain and longing. When men sense that there are others who care and want to know them and wish to be of support, their self-esteem begins to change. They have something to strive for in the presence of men who encourage them to reach out and get on the path. They begin to thrive and they blossom into being Spiritual Warriors.

Male Kinship and the Role of Allies

An evolutionary view of the father-son relationship reveals that the key problem in our age is not that once upon a time individual fathers were deeply intimate with sons, and now they are not. It is better summed up as once upon a time men in general were intimate with boys through male kinship systems involving fathers, uncles, grandfathers, and mentors; now those systems are pretty much broken down, leaving dad to be the only king a son has but forced to work most of the time, often at a job that makes him feel more like a mule than a king. So, without a proud, nurturing male kinship system to help him raise his son, his son may never get fully raised.

For most men struggling to make a living, satisfy wives and children, and reach their dreams, there is very little support. It is imperative these days that men develop good support systems for themselves through having a circle of friends and being involved in a group of men who are soul-searching. Historically, when fathers were inevitably gone, male mentors from the tribe—grandfathers, uncles, elder brothers, and other teachers filled in.

The mother's and wife's roles in a man's search for his own support system is crucial. Parents need to remain loving with each other and work together but also need to develop reasonable independence and autonomy from each other and cultivate more attachment and bonding to their own same-sex communities and communal systems. Space can serve as an antidote to distance and estrangement, so when mates champion each other's solitude and autonomy, they actually nurture the spirit of co-creativity that feeds true interdependent and sustaining relationships.

Male kinship is key to shaping the character and moral development of boys as they mature into conscious masculinity. Fathers are crucial to providing such support for the journey into manhood. So can uncles, grandfathers, older brothers, and close friends. As I've learned through my practice, good stepfathers can also make all the difference in a boy's development when his nuclear family has dissolved into an extended family structure. And whether or not there is a strong male relative in the family, other mentors can provide the bridge for a boy to cross as he cuts the ties with his parents and leaves home on the journey of self-discovery that helps him to forge his identity. These allies are the necessary guides that support the boy during his pilgrimage. In the mythology of princes and kings, which we find in cultures all over the world, the king is always part of a male kinship system that sustains him, his family, his sacred duty, and his children.

Being a step-parent can be quite tricky. It's often plagued with the sense that because you didn't sire the children, your contribution has less significance in their lives. However, step-fathers and step-grandfathers can be integral in the lives of the children that look up to them. Adults who channel loving attention to developing youngsters can help to shape the course of their lives, and it may significantly determine what results in the outcome. My editor, Sylvia Cary, whose ex-husband is deceased, shared with me that her current husband, who is step-dad to her now adult daughters and step-grandfather to the grandkids, plays a huge role in the family structure. The grandchildren even call him "Morfar" which means "mother's father" in Danish.

Single Fathers

The United States currently has a fifty percent divorce rate, leaving many single parents with the responsibility of becoming the breadwinner and nurturer. Even though most single parents are mothers, the number of single fathers is increasing rapidly. There have been publications that have suggested that fathers are not necessary to the process of raising healthy, well-adjusted children. The truth is that there is considerable evidence to the contrary. Author Michael Gurian, a good friend and colleague, has penned close to thirty books that have had quite an influence on my thinking regarding the role of fathers in the lives of their children. Gurian states,

> "Mothers and fathers are crucial to children of all species, in their own ways, and with various degrees of proximity and closeness to their offspring. There is no 'available science' that proves fathers are not as useful as mothers, just as there is no science that proves mothers are less useful than fathers."

In the United States today, fathers make up about twenty percent of single parents. Somewhere between one and two million American children are being raised by single dads at any given time. The role of fathers, married or single, has been changing. Today, fathers are more likely to help children in a classroom setting and do household chores than in the past. Historically, fathers were not socialized to be primary caregivers, although many men did raise children on their own due to high rates of maternal death during childbirth.

In the 1950s, the stereotypical values of parental roles were more rigidly defined. The man made the money, and the mother took care of the children. Now in the 21st century, researchers have found that a father's love for his children is just as important as a mother's love (Rohner and Veneziano, 2001). A parent's love, from either parent, is found to have a positive effect on their children's happiness, well-being, and social and academic success. Single fathers can act as positive role models to children. There are no factual studies that indicate that fathers are less capable of raising children than women. Also, no factual studies show that children raised by men are more likely to use drugs or engage in sex at an earlier age.

It is helpful for single fathers to be educated in what needs to be done in order to successfully raise children on their own. The three main elements that are essential in raising children are time, interaction, and maintaining healthy relationships. Children with fathers at home tend to do better in school, are less prone to depression, and are more successful in relationships (Sylvester & Reich 2000). Also, father-child interaction has been shown to promote a child's well-being, perceptual abilities, and competency for relatedness with others, even at a young age (Kraupe 1993). The bond between father and child is just as important as the mother's in the overall social and emotional development of a child. A 1996 study by McGill University found that fathers who spent time alone bonding with their children more than twice per week brought up the most compassionate adults.

When one of my patients, a single-father, needed to make the tough decision to send his son to a wilderness program and residential school, he had to take a long hard look at himself. His sense of his fathering was called into question. He also had to come to terms with not having given enough attention to his daughter. He was allowing his disdain for his ex-wife to get in the way of his desire to be more fully present to his children's needs. Through the support of his weekly men's group and due to his willingness to courageously examine his parenting and his motives, he discovered new dimensions to his manhood when he made the decision to step up and take a firm and commanding stand with his kids. Four years later his son is in college, holding down a job, and living on his own. His daughter is maturing and no longer plays her mother and father against each other.

Stay-At-Home Dads

The number of stay-at-home dads has been gradually increasing, especially in developed Western nations. Increasingly, disparaging stereotypes are giving way to a more positive portrayal in the media, especially in the United States. However, in some regions of the world the stay-at-home dad remains culturally unacceptable.

There are several reasons why some families feel that it would be more beneficial for the father to be the primary caregiver while the mother works outside of the home. The decision to use a stay-at-home dad arrangement is most commonly due to economic reasons. The current economic downturn has caused an unemployment rate on par with that of the Great Depression of the 1930s. Men en masse are out of work and can't find jobs. At the same time, women are progressing into higher-paying jobs.

Financial ramifications come into play when deciding whether the mother or father should become the stay-at-home parent. Many middle-aged men have become essentially unemployable, thereby causing a role reversal. In cases where the woman is the higher-paid it makes economic sense for her to continue to work while the man takes on the caregiver role. Also, the mother's job may offer the health care benefits for the family whereas the father's may not.

With the proliferation of telecommuting, many men are also able to work from home. In this regard, a father is contributing financially to the family while also acting as the primary caregiver of the family's children. Differences in schedules can also account for some of the stay-at-home dads. Sometimes, the mother works odd hours like, for example, a nurse that works the swing shift.

Fixed gender roles have become less prominent in the Western world in recent years, allowing men to make their own choices without regard to traditional gender-based roles. Some men who choose the role of stay-at-home dad may do so because they enjoy being an active part of their children's lives, while in other families, the mother wants to pursue her career. Some retired males who marry a younger woman decide to become stay-at-home dads while their wives work because they want a "second chance" to watch a child grow up in a second or third marriage. However, carrying the financial burden and dealing with children's attachment to the dad can be difficult on a working mother.

Some men struggle to find acceptance within the role of stay-at-home dad despite the many gains that have been made. Many worry about losing business skills and their "professional place in line." The role of stay-at-home dad is difficult for men who feel as though they had no option. It is hard for these men to adapt from being a financial provider in the family to being a homemaker. The men who willingly choose to become a stay-at-home dad are much more satisfied with their role in the family.

Robert Frank, a professor of child development at Oakton Community College in Illinois, conducted a study comparing households with a stay-at-home dad and households with a stay-at-home mom. His study concluded that women were still able to form a strong bond with their children despite working full-time outside of the home. Also, women working full time were often more engaged with their children on a day-to-day basis than their male counterparts. His study concluded that in a family with a stay-at-home dad arrangement, the maternal and paternal influences are equally strong. This contrasts with the more traditional family structure where the father works outside of the home and the mother stays home with the children. In this type of arrangement, the mother's influence is extremely strong, whereas the father's is relatively insignificant. The study found that both parents play an equal role in a child's development, but the stay-at-home dad arrangement is the most beneficial for the child.

It is becoming more important and more advantageous for men to establish fulfilling relationships with their children. They are beginning to value these relationships over financial gains. A survey conducted by Minnesota's Department for Families and Children's Services shows that men consider child-care to be far more important than a paycheck. Of 600 dads surveyed, a majority said their most important role was to "show love and affection" to kids. "Safety and protection" came next, "moral guidance," "taking time to play," and "teaching and encouraging." "Financial care" finished last.

Many men are now becoming more involved in their children's lives, and because of that many men now have a better understanding of what life is like for their child growing up in the current times. Because fathers are immersed in their children's lives, many of the so-called "manly" things men do are pushed aside for their children. This allows children, especially male children, to grow up without a misogynistic outlook on life given to them by their fathers. These children are more compassionate because they have learned compassion and caring from their fathers. These stay-at-home dads, however, are not embarrassed about themselves or their roles. They know that they are fulfilling their role as primary caregiver. Later in life the father will serve as a close friend of the teenager. As the children become young adults and begin raising families of their own, the father will be not only a good grandparent but a good source of advice as to how children should be raised.

Nick Rath, one of the men of our Sacred Path community who teaches parenting classes for the Los Angeles Unified School District as well as on our men's retreats, believes that the role of parents is to support children in growing up to become successful adults in the world. He doesn't use the word *raise* because he essentially believes that children will *rise up* when they have the proper guidance and support that helps them to realize that it is their own responsibility to grow and develop utilizing the opportunities that are available to them along the way.

Fathering: Lessons Learned, Lessons Taught

In Michael Gurian's book, *The Wonder of Boys: What Parents, Mentors and Educators Can Do to Shape Boys into Exceptional Men*, (Tarcher/Putnam, 1996) he states that, "Among all his other ways of nurturing a son, a father raises his son in the father's shadow, a shadow both dark yet also luminous, in which the son will learn essential lessons about how to live, first as a boy, then as a man. Fathers teach through modeling behavior. Whether it's through the mistakes he makes or through his successes, a father teaches the wisdom lessons potentially learned by how he expresses his beliefs, values, attitudes, and conduct. A father's manifest weaknesses and strengths help a son to develop his own character and personality." Gurian goes on to say, "Whether teaching a son through what-not-to-do examples, commandments for living, or why fences must be built, or what it means to have a sacred mission, the father blesses the son with a man's power to shape both his inner and outer world as a male."

Gurian concludes that,

> "Every son wants from his father to gain a sense of mission in life and receive permission from an elder male to pursue the mission; to feel a strong, loving masculine ground beneath his feet so that he will not, once he's an adult, have to say to his wife, his children, or to strangers, I don't know what a man is, please teach me; to be challenged toward a vision of faraway stars—impractical dreams and ambitions, that he may make, one day, possible; to learn what part of the sacred circle of human and spiritual life he will be responsible for; and to be mirrored by an intimate elder male and found, in that mirroring, to be a loving, wise, and powerful man."

The Role of Spiritual Warrior Fathers in the World Today

The picture a man displays through the role of fathering radiates outward as part of what gives existential meaning to individual and community life. Through the role, the person is connected to self, family, society, and earth. Without the role, the person would drift through life without purpose.

My friend, Malidoma Somé, a Shaman of the Dagara Tribe of the Burkina Faso area of western Africa, once told me that there was no word for depression in his tribe because everyone born into the tribe came to understand what their purpose and importance was to the whole of the community. Each was born into an integral system of interconnectedness so that no one felt estranged or unimportant.

Individuals were viewed with inquisitiveness and called upon to impart their own wisdom to benefit the tribe; ergo, depression was not symptomatic. Depression runs rampant and is endemic to our modern day culture and societal make-up.

Our boys, young men, and our mature men are calling on us to explore with clarity what the role of fathers should be. If we do not provide a sacred role for our boys as they grow, they are more likely to join a gang, abuse their lovers, abandon their children, subsist in emotional isolation, and become addicted, hyper-materialistic, lonely, and unhappy. A boy needs a structure and discipline in which to learn who he is. He needs to live a journey that has clear responsibilities and goals. He needs a role in life. Without these, without the role training that accompanies these, he does not know his sacred and important objectives in life.

Without the disciplined role that a father exudes, sons and daughters do not know how to gauge their actions and behavior that manifest their intentions, achievements, and successes. Especially in areas of responsible relationship, children will never quite know what they have accomplished while experimenting with the sacred tasks of love, caring, and commitment. When fathers are firm and commanding in their role structure, they provide a context made up of boundaries and limits. It gives their children something to lean against that is solid, has margins, and provides containment.

The male role of father should rise from the seed of this word: husbandry, which means to dwell. In ancient cultures a husband was a household dweller who felt a deep masculine bond to his home and land. Husbanding implied generating and maintaining stable relationships with self, family, community, culture, and earth.

Boys and men at their best will mature into a role in which they are not only required to but want to be good husbands and fathers—husbands and fathers of families, stewards of communities and cultures around the world.

Chapter 6

Mentoring

It is the task of a good man to help those in misfortune.

—Sophocles (497-406 BC)

MY BEST FRIEND, ALLY, and genuine mentor for the first twenty years of my life was my grandfather. His name was Lawrence Stewart, but everyone called him Stew. He was just that sort of a fellow, too, who would answer to a nickname like that. Scottish, six-foot two-inches, perpetually grinning, bald, and rugged; he was bigger than life itself. He had a huge lap that could hold both his dog and me at the same time.

Stew was a man's man who loved the great outdoors and cherished fishing and hunting as expressions of his personal relationship with the great outdoors. He normally wore moccasins, a deer hide jacket, suspenders, and a broad brimmed hat. The man loved his garden and was especially proud of his multicolored rose bushes. In the kitchen, he reined as king. From my boyish perspective, there was no match for some of the culinary surprises that he whipped up and there was no limit to the amount of ice cream we could consume on a single summer afternoon.

My grandfather was a self-taught carpenter and an artist who had a shop in the back yard that served as a sacred container for his special creations. The shop had all the right tools including every size nail and screw, and it was home for a vast array of paints and pastels of every hue. This space had no doubt been sanctified for a wizard to fashion the very things that would delight a young, aspiring apprentice.

As an ally, Stew accepted and validated me without question. He unconditionally loved me, and I knew that I was pleasing to him. He admired me and always seemed curious and interested in what I was thinking, dreaming, and doing. I could fantasize with him, and we would tell tales, spin yarns, make up stories, and even on occasion, act them out.

As a mentor, he taught me how to ride a horse, steer a boat, tie a fishhook, and whittle a piece of wood. One afternoon he took me to the Van Nuys airport and hired a small plane to take me flying. The pilot let me take the co-pilot's steering wheel and guide the plane for a while. It was a thrilling and memorable experience. Stew encouraged me to go for it, not to hold back but to stretch and reach for what I wanted. I felt his support and knew that he stood behind what I was doing. This provided the needed safety to attempt the new, the daring or even the seemingly impossible. Unquestionably, I felt that he was on my side.

My grandfather served me in many ways, not least among them was being a model of what a true friend and ally could be to another. He stood for loyalty and devotion. He displayed strength and courage. He was commanding while avoiding being demanding. He had a gentle side and even a vulnerable side that I saw from time to time. His compassion and understanding always revealed the depth of his caring. He told me his truth and made room for mine.

Stew displayed the traits of a man who had grown up during the Depression and had learned to make it on his own and fight for what he knew was right. Even his John Wayne-like characteristics, which have grown less fashionable over time, were steeped in tradition and grounded in his own personal history. As a high-ranking Mason he embraced the same daring pioneer spirit that helped to guide the founding fathers of this country. He represented freedom for me, the freedom to be myself, no matter what. My grandfather made an impact on me, leaving an impression that will be felt for my entire life. The legacy that he passed on has given me the courage to embark on the journey and the strength to endure the tests along the way. I think the pain of his death was too overwhelming for me at the time, so I avoided authentically grieving the loss until I was around the age of forty. It was in the midst of my midlife crisis that I finally allowed myself to realize how deeply I had missed him and how much I would have liked to have his soothing support during such a challenging time in my life.

When I talk with others, they frequently convey stories about a special relationship with a grandparent or another elder. An honoring is expressed as they speak of their mentors with respect and appreciation. Sylvia Cary, my writing coach and editor, told me about an important mentor during her younger years. She shared,

> "I had a step-grandfather who played that role for me. He was a gun expert who wrote gun articles for *True* Magazine. His name was Lucian Cary. He and my step-grandmother lived on 125 acres in upper Connecticut, and he'd take me out and show me how to shoot clay pigeons and how to make bullets from molten lead, and I used to make dollhouse furniture in their barn using all his shop equipment. I still have a few items I made. I never knew my other grandfathers. Both died before I was born. So my cranky grandfather Lucian was the one who filled this role for me, even though I was a girl. But that didn't seem to matter to him that I was 'just a girl.' He was my mentor all the same."

Mentors

"Mentor" first appears in Homer's *Odyssey* as a loyal adviser of Odysseus who was entrusted with the care and education of Telemachus, the son of Odysseus and Penelope. Telemachus' name in Greek means "far from battle," perhaps reflecting his absence from the Trojan War.

Odysseus was one of the most influential Greek champions during the Trojan War. When he had been absent for over ten years, Penelope was being urged to marry one of the insolent and unruly suitors who infested their home. As a young man, Telemachus was much favored by the goddess Athena. When Athena visited Telemachus she took the disguise of Mentor to hide herself from the suitors of Telemachus' mother. As Mentor, the goddess encouraged Telemachus to stand up against the suitors and go abroad to find out what happened to his father. With Athena's help, he sailed to Pylos and then to Lacedaemon, to inquire after his father's fate. On the journey back to Ithaca, Athena advised him to return by a different route, in order to avoid an ambush planned by the disgruntled suitors.

By the time Telemachus got back to Ithaca, he was a much more self-confident and assertive young man. He got to prove his newly acquired maturity when he joined Odysseus in slaughtering the suitors and then standing up to their outraged relatives in the final scene of the Odyssey.

Because of Mentor's relationship with Telemachus, and the disguised Athena's encouragement and practical plans for dealing with personal dilemmas, the name Mentor has been adopted in English as a term meaning someone who imparts wisdom to and shares knowledge with a less experienced colleague.

A Mentor's Skills

Throughout history, a mentor has been a wise and trusted counselor, usually at least ten to fifteen years older than his protégé or student.

The mentor has skill and has performed his craft to a level of mastery. He, as an example or model, passes on his skill and shows the student how dreams can be realized.

The mentor recognizes the meaningful issues in the student. He enhances the experience for the younger man who has already achieved something and is looking for more. The "puer," which is Latin for "boy," is an uninitiated or naïve male who longs for someone to acknowledge his gifts, to validate him, and to bestow a blessing. The father often misses this opportunity, since the role of provider usually takes him away from the house. When the father is away, the house is turned over to the mentor.

It is not traditionally the father's job to see to his son's soul, nor is it the mentor's job to put a roof over the boy's head or to protect him. The mentor provides a bridge away from the father, guiding the young man to cut the parental ties and bond with nature. The mentor sees the boy's spirit and gives him a name. He opens the world of the boy's interest and guides him in finding his direction.

There are countless numbers of young men in this country who are starving from father-hunger and who have never experienced the mutual admiration inherent in a mentoring relationship. Due to the breakdown of the nuclear family over the last forty years, family members have drifted apart and are now suffering the pain of that alienation and isolation. We have a vast generation of men going through midlife and careening from crisis to crisis, longing for the understanding, wisdom, and guidance of a ritual elder. Many men remain clueless concerning their needs, and yet there are those who are searching for greater understanding of what it means to be a balanced male in a changing world and are eager for the spiritual initiation into conscious manhood.

With so much importance these days directed toward the young and the youthful lifestyle in this country, I have observed a growing tendency to ignore or even neglect our ritual elders as unpleasant reminders of aging and mortality. Many of our seniors have been passed over and have tended to lose sight of their own intrinsic worth. I sincerely encourage that we don't forget the inherent value of the grandfather as a natural resource but, rather, commission our elders to pass on their history through mentoring their offspring.

Walter's Journey into the Wilderness

In the early phase of my work on this book, one of the Elders in our Sacred Path Community, Walter Atkinson, had been diagnosed with cancer and his condition had turned grave. The cancer had metastasized to his lungs, brain, and liver. He'd been undergoing chemotherapy and had been in and out of the hospital. All of this was starkly similar to my father's battle with cancer, and Walter was fighting his in a way that truly reminded me of my father's vigilant stand against the disease. Walter's physicians had informed him that he had about one year to live.

During his last year Walter worked diligently on his book, *The Wilderness*, and prepared for a Call to Adventure Retreat, scheduled for the spring, in which he wanted to initiate his grandson, Benjamin, into manhood. Walter's passion had been focused on mentoring and creating rites of passage for youth into adulthood.

I had known Walter for about a dozen years. He attended the retreats on a regular basis and served on the Wisdom Council Staff as a team leader for our groups or tribes, as they have been called. The men had come to admire and respect Walter as a beloved Elder and ally. Walter loved the younger fellas that participated with us, and he generously brought the energy of the grandfather to them.

In 1998, I had transferred to Walter the 501c3 corporate status of the Men's Center of Los Angeles, which had been founded as a non-profit public benefit corporation in 1988. I had come to the conclusion that I could no longer serve as CEO of the corporation due to the increasing demands of my private practice and had been looking for someone to step forward to take over for me as administrator; otherwise, I would need to shut it down. Since I had no volunteers, after careful consideration, I decided to give the 501c3 corporate shell to someone, or to an organization, that could make good use of it.

I knew that Walter had a vision for creating a school that would provide rites of passage initiation for youth into adulthood. We discussed the matter and decided that Walter would become the CEO of a newly formed non-profit corporation—so the Millennium Oaks Institute was founded. I came on the board as Director of Project Development. Our unified objective was to initially create rites of passage programs for youth and eventually launch a school with this focus as its foundation.

Two years later, another one of our men, Tim Cook, approached me with an idea he had for his Master's Thesis. I had come to know Tim as a robust, passionate man who cared deeply about "menswork" and who displayed a special interest in older men mentoring younger men. He wanted to research rites of passage initiatory rituals for boys into manhood. I had already been considering setting up a retreat for boys to parallel our Sacred Path Retreat for men. I had wanted to call it the Odyssey Youth Mentoring Project, after the epic poem attributed to Homer.

Years before, I had heard that message that I described at the beginning of this book—that same inner voice that spoke to me about other matters of importance—telling me that if I were to "bring good men together and help to bring out the best in them" they would in turn give back through devoted service to other men. I felt that we had enough men, after ten years of retreats, to staff a retreat for youth.

Tim and I decided to combine his thesis research with my concept for a youth oriented retreat. He invited me to sit on his thesis committee as an outside advisor. I was honored to participate on his journey. We then spoke with Walter concerning his vision for rites of passage and decided to co-sponsor a retreat through the Millennium Oaks Institute in association with The Men's Center of Los Angeles. Tim suggested that we name it Call to Adventure, after the second of the twelve stages of the initiatory journey into manhood as outlined by mythologist, Joseph Campbell.

Timothy "Whispering Eagle" Aguilar, Shaman and spiritual teacher, had been working with me as a facilitator for our Sacred Path Men's Retreats. He also had a strong connection with our vision for initiating boys into manhood. He was enthusiastic about the creation of a separate retreat for youth.

As a collaborative result of the occasionally strained synergy of the four diverse characters of Tim, Walter, Timothy, and yours truly, a mutual vision of a rites of passage retreat for boys was born. The first Call to Adventure Retreat was convened in the spring of 2000. It was deemed to be a huge success in every way but financially. Actually, we broke even, so it couldn't really be considered a financial failure. Our second CTA Retreat in 2002 provided the same results. We were quite satisfied with the work that we were doing with boys, especially offering the retreat through scholarship to boys who were less fortunate.

In April of 2004, we held a combined Sacred Path Retreat for men and a Call to Adventure Retreat offering a rites of passage experience for eighty-five men and youth. With the knowledge that this would undoubtedly be the last CTA Retreat that Walter would attend, we approached the event with a mixture of emotions. It was a blend of somberness, sadness, and jubilant celebration.

Walter's two grown sons, Charlie and Tom, including Tom's son, Benjamin, flew out from the East Coast to attend. For years, Walter had looked forward to Benjamin turning thirteen so that he could participate in the Call to Adventure. The time had finally come. Little did we know at the time that when the occasion would finally arrive, it would serve as one of the most memorable experiences of completion that any of us had ever witnessed.

Walter, with the help of a group of dedicated men and women, designed and crafted a replica (built to scale) of a bridge for the participants to cross as a ritual ceremony at the conclusion of the retreat. This would signify that the youth had crossed over from boyhood to manhood. Walter graciously invited any man who so desired to make the tricky crossing. We knew that there were plenty of men who wanted to enjoy the experience of being welcomed personally by Walter into conscious manhood.

Everyone, all eighty-five of us, crossed the ritual bridge and was greeted by Walter as each one stepped back onto terra firma. He lovingly placed his hands on each man's shoulders, looking each squarely in the eyes and bestowing a blessing that shall never be forgotten. Watching Walter bless Benjamin was one of those Kodak moments, a snapshot that any one of us can retrieve at will.

I was one of the last to cross. As Walter and I hugged after he bestowed his blessing on me, we agreed that the bridge was the perfect ritual to cap off an incredible retreat. This was the culmination of his dream, the ability to welcome his grandson and two sons into manhood and to leave a legacy for the men to carry on in his name. After that I had a feeling that it would not be long before Walter would make his transition from this world to the next.

Walter was in and out of the hospital following the retreat. On one of his stays in the hospital I visited with him while I was en route to be a guest on a radio show. I helped him put on his slippers and robe so that we could take a walk around the hallway. With my right hand, I pushed a stand on wheels that held his intravenous feeding bottles, and I placed my left arm around his waist to steady him as we trudged the circular corridor. It was a close and tender moment for us as we discussed a variety of topics including the Hubble Telescope, other engineering feats, and of course men's work and rites of passage for youth. Walter's mind was sharp and his sense of humor was intact as I chided him that "he was still an ornery cuss." Walter and I would occasionally bang our hard heads together, but we always retained a respect for each other as we authentically offered our differences of opinion. We frequently shared a good laugh, and I loved to tease him and watch him erupt with fits of joy.

After Walter's last hospitalization, a particularly brutal three-week bout in the Intensive Care Unit, he was barely able to fly to New Hampshire. This episode was nearly his undoing. He wanted to get back to New Hampshire for Benjamin's brother Mathew's birthday and to the cabin on the lake where he so loved to visit each summer for a month with his entire family. This time it would be for the final farewell.

One of our men, Dan Stanton, a longstanding and highly dedicated member of our Community, sent this letter to me after a visit with Walter just a few days before Walter's passing. He requested that I forward it to all the men:

Tuesday, July 27, 2004

Dear Brothers,

I visited Walter yesterday at his New Hampshire lake cabin that they affectionately call the "The Camp." Walter's sons Charlie and Tom were there as well as his daughter Liz, daughter-in-law, and grandson Ben. During the several hours that I visited Walter, nurses, neighbors, and friends stopped by to see Walter and his family.

The Camp is in a beautiful location next to a large natural lake with the sounds of loons in the air. There are blueberry bushes all around the cabin. The air was cool for a July summer day and the humidity almost non-existent. Oak and maple trees can be found throughout the area and little chipmunks were chattering and scavenging everywhere you looked. In the cabin a bed was set up in the main living area facing the windows overlooking the lake. Next to the bed was a wheelchair and small folding table with a laptop setup and handwritten notes containing changes for Walter's book "The Wilderness."

Walter was resting comfortably dozing in and out as we sat around his bed. His skin and eyes were extremely yellow, but his hands were very soft to the touch. His breathing was very raspy, but his mind was still alert. We talked about family, especially his grandson, about the men's work, the Call to Adventure, and his book. In between taking droplets of water from his daughter, he would talk, and we would listen. Continuing the work of the Call to Adventure (C2A) is really important to Walter. He felt that the combined C2A and Sacred Path Retreat was a huge success. He would have liked to see more talking stick and community time with the young men; otherwise he felt everything was perfect. He informed me that his grandson Ben is one of our biggest supporters of C2A and that he would like to see a C2A event on the east coast. Walter then asked me how I felt about continuing the C2A in New England. I told him that it is a passion I have and that I would be honored to continue this worthy endeavor. I told Walter that several men had approached me from the Wisdom Council, during the last retreat, offering their assistance and participation when we were ready to proceed.

Walter then asked Charlie to make sure that I received the pictures and plans for the "The Bridge to Manhood," several of his talking sticks, and a few other items that he wanted to remain with the C2A. Ben then came over, put his hand on my shoulder and said, "When you're ready to begin the planning, I will be there."

The rest of the morning continued with sharing memories, stories, laughing, and crying. When the nurse arrived to check on

Walter, Ben and I went outside, so he could show me around. We walked to the lake and stood looking across at a few sailboats and loons that were enjoying the warm water of the lake. The water was crystal clear. Ben asked me if I wanted to pick some blueberries along the coast, and I said, "sure," and he said, "Take off your shoes and follow me." Before I knew it, we were walking in the lake along the rocky bottom water, heading towards some bushes along the bank. There were thousands of beautiful blueberries. Ben quickly pointed out that the dark berries next to the blueberries are called "Dog Berries." They have a dark juice instead of the light color juice of the blueberry. He said if you eat one of the "Dog Berries" you'd be sick within two minutes. Enough blueberries were picked to make a pie later in the evening. Ben then showed me where his grandpa had setup a sacred space area within the trees. This is a favorite camping site that the men of the family enjoy. There was a sitting area on rocks and a circle of stones for a fire-pit. It was a very peaceful and lovely spot amongst the trees.

Back inside we visited a little longer. Walter was beginning to get really sleepy because the nurse started giving him morphine to keep him comfortable. The family was instructed on how to use the morphine and was given a phone number for a nursing service that was available twenty-four hours per day in the event they need immediate help. Walter and I held hands, and I asked him if there was any message that he wanted me to pass on to his fellow brothers in California. He said, "Yes, please tell them good-bye for me and to light candles for me when I am gone." We then hugged and told each other how much we loved one another. So my brothers, please light your candles and think of Walter. He is and was a good man that gave to others and tried to be the best person he could. He touched the hearts of many young men and brothers. He has a wonderful loving family that is taking care of him during his final hours in a place he loves. We all should be so lucky to have such a place to spend our remaining time before we leave this world.

God Bless & Namaste,
Your brother from New England,
Daniel

P.S. One additional comment: A strange thing happened to me when I was about five miles from Walter's cabin. I was driving along the two lane road when a bird flew in the open window of my van, just past my head, and crashed into the inside passenger door. I pulled over and found that a yellow finch had flown in and died when it hit the door. After Ben had shown me around the "The Camp," I told him what had happened when I arrived, and he helped me bury the beautiful bird near Walter's sacred area. We placed one of the stones to mark the spot and Ben placed four sticks around the stone to mark the four directions, just like he learned at the sweat lodge at the C2A. We then said a blessing and went back into see his grandpa. We did not understand why that had happened. Was it because I needed to pull off of the road at that moment? Was it because it was an opportunity to share death with Ben, before his grandfather passed away? Or was it just a sign that the color of the bird and the state of Walter provided a connection or statement that the end was coming soon? We'll never know, but Ben and I were able to share the moment that was very special to both of us.

Walter had a brief phone conversation on Saturday, July 24th with my son, Ian. The two had grown quite close over the years. Walter took a special interest in Ian and was very much a grandfather figure to him. They had even spent time together outside of the men's community visiting a gem show one day and sharing a meal from time to time. After his conversation with Walter, Ian called me in deep grief. Their goodbyes had left him bereft. This was essentially the third grandfather he had to bid farewell to in the past two years. My wife's father had died in December of 2002, and my father had passed away in June of 2003. Ian had been pretty broken up when they were speaking the day before. I affirmed how much he loved him. He knew and said he loved him too. He was so glad to see how Ian had matured into manhood and felt that he was a good example for the younger boys.

We shared memorable experiences from past retreats. He particularly loved the scenes of Conrad and Mathew as they stood together in the center of the community and spoke to each other from the depths of their hearts, man to man. He thought that his speaking to Benjamin in front of the men had served to reinforce the importance of the grandfathers in the lives of grandsons and elders in the lives of younger men. I assured him that it was an indelible imprint in the minds and souls of all of us and something that would inspire us to attract more grandfather elders into our community.

Even though his book was not finished, he was done with it. He had written as much as he could in the time he was given. He had made notes for its publication and for four sequels to be penned by other authors. *The Wilderness* was the synthesis of a life's journey, the culmination of the experiences and lessons that had served to impact and shape the man who lived his life as Walter Atkinson, our beloved elder, father, grandfather, mentor, and friend.

I thanked Walter for everything that he had been to us and given of himself so elegantly. I told him that I loved him, and he said he loved me as well. We said our goodbyes. We were complete.

Walter passed away peacefully in his sleep at 4:00 pm on Tuesday, July 27th, 2004. In his memory, we created the Walter Atkinson Memorial Scholarship Fund to raise money, through donations, that allows youth in need to attend our retreats. Walter is missed, and yet his legacy lives on as a guiding light for our rights of passage work in the world.

Coach

Being a coach for your children and others when they are engaging in sports is one way to be a mentor. We have a lot to learn from those who perform this role well. I have been impressed with how Steve Branker, Associate Director of the Men's Center, has used his coaching skills to gain the trust and attention of the boys that attend our Call to Adventure, Rites of Passage Retreats. Steve works with a basketball, tossing it to one boy after the other, while he speaks to them about important matters like disavowing drugs, gang involvement, violence, and other matters of conduct and character. The boys have to keep their ears open and their eyes on him since they never know if the ball is coming to them.

As a USC guy myself, I had long admired football coaches like John McKay, John Robinson, and of course, Pete Carroll, who rebuilt our football program after over fifteen years of lackluster coaching and far too many losses.

Though we're supposed to be cross-town rivals and not like anything having to do with the other program I freely admit that one man I had long admired as being a model of a truly good man and mentor to countless many is legendary UCLA basketball coach—"the Wizard of Westwood"—John Wooden, who won ten NCAA basketball championships at UCLA, the last in 1975. Nobody has ever come within six of him. He won eighty-eight straight games between January 30, 1971, and January 17, 1974. Nobody has come within forty-two since. When you hear the word coach it has almost become synonymous with John Wooden who consistently demonstrated the characteristics that had brought him the well-deserved acknowledgment throughout the years. His 1997 book, *Wooden:*

A lifetime of Observations and Reflections On and Off the Court (McGraw-Hill, 1977) is one of the top-selling titles of its kind.

His suggestions were often disarmingly simple—lessons culled from childhood on an early twentieth century farm in Centerton, Indiana. As one admirer put it, "There has never been another coach like John Wooden. He is quiet as April snow and square as a game of checkers; loyal to one woman, one school, one way; walking around campus in his sensible shoes and Jimmy Stewart morals."

Coach Wooden was a living link to an era in which wisdom was hard-won and time-tested. Wooden said, "I tried to rely on the teachings of my father to begin with." One of his key precepts is "Don't be too concerned with regard to things over which you have no control, because that will eventually have an adverse effect on things over which you have control." "Discipline yourself, and others won't need to," Coach would say. "Never lie, never cheat, never steal," and, "Earn the right to be proud and confident."

He believed the things within a person's control, such as attention to detail and dedication to hard work, are more important than the talents with which someone is born. His credo is available to everyone, and it comes down simply to hard work and preparation, both mental and physical. He surmised that failure is not making the effort to execute near your own particular level of competition. One of his oft-used expressions is: "Failing to prepare is preparing to fail. Now, in some cases, the other fellow is just better than you are, and that's no failure." He admired the "everyman" who achieves excellence through steadiness and continual effort and belief in oneself: "In times of crisis, the best players won't start forcing things and getting away from what got them there in the first place. I believe it's the confidence they have in themselves, without being over-confident. The better ones believe in themselves, probably more than anything else."

Many a father has been known to teach his son and daughter that

Coach's "Pyramid of Success" was responsible for building the success of a sports team by building the character of each of the players. It was the sense that Coach understood something essential about character, not just basketball. He was first and foremost a teacher of life and championed the time-honored elements of industriousness, friendship, loyalty, cooperation, and enthusiasm that formed the foundation of the pyramid with success at its peak.

Coach had his rules and expected his players to abide by them. For example, no long hair and no facial hair. "They take too long to dry, and you could catch cold leaving the gym," he'd say. That one drove his players bonkers. One day, All-America center Bill Walton showed up with a full beard. "It's my right," he insisted. Wooden asked if he believed that strongly. Walton said he did. "That's good, Bill," Coach said. "I admire people who have strong beliefs and stick by them, I really do. We're going to miss you." Walton shaved right then and there. Throughout the years Walton called once a week to tell Coach he loved him.

In his personal life, Coach Wooden lived the code that he taught. He was humble, self-effacing, always dignified, and gentle-spoken. Most of all he was a man of devout faith. It is said that his sharpest curse, uttered during the heat of battle on the hardwood, is familiar to any Midwesterner: "Goodness gracious sakes alive."

During the last three decades of his life Coach lived modestly in a condo in the San Fernando Valley. It was there that he wrote a letter each month to his wife, Nel, of fifty-three years who had died in 1985. He placed each letter on her pillow. Following her death he continued to sleep on his side of the bed next to where he had carefully laid out her nightgown on her side of the bed. "I'm not afraid to die," he would say. "Death is my only chance to be with her again."

I was touched by the devotion he felt for Nel and quite moved by the last story I had heard about him concerning the day before he left us. His son had come to visit him in the hospital, and Coach asked if he would shave him. "Of course, Dad," his son said. "I want to look good for your mother when I see her," Coach expressed.

When a Mentor Appears

I have been quite fortunate to have had many mentors over the years. Some of them have played minor roles, and others have made a more significant influence on shaping my growth and development as a man. During my younger formative years there were certain teachers, coaches, camp counselors, and adult friends of the family that made a positive impact on me.

When I was in high school during the early 1960s at Notre Dame in the San Fernando Valley, two of the Brothers of Holy Cross helped me get through that part of my four-year education relatively unfettered. Brother Leonard, my religion and algebra teacher, and Brother Marcel, one of my instructors for Latin, who was also the Prefect of Discipline, went above the call of duty to provide some much needed mentorship. The turbulent teenage years can be quite tricky for boys, but with structure and guidance the path becomes less problematic.

Brother Leonard and I would play handball, take grueling bicycle rides, and don boxing gloves and spar. The rule was that he could block with both gloves but could only hit with his left. Nonetheless, he would get the better of me, but I learned to take a punch. Brother Leonard became a missionary and teaches in South America. Brother Marcel, an avid fan, took me to my first hockey game. Marcel left the order after Vatican II and moved back to his hometown in New Orleans. He just turned eighty, and we exchange Christmas cards every year.

Following high school I spent a year and a half at Pierce Community College getting my grades up so that I could attend the University of Southern California. My first psychology professor, Richard Lees, and I developed a close relationship. He encouraged me to move out of my parent's home at age nineteen and into my own bachelor style apartment, moving from the San Fernando Valley to the Westside. He and I spent time together working out in the gym and enjoying the beach scene in the South Bay. I was developing a sense of autonomy and the confidence to explore life on a broader horizon.

I transferred to USC in 1967 as a mid-year sophomore. I was twenty-one years of age. One of my classes at USC was a particularly popular course in abnormal psychology taught by Dr. Leonard Olinger. After a few weeks, I asked Dr. Olinger if I might speak with him after class. When the other students had left the classroom, I approached him stating that the text for the course read just as if it could have been my own autobiography.

I couldn't hide my dismay with how the personal issues with which I had been coping were becoming unbearable. I had recently married, and I knew that my relationship with my wife was severely strained as a result of my emotionally labile temperament. Dr. Olinger, a wise, kind, and caring man, offered to remain after class for the next several weeks providing free therapy for me. In my desire to repay him, I offered to assist him with the grading of papers and preparation for class. He arranged for me to be paid as his teaching assistant and then subsequently as his psychology intern.

A true mentor/protégé relationship commenced which resulted in my coming to know myself better and helped me in making significant strides in personal and professional development. It was to a large degree a result of this relationship that I decided to make a course correction shifting my career objective from medicine to psychology.

I have had the privilege and pleasure of maintaining a connection with Len over the years, forty-five to be exact. I know he'd prefer that I keep his age between the two of us, and even at his age I can attest that he's as sharp as ever. He is still practicing, treating fifteen patients a week in the office and on the phone. When we meet for lunch I love to remind him of the lessons that he taught me. There are so many stories that I can vividly recall and recount. One of my favorites was an occasion one night after class that was convened in a building in downtown Los Angeles.

It was about 10 pm as we left the building and passed by the homeless who were preparing to spend the night dug into some make-shift shelter on the street. I tended not to make contact with them in order to maintain a boundary. However, one fella asked me if I could spare a quarter. I declined, and he said, "Well sir, that is your prerogative, thank you anyway." Dr. Olinger and I walked a few yards past the man and then he asked me if I heard how the homeless man had pronounced the word "prerogative."

I answered, "Yes," and queried him as to the significance.

He said, "He pronounced it correctly demonstrating that he was undoubtedly an educated person. Many people, even if they often use the word in their vocabulary, will pronounce it, '*perogative.*'"

Dr. Olinger said, "Follow me" and turned to walk back toward the homeless man. He reached into his pocket and pulled out a dollar bill and gave it to him. The man thanked him. "May I ask you a question?" Dr. Olinger asked him.

"Of course, sir," the man responded.

Dr. Olinger then asked, "I'd like to know what you did before you became homeless."

The man paused, dropped his head for a brief moment, and said, "I was a doctor; in fact, I was a surgeon."

Dr. Olinger then asked if he had been married and had a family.

"Yes, sir, I was married and have three children, though I've lost touch with them."

"What happened?" Dr. Olinger asked.

"I couldn't control the booze. It just took over my life, and I lost everything."

We spoke with him for a few more minutes, and as we walked to our cars, Dr. Olinger said, "You see you never know the circumstances that can cause one to fall from a higher station in life and wind up going down and out. I'm sure there are countless others just like him living on the streets with wrenching stories to tell about the tragedies that had toppled them." He went on, "You can learn a lot about someone just by listening to how they speak, including the words they use and how they pronounce them."

After completing my Bachelor's degree I was admitted to the counseling psychology department in the school of education at USC. I was awarded a full fellowship plus a monthly stipend to pursue my Masters of Science and Doctoral degrees specializing in rehabilitation psychology. In contrast to the undergraduate teachers, who had often been quite remote and removed, the professors in the graduate programs came across more as guides on a mutual exploratory mission. Throughout my four-year program to attain my Ph.D. my professors were accessible and were more like friends and companions on the journey of self-discovery.

In 1969 I met Dr. Leo Buscaglia, a professor in the special Education department. He was also teaching an experimental college course on the topic of love. Leo, as he preferred to be called by everyone, was a remarkable fellow who had a child-like curiosity for everything and passionate enthusiasm especially for education. He was deemed to be the professor of the year, several years running. He, along with Leonard Olinger, sat on my doctoral committee and we became close friends.

Leo and I would have lunch together many days of the week after going for a run or taking an on-campus yoga class. He encouraged me to stretch beyond my ordinary reality seeking the extraordinary wherever it could be found. He opened his life to me, expanding my world-view while introducing me to theatre, opera, and the philharmonic. Primarily, he encouraged all of us to be more loving and caring of each other. Leo was renowned for giving great hugs. You could always tell those that had come under his influence because they would joyously greet each other with big hugs. Leo passed away in June of 1998, but his legacy and my memories of him will always live on in my heart.

During the same period of time I was introduced to Dr. Gary Fisher. He was one of a group of men, including Timothy Leary, Dr. Richard Alpert (aka Baba Ram Dass who I credit as starting me on my spiritual quest when I read his ground breaking book, *Be Here Now*), and Aldous Huxley who were experimenting with psychedelics. Gary had published approximately 200 journal articles concerning the use of LSD in the treatment of severely disturbed patients. He also conducted LSD sessions selectively for those in his private practice seeking to journey deeply within their psyches. He invited me to sit in on some of the sessions he was conducting and also facilitated a session for me as well.

As our friendship grew, Gary's mentorship was instrumental in helping me to expand the further realms of my own consciousness. He became a painter in his later years, and a half dozen of his art works adorn our walls. Gary passed away just after the holidays in 2012 following his eightieth birthday. We had an opportunity to sit together for a few hours prior to his death and reflect on the forty-three years that we were friends. We were complete.

In 1974 I handed in my doctoral dissertation and graduated from USC with a Ph.D. in Counseling Psychology. The topic of my dissertation was *The Effects of Yoga Therapy on Self-Concept, Conflict Resolution and Emotional Adjustment*. The research was performed through the Kundalini Research Institute, and I had significant results from my study evidencing the value of practicing Kundalini yoga therapy to support one's personal well-being. I taught hatha and Kundalini yoga for about five years as an extension of my psychotherapy practice. Yoga is still very much a part of my life today.

In 1975 I met Leonard Orr at a Humanistic Psychology Conference held on the campus of UC Berkeley. Leonard was exploring the power of conscious breathing and had coined the term *"rebirthing"* due to his awareness that circular breathing could unlock the effects of traumatic events, including birth trauma, held in one's cellular memory. I was eager to experience the process and found it to be as powerfully effective in inducing an altered state of consciousness as the psychoactive elements I was working with at the time. Rebirthing has also been referred to as Maha yoga or supreme yoga.

I went on to support Leonard in his pioneering work and along with two associates created Holistic Arts Productions and began to host Leonard's Rebirthing Trainings in Los Angeles. We established the Rebirthing LA Community and then hosted Sondra Ray's Loving Relationship Training becoming the LA training center for Leonard and Sondra's work. I joined the ranks of certified rebirthers and began offering my own workshops and trainings as well.

Sacred Breathing Sessions became central to the therapeutic work that I was facilitating through my psychotherapy practice, seminars, practicums, and retreats. Learning Leonard's concepts regarding spiritual purification through the elements of earth, air, water, and fire has served as a tremendous influence on my life personally and professionally. Leonard and I still have a close relationship. His mentoring has been instrumental through providing an integration of the eastern approach to expanded consciousness with the more western concepts for mental health and psychological well-being.

Though it's more common and usually more comfortable for younger males to be mentored by older men, there are occasions when a good mentor relationship can be forged between a male and a female. I had found comfort from the wise counsel of a teacher that I had come to know quite well. When I completed my Ph.D. in 1974

I entered a four-year course of study in metaphysics concentrating on the Essene Teachings. Dr. Beverly Gaard had become a trusted confidant and mentor to me. I would turn to her for spiritual guidance. My first marriage was ending, and it was largely through Dr. Gaard's loving support and guidance that I found my way through the dark morass of confusing choices and into the light of personal reconciliation.

In the field of men's work, I can attribute my relationship with men like Robert Bly, Michael Meade, James Hillman, Robert Moore, and others as profoundly instrumental in shaping my personal growth into conscious manhood. They also had a significant influence on the development of my professional interests in the study of the psychology of men, my therapeutic treatment of men in my practice as well as my support of men within The Sacred Path community.

The men on The Sacred Path Wisdom Council who comprise the team that staffs the retreats have learned the value of mutually mentoring each other. They model the importance of men being "their brother's keepers." They are accountability partners, learning about each other's challenges and tripping points as well as providing a leg up on their intentions and goals. They essentially hold their brothers' feet to the fire, encouraging and supporting them so that they bring out the best in each other and live their lives to the fullest.

In conclusion, even when one has a good relationship with his father, a father cannot provide what a mentor provides and vice versa. A father that knows this fact will turn his son over to a close friend to mentor him, not only on a career path but also most importantly in the ways of the world. It has been far more typical, due to the widespread lack of a father's guidance in the life of a son, for young men to seek out their own mentors.

Sometimes an older guide may choose a worthy candidate to mentor. The right pairing can make all the difference in the outcome of a mentor relationship. Even older men that haven't had a mentor when they were younger can seek out one at this stage of their life. I encourage you to choose wisely and by all means allow yourself to have one or more mentors during your lifetime and don't forget Robert Moore's admonition to find younger men to admire. Just as it's important to be mentored, you'll come to realize that it's vitally important to another to have found you as his mentor.

> *"If you're a young man and you're not being admired by an older man, you're being hurt."*
> —Robert Moore—*King, Warrior, Magician, Lover (1991)*

Part II

A RETURN TO CHIVALRY

A Return to Chivalry: The Six Challenges

I'M SURE YOU'VE HEARD of the Knights of the Round Table. The legendary Knights were men of courage, honor, dignity, courtesy and nobleness, valiant against obstacles standing in the way of their noble pursuits. To support their quests, to foster their sense of brotherhood, and to govern how they dealt with other men and with women, the Knights developed a code of conduct. They called it chivalry, and they knew its power.

Today's men can be knights, too. They can adopt a code of chivalry. But unfortunately, unlike their forebears who had rites and tasks to perform to meet the test of manhood, today's men have no clearly defined precepts or goals — practical, spiritual, or psychological — to help them to reinforce their belief that they can indeed be chivalrous.

I am struck by how the men I work with are fascinated with the idea of chivalry and how starved they are for a code of conduct that can sustain and guide them. Women are struck by the idea too. As one female client of mine told me about her husband, "I fell in love with Todd because he was truly my knight in shining armor. I had never been with or met another man, for that matter, who embraced the qualities of a well-bred gentleman. Todd is like someone from another era when men knew how to treat a woman with respect and take a stand on principle. My girlfriends adore him and think that I'm the luckiest woman in the world."

A chivalrous man lives a life of honor. He is recognized in the world as being a man of consequence guided by his principles and integrity, meaning that he is well-integrated and balanced in body, mind, and spirit. He can enact his intentions with the women in his life, his children, coworkers and friends in a caring, life-affirming way.

A chivalrous man operates from a set of personal ethics and standards that ground his actions in the world. He is loyal and trustworthy and can be counted on to do what he says he will do. It is said that the measure of a man is whether he follows through with what he says he will do. He is truthful and virtuous and operates using a moral compass. He knows how to locate his inner North Star. He is authentic, resilient, and flexible while being enduring and durable. And because he possesses these characteristics, he is respectful and admired by others. Chivalrous men take a stand for what they believe in and are committed through their actions to make a difference in what is meaningful to them.

As men explore the chivalrous path of their unfolding manhood, they meet six different challenges. Confronting these six challenges is what solidifies a man's commitment to chivalry and fortifies him in stressful times when his manhood is being tested or attacked. In the following six chapters, I lay out these challenges and show how men can begin to apply these precepts to the tests they face in their private, romantic, professional, and spiritual lives. I encourage men to challenge themselves to achieve:

1. **Self-Discipline**
2. **Positive Intentionality**
3. **Valor**
4. **Honor**
5. **Compassion**
6. **Joy**

CHAPTER 7

Self-Discipline

Mental toughness is many things and rather difficult to explain. Its qualities are sacrifice and self-denial. Also, most importantly, it is combined with a perfectly disciplined will that refuses to give in. It's a state of mind—you could call it character in action.

—Vince Lombardi (1913 – 1970)

ARE YOU SELF-DISCIPLINED? When you think of the term, what comes to mind? Does it make you think of your childhood and bring up memories of how you were disciplined by your parents? If you had a Catholic school education, does the word "discipline" conjure up images of being reproached by the nuns, serving detention, or being called on the carpet for a stern talk delivered by a priest? If you've been an athlete and have competed in sports, you most likely remember the admonitions and commanding guidance of a coach. The word may even stir up uncomfortable emotions surrounding a time when you had a run-in with the law and had to suffer the consequences. In all of these instances, however, "discipline" is something that resides outside of you. It is measured and delivered to you by someone external to you.

The word *discipline* can also be defined as living a life in a rigorous manner that includes establishment of appropriate limits and boundaries, self-control, and self-reliance as well as self-management in the areas of physical health and emotional, mental, and spiritual well-being. It also includes clear communications, personal responsibility around agreements, keeping commitments, and successful completions in the area of inter-relationships. Here, "discipline" resides within you. It is measured and delivered to you by you.

Living a disciplined life requires that you first abide by the Buddhist proscription *Do no harm to oneself or another.* It requires the elimination of negative behaviors in the form of disorders of conduct, addictions, dependencies, and toxic indulgences. It also necessitates your evolution beyond the trappings of false or inauthentic displays of masculinity, such as excessive involvement with competitive activities; hyper-sexuality and misogyny; over-achievement and over-indulgence in materialistic pursuits; and other abuses of control and power.

You must prepare yourself for the journey into authentic masculinity or conscious manhood by a most careful self-examination, taking a rigorous inventory of your life and assessing the degree to which you may be invested in behaviors that are dysfunctional and destructive. It is imperative that you heal the underlying causes of any acting-out behaviors that are addictive and reckless. This may require mood regulation, temperament management, character transformation, and attitude adjustment. To facilitate this endeavor, psychotherapy, including psychopharmacology as needed, can help you identify the source of the problem and ameliorate the symptoms through addressing the unresolved emotional issues and neurological concerns, if present. Self-help recovery programs, to assist with overcoming addictive behaviors, are a valuable resource.

A Basic Set of Tools

In the opening of his groundbreaking book, *The Road Less Traveled: A New Psychology of Love, Traditional Values and Spiritual Growth* (Simon and Shuster, 1978), psychiatrist M. Scott Peck, MD, exclaimed that, "Life is difficult! Life is a series of problems. Do we want to moan about them or solve them? Do we want to teach our children to solve them?" He suggests that, "Discipline is the basic set of tools we require to solve life's problems. Without discipline we can solve nothing. With only some discipline we can solve only some problems. With total discipline we can solve all problems."

One of my clients has been dealing with the challenges presented by his two teenage sons. One of the boys has gotten involved with drugs and has been through a twenty-eight-day in-patient rehabilitation program and is now residing in a sober living environment. The road to rehab was a bumpy one for this boy. His character disorder manifested in his dropping out of high school and run-ins with the law, including perpetual lying and stealing to support his drug habit. The other son has had a chronic bi-polar mood disorder that fluctuates between extreme highs and lows with an attention deficit hyperactive disorder and obsessive compulsivity. This boy has also incurred problems at school and within his peer group. Both boys are being treated with psychotropic medications and are in therapy.

The father feels guilty for not having been more active in his sons' lives when they were younger. Faced with all of these problems, it made matters worse that he was not around enough to provide the support needed to stabilize the family unit. He worked long hours to nurture a growing business as well as to avoid a discordant relationship with his wife. He was often too busy to attend his sons' sports activities and was frequently out of town when other important events were taking place. The boys have made it known through their acting out behavior that they have felt like after-thoughts in their father's consciousness. It took their problems to attract attention to the bigger issue at stake—that the whole family was in trouble. As the boys' symptoms got worse, so did the parents' relationship, sending the family dynamic into a tailspin. All members of the family are now in therapy comprising individual, family, marital, and group counseling.

My client had to come to terms with the choices that he had made and the ways that he avoided being accountable for the issues that were brewing on the home front. Through therapy he has awakened to the realization that it was not too late to grab the wheel and make a course correction for his family. He now realizes that personal discipline is required in order to return order to the family structure and have the kind of future that he wants.

Becoming Your Own Pilot

In the introduction to his book *The Good Son: Shaping the Moral Development of Boys and Young Men* (Tarcher/Putnam, 1999), author Michael Gurian shares his vision of parenting that he hopes will guide and inspire parents when it comes to the discipline and moral development of their offspring: "Initially it is by receiving the gift of discipline from parents and intimate caregivers that children learn how to contain, manage, regulate, and channel their physical and emotional energy. After years of childhood and adolescence experience, children develop self-discipline. They become their own conscience, their own physical and mental pilot. And when a human community is teaching morality and self-discipline well, its children learn to control not just their own drives, but to channel their physical, emotional, and mental energy toward the highest good: the compassionate life."

Living a disciplined life does not demand a rigid and overly controlled existence. The truth is that when you have self-discipline you can create the parameters that allow for a modicum of control and an abundance of personal freedom. Individuals who are self-disciplined not only provide more freedom for themselves they also create an atmosphere in which others feel safe enough to exercise the fullness of their own personal freedom. When you are practicing self-discipline you feel better; you feel uncomfortable when you are *not* self-disciplined and piloting your own journey through life.

Self-discipline expresses itself in your ability to take on tasks and bring them to fruition in a constructive and timely manner. It requires minimal procrastination and the sufficient execution of the task to bring it to successful completion. This also implies that you can maintain a commitment to fulfill the obligation to the mutual benefit of all concerned.

Often we find it effortless to be self-disciplined in some areas of our life and a struggle to exercise discipline in other areas. It's true that self-discipline can be elusive and cagey when it comes to our ability to be consistent and maintain continuity in affording balance, stability, and prudence.

It's important that we do the best we can do to handle the tough areas that challenge our self-discipline and be forgiving of ourselves for our human frailties and imperfections where our best does not seem to be good enough. And we shouldn't give up on ourselves when we fail; be mindful to keep the faith and try again.

Being disciplined implies that you are mindful of taking care of yourself with the intention of maintaining a healthy lifestyle and sustaining longevity. It requires consistent exercise, dietary consciousness, rest, relaxation, moderate consumption, and the avoidance of excesses that may prove harmful. Self-discipline is essentially synonymous with self-control and knowing when to refrain. It may require practice in achieving the right balance between letting go and holding on.

Self-Discipline Requires Practice

When you engage in a spiritual practice you are dedicating yourself to live a life that is centered on a set of principles and exercises established to guide you along the path to enlightenment. The reason it's referred to as a spiritual *practice* is because you have to practice in order to make progress. For example, if you commit to meditate, pray, and do yoga daily you will certainly find yourself creating reasons or excuses to avoid the practice from time to time. If you skip it enough times, before too long, you will discover that you have let it slip away entirely. However, if you remain self-disciplined in your commitment to your daily practice you will find that, over time, you will achieve the goals that you set for yourself.

Self-discipline is often like juggling, keeping five balls in the air at once. The term "self-discipline" clearly covers a lot of territory. It might help if you consider how you relate to self-discipline in each of these areas of your life:

1) Self-Discipline and Work
2) Self-Discipline and Health (physical and emotional)
3) Self-Discipline and Family/Friends
4) Self-Discipline and Community
5) Self-Discipline and Spirituality

Living a disciplined life may require hard work and well-placed efforts. It calls upon us to be discerning and to make wise decisions and judgment calls regarding where we will invest our energies to maximize the best outcome with the appropriate amount of effort and energetic expenditure. We need to distinguish what we can control from what we can't control, and between when we need to sustain the effort and when we need to let go and surrender to the outcome that is beyond our control.

Lastly, knowing that we are committed to the path of the Spiritual Warrior requires that we possess the self-confidence to believe that we have the ability and the capacity to get the job done, whatever that entails.

Chapter 8

Positive Intention

If you can change your mind, you can change your life. What you believe creates the actual fact. The greatest revolution of my generation is to discover that individuals, by changing their inner attitudes of mind, can change the outer aspects of their lives.
—William James (*The Will to Believe,* 1897)

WHEN YOU OBSERVE THE results that are created in your life, you can usually trace back the cause and effect relationship within your thought pattern. It's typical that one's thinking will reveal the clues as to why someone is manifesting certain outcomes. For instance, when a person doesn't have enough of what he wants in his life, it's probable that at the core of his belief system is the notion that he's not good enough. In fact, this particular belief is widespread. I find that many people feel that they're not good enough and therefore feel that they're not deserving of what they want or need to support their preferred lifestyles.

When one has a belief such as, "I'm not good enough," it's normal for other beliefs that contain the theme of "not enough" to stem from this central thought, just like spokes on a wagon wheel that radiate outward from a hub. It could be said that the hub of one's thinking is the core law or central belief that is held as the ultimate truth. The spokes represent the beliefs that generate from the law, and the rim of the wheel is what manifests or results from the belief system. One's belief system, just like the wheel, is what moves us through life. Whether the ride is smooth or bumpy will depend upon the configuration of our thought pattern.

If you believe that you're not good enough you will also typically believe that you don't have enough money, enough time, enough friends, enough fun, and so forth. And the truth is, since thought is creative, you will unwittingly create the self-fulfilling prophesy that provides the evidence that you do not, in fact, have enough.

Another way of looking at it would be to visualize yourself sitting on the shore of a placid lake. If you picked up a pebble and tossed it into the lake, where it entered the water could be likened to the core or central theme of your belief system, and the ripples that generate from the main splash-point are like the beliefs that radiate out from the central belief or core law.

Your Thoughts Reveal Your Beliefs

I make it a point to listen to how my clients express themselves as they explain to me how their lives are not working. They provide example after example of the problems and challenges they are facing. I notice that the clues to what's happening to them can be traced back through their expressed thoughts to their system of beliefs that are reflected by their self-esteem or identity.

One patient came into his sessions with a whole tale of woe predicated upon his feeling like a victim in the world. He attempted to convince me that the world was just not giving him a fair shake; that the world was full of people who just wanted to take advantage of him; that he will never be able to get ahead because people are always victimizing him and stepping on him—and on and on the story went. And of course, he was right. Since we tend to create our own personal realities, he got to be right, but he didn't get to win.

What I discovered after further discussions with him was that his father was a highly judgmental and critical authority figure who had opinions concerning everything and everyone. He was a fault-finder who didn't trust people and didn't keep it a secret that he had little regard for anyone who wanted to sell you something or those "know-it-alls" who were in positions of power over you. He would broadcast his negative rhetoric as often as possible. My client had inculcated the message as though it were gospel and made it his own mantra. He was living his life according to his father's prescription for protecting yourself from a hostile and unsafe world.

When someone has a belief system that has at its core the thought that "people are out to get me" or "people are not to be trusted" or "people just care about themselves," they will tend to see that evidence mirrored back to them wherever they go. It would be going too far to say that there aren't real victims in the world. It would seem off base to generalize that all people who live in impoverished areas of the world have created their condition through a consciousness of poverty or scarcity, or that people who have been inundated by tragic events, such as hurricanes, earthquakes, or other disasters, have brought it on themselves through a lack of positive intentionality. Certainly a positive person can be victimized by someone who is out to take advantage of his vulnerability, or one can be harmed by being caught off-guard by an unfortunate event. Bad things do happen to good people.

But what we want to accomplish here is to create a context in which one becomes more aware of his state of mind and the effect that it is having on his life. This is the practice of mindfulness.

In the case of another male client who had a negative belief system, I discovered where his core law had originated. He, in fact, had been victimized when he was a child. The clues were contained in his personal story of how he had been molested by one of his mother's boyfriends after his parents' divorce when he was very young. The molestation went on for several months, and he was intimidated into not telling a soul about it for fear that no one would ever believe him and that his mother would be angry with him for telling lies. This caused him to feel unsafe in the world and to generalize his terror of the man who "perpetrated" him onto the world in general—and particularly to fear and distrust all men. His core belief was that, "Men take advantage and hurt me."

Through therapy, I was able to help this client heal the abusive and traumatic events that conditioned him to fear men. He wanted to be able to make a distinction between the person who abused him and those who are not dangerous. His intention was to be free of the post-traumatic conditioning that caused a myriad of symptoms that interfered with his being able to live in the world feeling comfortable within his own skin. Through his commitment to the work, he evidenced the ability to turn his intention into a new set of results. His new intention was to find men who were kind, caring, and compassionate toward him. He created an affirmation that expressed, "I am willing to experience that there are good men in the world who will positively support me." He transformed the experience of being a victim into the empowering experience of being a survivor.

Change Your Thinking, Change Your Life

The key to transforming what results you get in your life is supported by your ability to transform your mind. In other words, change your thinking; change your life. If you want to make a positive difference in your life, pay attention to your thoughts and turn the negatives into positives and affirm the results that you desire to transpire. Where there is post-traumatic conditioning, seek counseling to heal the original causality so that there is less resistance to the process of transforming your belief system.

Intention is essentially about allowance and resistance. Every action either flows effortlessly or meets some impediment to the smooth resolution of the action state. And every action begins with an intention irrespective of whether you are consciously aware or operating unconsciously. Therefore, whatever the outcome one manifests, the course of its evolution followed some well-designed or ill-conceived intention.

Every thought that you have is either promoting a positive or negative result. Thoughts are powerful and creative. Therefore, every manifestation of our thoughts expresses the structure of how we imagined or conceived the outcome. In other words, we are the architects of our reality, the authors of our own existence—however we may choose to express it. Energy flows in the direction of our thoughts. Energy becomes what we think.

A Spiritual Warrior strives to be well intentioned. He is mindful of how his thoughts shape his actions in the world. He desires the best outcome that has the best chance of manifesting as a positive materialization of a well-crafted intention.

Just Let Go...Or Not

It's been my experience as a psychotherapist that it's not easy for men to "just let go." We are conditioned to hold on and stay the course, no matter what. It's like the old joke about a man out mountain climbing who loses his footing and finds himself hanging precariously over an abyss, clutching a flimsy tree limb.

"Is anyone up there?" he calls out, desperately hoping for aid from someone on the rocks above.

Suddenly he hears a booming voice, seemingly from the heavens, "Yes, my son, I am here."

"Is that you, God?" the climber asks.

"Yes, my son," says the voice.

"Help me, God, save me!" the climber yells.

"Certainly, my son, all you need do is let go."

There is a moment of silence, and then the climber's voice again, "Is anyone else up there?"

The reason this joke makes us chuckle is its familiar call to surrender and our equally familiar resistance to it. What our spiritual teachers have told us—like God's voice in the joke—is that if we want to leave behind places where we may be stuck and move into richer life experiences, we must risk discomfort and confusion, trusting to what we don't know and can't explain. We all have dangled from some sort of cliff, hoping to be saved, without realizing in the moment that all we need to do is to have faith and let go.

How do we learn to "just let go?" Since our thoughts precede our actions, we need to turn our attention to how our intentions influence our behavior. On the continuum of moving your thoughts from the lowest potential, that is called *doubt,* to their highest potential, that is called *knowledg*e, we move through hope, faith, and belief. Doubt constitutes the resistance to the positive flow of your intentions that we spoke about earlier. Hope is passive and usually causes one to wait to see what might happen. Often people wait and wait, hoping that something will come along that will prove to them that it is safe enough or worthwhile enough to take action.

Leap of Faith

On the other hand, faith is an active process that impels you to take some action to implement your intention into manifestation. Your head can only take you so far. In order to get somewhere you need to be willing to step out and risk; therefore, the significance of the "leap of faith." Belief is what follows from the experience that is derived from the action of faith. And, the ability to replicate the experience is what provides the knowledge that affirms or validates that your intention has come to fruition. There is nothing more powerful than the confidence that comes from knowing that you can do something.

Knowledge is power and knowing that you know is all-powerful.

One of the Spiritual Warriors in our community, Dan Stanton, had become a member of The Sacred Path Community as a result of the committed work he had accomplished through his therapy. It was his wife, Hannah, who had heard of my work with men and called one day to say that her husband was a good man and needed some mentoring to further evolve into mature manhood. Dan and I met and commenced a great relationship that grew and expanded over time.

Dan took the leap of faith in the summer of 1997. He had transformed his life through his dedication to men's work and was very committed to his desire to give back to men, and especially through rites of passage initiatory experiences helping boys grow and develop on the path leading to conscious manhood. Earlier that same year, we held a retreat called Window to Your Soul and invited Robert Bly, poet and author of the best selling book *Iron John: A Book About Men* (Addison-Wesley Publishing Co., 1990), to be our special guest presenter.

It was an honor to have Robert join us, especially because I had asked him periodically over a ten-year period if he would be willing to participate in one of the Men's Center's Sacred Path retreats, and he had always declined. It had become a kind of rite of passage for me to stay the course and not lose faith that he would one day say yes. I also think he was waiting to see the appearance of gray in my beard.

During the ritual ceremony late in the third day of the retreat Dan asked Robert if he would give him the blessing that only an esteemed elder can bestow on a man wishing to be initiated into manhood. Robert gladly responded to Dan's request and gave him a profound blessing that resonated throughout Dan's entire being.

Later that night Dan had a dream of riding his bike across the country to draw attention to and raise money for cancer research.

Dan's wife, Hannah, had lost a number of her family members to cancer, and Dan was quite moved by the loss. He reported his dream to the men the following morning and made the commitment to direct his faith into the design and execution of a bike-riding campaign to raise consciousness and money to support cancer research.

That summer Dan's leap of faith translated into an experience that gave him the knowledge that he could fulfill his dream. He gathered family members and friends to his side requesting their support of his vision. Hannah volunteered to drive the van and a few of the others volunteered to ride their bikes with Dan. The team began to train and get into condition for the 3,000-mile trip. They mapped out the journey and established the stops. Dan also created a promotional campaign to draw media attention that could bring awareness to what he was doing. As a result of his positive intention, he was able to raise several thousand dollars in corporate and personal donations, and he did indeed call attention to his vision for a world that is eventually cancer-free.

The ride was not always smooth. There were hills to climb, valleys to cross, and bumps in the road. Challenges came and went, and his relationship with his family was tested. They all hung together, learning from the lessons that presented themselves, turning tempting times for negativity into opportunities to conduct themselves through the power of positive thinking accompanied by right action. The Ride Across America was successful in more ways than one and will be remembered by the Stantons as a milestone of what can be accomplished when you are positively intentioned.

Chapter 9

Valor

The ultimate measure of a man is not where he stands in moments of comfort and convenience, but where he stands at times of challenge and controversy.

—Martin Luther King, Jr. (1929–1968)

THE LEGENDARY KNIGHTS WERE indeed perceived to be valiant and to possess valor in the face of obstacles standing in the way of their noble pursuits. They protected ladies and damsels, honored and fought for kings, and undertook dangerous quests. The Round Table was founded on the principles of patience, humility, and meekness. The equality, unity, and comradeship of the Order and singleness of the purpose of all the knights united them in the Fraternity of God. The Order's dominant idea was the love of God expressed through its noble deeds. The cross in the emblem that was given to the knights by King Arthur, when each was initiated into the Order, was to remind them that they were to live pure and stainless lives, to be chivalrous, to strive after perfection and thus attain the Holy Grail.

What does it take to implement the power of your intentions? It takes faith, which is comprised of courage, determination and trust.

It takes courage to be willing to risk sticking your neck out to move forward with your intention. It takes determination to be willing to stay with it through the process of its evolution into form. And it takes trust to be willing to believe in yourself and your ability to manifest your endeavor.

We may conclude that, for you to be faithful to your intention and to a cause greater than yourself, it requires *valor*. Certainly, when you are intrepid or courageously engaged in the pursuit of a mission with a worthwhile endeavor, that would qualify you as being valiant. To be intrepid means that you are willing to feel the fear and to do what you are called to do anyway. You don't let the fear hold you back; you take it with you.

When I was a youngster I suffered from a lot of anxiety and would typically let my fear hold me back. I would go to extremes to create excuses to hopefully legitimize why I couldn't follow through with things that scared me. Eventually, I had the presence of mind to make an agreement with my fear. I told it that I would no longer allow it to hold me back and that it could come along with me or stay behind, but I would no longer allow it to have the power over me to keep me from moving forward with my life.

Certainly it's important to set appropriate limits and boundaries. We don't have to do everything in order to prove that we're courageous or manly. It's just as important what we say "no" to as it is what we say "yes" to, and that distinction can help to keep us safe and secure.

In the mid-1970s, when I experienced the rebirthing process, I learned a lot more about my fears and what had caused them. I also learned that breathing into fear allows it to transmute into excitement. It occurred to me at the time that fear was really excitement without breath and that it was a lot easier to get off of my heels and onto my toes when I didn't hold my breath.

Susan Jeffers, Ph.D., in her breakthrough book, *Feel the Fear and Do it Anyway* (Random House, 1987), published twenty-five years ago, asks her readers to ponder the question, "What is it for you? Fear of public speaking, asserting yourself, making decisions, intimacy, changing jobs, being alone, aging, driving, losing a loved one, ending a relationship?" She goes on to state, "Fear seems to be epidemic in our society. We fear beginnings; we fear endings. We fear changing; we fear 'staying stuck.' We fear success; we fear failure. We fear living; we fear dying." Dr. Jeffers posits that, "...fear is primarily an educational problem, and that by reeducating the mind, we can accept fear as simply a fact of life rather than a barrier to success." What she discovered is that, "At the bottom of every one of our fears is simply the fear that we can't handle whatever life may bring us." She realized that, "If we knew we could handle anything that came our way, what would we possibly have to fear? The answer is: NOTHING!" Dr. Jeffers concludes that, "All we have to do to diminish our fear is to develop more trust in our ability to handle whatever comes our way!"

Perhaps what the world is seeking now is a modern day Knights of the Round Table that champions a return to the noble traits and principles that serve to teach and encourage men to embody the values set forth in the days of Camelot. The movie *Braveheart*, one of my favorites, immediately comes to mind. The role of William Wallace (played by Mel Gibson) embodied the attributes of a valiant warrior. His chivalry, displayed as a warrior vindicating the death of his beloved while he fought bravely for freedom, was stunning. The role of Nathan Algren (played by Tom Cruise) in the movie *The Last Samurai* also revealed a passionate commitment to the principals of living a life dedicated to valor.

A Gentle Man: The Way of the Peaceful Warrior

Valor is expressed in a variety of ways, and valiant men may manifest their valor in gentle and peaceful ways as well. Jesus Christ, Mahatma Gandhi, and Martin Luther King are vivid examples. A few years ago we held a Sacred Path Retreat on the theme of the Warrior, one of the four archetypes of the mature masculine: the King, Warrior, Lover, and Magician. I spoke about a man who I had come to admire as a gentle warrior, a spiritual warrior—the late Fred Rogers. Yes, the same Fred Rogers who was for years the host of the long-running children's TV show, *Mr. Rogers' Neighborhood.* He provided gentle leadership and soothing comfort to his young viewers during painful times, such as when President John Kennedy was assassinated. His reassuring guidance, presented in simple verses of wisdom, has held meaning for us long after his show went off the air.

In the book, *The World According to Mister Rogers: Important Things to Remember by Fred Rogers* (Hyperion Books, New York, 2003), Rogers reminded us that, "Most of us, I believe, admire strength. It's something we tend to respect in others. We desire it for ourselves, and wish it for our children. Sometimes, though, I wonder if we confuse strength with other words—like aggression and even violence. Real strength is neither male nor female. It is, quite simply, one of the finest characteristics that any human being can possess."

America's real heroes don't flaunt the good they do. They go quietly about their daily lives, doing what they do best. They have earned our respect, often for the unassuming manner in which they make a difference in the world. Mr. Rogers also said, "The thing I remember best about successful people I've met all through the years is their obvious delight in what they're doing...and it seems to have very little to do with worldly success. They just love what they're doing, and they love it in front of others."

Look around and see if you can find one of those heroes in your midst. Often, they are the ones you'd least suspect but would most like to have on your side if anything ever happened. Take the time to thank anyone who has made a difference in your life. With encouragement they could be the next Mr. Rogers.

A few years ago as I was thinking about some of the good men that I had come to know intimately through The Sacred Path, it occurred to me that our community of men was comprised of monks who resided outside of a monastery. In fact, many of these men are husbands and fathers, and yet they imbued a kind of radiance that I found to be very monk-like. When I mentioned to them that we seemed to have a community of monks who live in the world—sometimes referred to as "householders"—it resonated with a unanimous acknowledgement of agreement.

A Monk in the World

Soon after that I came across an interview with Brother Wayne Teasdale (1945–2004), a lay monk who taught at DePaul University, Columbia College, and the Catholic Theological Union. Brother Teasdale had lived in a monastery for over fifteen years prior to reentering the world. He wrote a few books, including one titled *A Monk in the World* (New World Library, 2002), in which he expressed that being a monk in the world requires embracing a spirituality of engagement and not one of withdrawal. He reinforced that it was not a spirituality where you are off in a cave somewhere praying.

There are times for retreat and solitary prayer and meditation. Jesus and other great spiritual figures went off for periods by themselves. There are times when we need to do that, and there are individuals who need to do that for their entire lives. But Brother Teasdale's message was that there is a social dimension in our lives that we need to be concerned about and should not leave to other people to do for us. We need to be valiantly engaged spiritually, and that is one of the most important aspects of living as a monk in the world.

His Holiness the Dalai Lama has also encouraged people to increase their personal value in the world by being actively involved in what he refers to as "secular ethics." He states that this does not require any particular religious orientation. It is merely a sense of caring about community while engaging responsibly with the recognition that all human beings, all of humanity, are members of the same human family. Regardless of one's nationality, religious faith, color, educational background, financial standing, or whether one is able-bodied or disabled, every one of us is the same. His Holiness stresses that, in order to achieve a happy life, one must give serious consideration to the welfare of others. His message to us is one of spiritual valor as he underscores that we need to devote more effort to spreading the oneness of all humanity.

Another good man that we admired for his courage and perseverance, Christopher Reeve, was certainly valiant in his fight to overcome the crippling accident that left him paralyzed and confined to a wheelchair. Acting was his job, but he found his vocation when he was thrown from his horse and survived to go on to become a model of faith and the power of intention. It is as though he was destined to rise up to become a Spiritual Warrior that could take on the challenge of dealing valiantly with such a lesson.

Reeve became a real-life Superman by holding to a set of core beliefs that empowered him to strive for total recovery. He had a dogged certainty that the grace of something higher emerges when we muster the will to face our tragedies. He upheld the belief that our minds wield a crucial measure of control over the health of our bodies. And, until the day he died, he embraced the principle that we have the potential to grow beyond what we are told is possible.

The poet, Rainer Maria Rilke, wrote, "We must hold to what is difficult." We must confront our challenges with valor. If we fail to do so, allowing ourselves to remain behind our walls, we may miss a powerful opportunity to expand and to blossom. There is a divine energy at work in the universe that wants to take us toward boundless existence. It is up to us to let go and get into the flow, allowing for the energy to fill us with divine creativity and universal intelligence. It's up to each and every one of us to become all of that which we are destined to be.

CHAPTER 10

Honor

Nothing deters a good man from doing what is honorable.
—Seneca (5 BC – 65 AD)

AN HONORABLE MAN IS one who is recognized in the world as being a man of principal and integrity—meaning that he is well-integrated and balanced in body, mind, and spirit. One definition of integrity is that it's how a man conducts his life even when he thinks no one is watching.

An honorable man operates from a set of personal ethics and standards that guide his actions in the world. He is loyal and trustworthy and can be counted on to do what he says he will do. He is truthful and virtuous and operates using a moral compass that allows him to stay on track. He knows where to find the North Star as his guiding light. He is authentic, resilient, and flexible while being enduring and durable. And because he possesses these characteristics, he is respected and admired by others.

Honorable men are prone to take a stand for what they believe in and are committed through their actions to make a difference in what is meaningful to them. We have many examples throughout history of men of honor who were searching for a better way. They have been agents of change who have attempted, through their ethical actions, to reshape society in a more positive direction.

Many diverse leaders have appeared on the scene to inspire us. Mahatma Gandhi shared with us a vision of peace and freedom through the transformational path of nonviolence, modeling an honorable and resolute commitment to excellence based on a call to take action through spiritual courage. His words, "Be the change you want to see in the world," challenged us to move beyond the human cycle of unmet expectations and disappointment (from looking outside ourselves for our good) and instead turn within to realize and express the goodness that lies inside each of us.

Jesus the Christ personified and served a love so great that he never hesitated to teach the power of that love that he honored so mightily with his whole body and soul. "Love thy neighbor as thyself" was his commandment. For Dr. Martin Luther King, Jr., this theme was his vision of a new world: "Our goal is to create a beloved community, and this will require a qualitative change in our souls as well as a quantitative change in our lives." Anthropologist Dr. Margaret Mead reminds us, "Never doubt that a small group of thoughtful, committed citizens can change the world; indeed it is the only thing that ever has." What these statements address is the reality that we must learn to come together as one spiritually united family and dedicate ourselves to an expansive, common vision that encompasses the collective good, while surpassing our own individual desires.

Today, many people are still searching. Perhaps it's a result of an unfulfilled spiritual longing. Many say they want more out of their lives. They want meaning, clarity of values, purpose, and a strong sense that their lives are worth living. Living an honorable life can bring a person to a spiritual place in which his ethics are inherent in every act that defines his day. Living ethically is to be an active, responsive member of your community. Living ethically is living morally and in an honorable way; it's living with spiritual values.

A Moral Compass

In his book, Michael Gurian (mentioned earlier) states, "Morality is and always has been the living human community's Code of Compassion. Moral values are humanity's insurance policy that compassion will prevail in human interactions, whether parent-child, adult-adult, child-child, or nation-nation. Every rule, law, or honor code exists, at its most fundamental level, to ensure that we human beings act compassionately toward one another. When we act 'morally,' we will always discover when we have acted without compassion...By consciously developing a child's natural compassion through moral education we provide the child a focus for their empathy and sensitivity, as well as frameworks by which to show honorable compassion even when they're angry."

This is the beginning of transcending one's individual needs and going beyond the self to think of someone else as having valid concerns that invite a response. In this process one can grow into becoming a more spiritual person. By stretching beyond a concern for yourself, you begin the process of personal transcendence, which is the starting point of discovering a spiritual existence. To live an ethical life, you have to have a spiritual sensibility and outlook. You have to be capable of thinking of someone else and not just yourself.

A condition that has rampantly grown in our culture today is that of narcissism. It is pervasive in our society and has taken on malignant characteristics. I see it all around me, but of course I reside in Hollywood, California, a community that has long been a magnetic Mecca for those who are self-absorbed and seeking to manufacture a captivating persona. Narcissists are extremely concerned about their own identities and are possessed by a craving to be recognized as someone special.

The irony is that the person who can move beyond his narcissism can actually find an authentic identity that is honorable. By getting out of himself and going out into the world, he actually becomes somebody. Many creative and admired people have become somebody simply by responding with an open heart to a situation of need. In other words, you find yourself by losing yourself. I've heard it said that Buddha reminded us, "It is enough to be nobody special." In kind, Gandhi encouraged, "What you do may not be important, but it is important that you do it."

A Code of Ethics

Thomas Moore, author of several books including *Care of the Soul* (Harper/Collins, 1992) and *The Soul's Religion* (Harper/Collins, 2002) states that, "Ethics simply means responding positively, creatively, and compassionately to the world in which you live. This means that you have to risk stepping outside the safe and protected world you have made for yourself...Part of being ethical is to stretch—another word for transcendence. If you can give yourself to your world, you are being ethical. This is the teaching and example of the Buddha, the Bodhisattvas, Jesus, Mohammed, and all religious leaders and saints." Moore goes on to say:

> "Remember, ethics is not a set of rules, not something to keep you from enjoying life. Just the opposite: Working ethically allows you to feel your mature innocence, be loved by your community, feel that you are making a genuine contribution, and that your life has meaning. These are the ultimate joys and rewards. Without them, you will get caught in addictions to alcohol, drugs, and sex. As a human being, you have to love. If you don't really love people, you will fall in love with a drink or a mere body for sex...
>
> "Here is one of my key points: Ethics is not acting on principle alone; it is acting from the sheer joy of life, from

being part of life and being creative in this life, instead of being literally destructive. It is sometimes ethical to criticize and withdraw; and those acts may be the best contribution you can make. As a person you should be ethical because in that way you become more of who you are. In that kind of act, you will find the deepest joy and sense of fulfillment…

"You have to reach the point where you realize that you are not important. You are a speck in the great design of things. You can add to the immense flow of life taking place around you, or you can obstruct it. It's your choice. And that's ethics. By being ethical habitually, you grow into a real person. That, and not a narcissistic feeling of being virtuous or better than others, is the reward."

Part of honorable behavior is simply doing the right thing. And that includes being a force for good in the world. Dan Stradford, in his book, *The Men's Code of Honor: 66 Principles that Make a Man* (Whisper Canyon Publishing, 2012) states, "In short, honorable behavior is its own reward. And the gratification of the honorable life tends to reinforce good behaviors, making it easier to choose the honorable path as time goes on."

Consider for a moment the person or people that you personally know who are living a life of honor. Are there any family members who come to mind? How about friends, including people who have influenced you such as teachers, college professors, counselors, or others who have been in positions of authority? Did you think of yourself? Do you consider yourself to be an honorable person? If not, what's missing and what do you need to do to remedy the situation?

"The greatest way to live with honor in this world is to be what we pretend to be."
—Socrates (469 - 399 BC)

CHAPTER 11

Compassion

The best portion of a good man's life is his little, nameless, unremembered acts of kindness and of love.

—William Wordsworth (1770 - 1850)

BUDDHA TAUGHT WHAT HE referred to as "the First Noble Truth," that ignorance leads to suffering and that enlightenment leads to non-suffering. He explained that when one is enlightened and is no longer living in ignorance, one has finally arrived at the understanding that the path leading to the enlightened state of consciousness is paved with the good acts of compassionate giving. We could also say that the path to compassionate giving leads one to the understanding that contributing to another's well-being produces the pleasurable feeling of enjoyment.

Compassion, though, isn't just sentimental or sympathetic. It is a state of consciousness in which one feels connected to everyone and everything, everywhere. In fact, research experiments reveal that all sentient beings are connected to each other—what the physicists might call "non-locality." It can be said that non-locality, in a sense, makes compassion itself the ground of everything. Marc Ian Barasch details the research in his book *Field Notes on the Compassionate Life: A Search for the Soul of Kindness* (Rodale Press, 2005).

Barasch speaks of a researcher named John Haidt, "who has shown there is an automatic, involuntary physiological response when we see someone being noble or selfless or showing extraordinary or even ordinary helping behaviors toward another. The vagus nerve, connecting the brain to cardiac tissue, seems to become activated, and we get that sensation of our heart soaring, of being just choked-up with tenderness. We're designed, as creatures, to rejoice in each other's caring."

Confucius taught the concept of Jen or "good-heartedness." He believed that all people are basically good at heart and that people will naturally help other people if they can. If you reflect on the best moments in your life, they were probably when you were being altruistic or experienced some random act of kindness extended to you from someone. Empathy toward another generally elicits an act of kindness. Kindness is like an elixir that takes the pain out of life. Many potentially volatile situations can be quelled with just a little kindness. Gandhi referred to humans' natural state of compassion occurring when violence has subsided from our hearts. We can release negativity in the form of resentments and aggressive thoughts toward self or another through the act of forgiveness.

Forgiveness: The Milk of Human Kindness

Forgiveness is a powerful and profound demonstration of kindness. We especially need to forgive ourselves. In fact, we don't understand forgiveness until we've forgiven ourselves.

Metta Practice: In the Buddhist tradition, we begin with the practice of Metta. It says that you might have to develop some kindness toward yourself in order to be kind to others. You start with the understanding that you're fighting the great battle of your own suffering. We tend to be very hard on ourselves. In Metta practice you start with yourself and then you extend that feeling of loving-kindness to people who are very close to you, such as family members, and then you take that loving feeling of closeness and extend it to neighbors, to strangers, and ultimately, you practice extending it to those you consider to be your supposed enemies. In this regard you expand your capacity for seeing more and more people as being within the circle of "us" rather than outside the circle as "them."

Jesus said, "But I say to you, love your enemies, bless anyone who curses you, and do good to anyone who hates you; and pray for those who carry you away by force and persecute you..." (Matthew 5:44) Jesus here emphasizes not to demonize or dehumanize an enemy. Acting on hate only creates more hate and then force and violence come into greater play. He taught love as a practical means to win over anyone who was opposing true harmony and peace. Teaching his disciples and followers to "love their enemies" was a valiant expression that was intended to transform the hearts and minds of people everywhere. Jesus taught love as the primary path for reconciliation and for the genuine manifestation of God's kingdom on earth.

Forgiveness is such a simple gift and actually such an easy act to bestow on another. It only requires a change of mind and a change of heart. It means allowing oneself the joy and privilege of being able to listen to the voice of God in our lives instead of placing ourselves under the tyranny of the ego. The ego-centered life is a very claustrophobic one.

Tonglen: There is another Buddhist practice called Tonglen. In this practice you imagine breathing in others' suffering and breathing out your own experience of well-being. Through this exercise you discover that you're able to accept others' troubles more readily because in a way they are really your own, and your happiness and the happiness of another, in the same sense, is the same. So our fundamental nature is that of loving-kindness, empathy, and compassion. In the Buddhist view, any other reaction is an overriding of this natural state of being.

No act of kindness, no matter how small, is ever wasted. We're missing the point if we do nothing because we believe we can only do a little. Every act of kindness creates a ripple, like a pebble in the water. The effect goes on and on, extending far beyond the single act. The best portion of a good person's life is expressed in his little, random, and nameless acts of kindness.

A Way Out of your Dismay

No matter how confused you may feel or how upset you are because you think the world has mistreated you, there is always a way out of your dismay. It is by following the path of kindness. It may be known by other names, such as courtesy, altruism, charity, mercy, grace, or hospitality; and yet it all simply comes down to compassionate kindness.

His Holiness the Dalai Lama made himself available for a private interview with Roger Teel for *Science of Mind: Change Your Thinking, Change Your Life* (Science of Mind Publishing, January 2005, Vol. 78 No. 1) during the Third Synthesis Dialogues, held during summer 2004 in Rome. His Holiness was asked what are the most important spiritual practices one should cultivate. His response was, "Important practices to develop are those of compassion and forgiveness." He said, "I think the positive results from the practice of compassion flow first to the practitioner himself...when you are compassionate, you definitely gain a great immediate benefit; the benefit to the other person will depend on his own sort of thinking or circumstances. The practice of forgiveness is the same. When you forgive, you immediately get something of immense value. If, instead, you feel hateful or you desire revenge, then you are the primary casualty. Anger, hatred, jealousy, these emotions themselves will not harm another. But they instantly harm your own peace of mind…"

His Holiness recounted a story during the interview that vividly portrayed the dedication of a monk to his commitment to live a compassionate life: "This story is about my old friend, a Tibetan monk who spent eighteen years in a Chinese prison, a Chinese gulag. After he came to India, we had a long, casual talk, and he mentioned to me that during those eighteen years, on a few occasions, he faced danger. I asked him, what kind of danger? I thought maybe he meant danger to his life. He told me that on a few occasions, he faced the danger of losing compassion toward the Chinese. And I thought, that's really wonderful. I don't know if I could practice like that. That monk, he is not a scholar; not a really well-known practitioner, he's just an ordinary monk. But the Tibetan tradition is so strongly based in compassion that for him, the concept of compassion is deeply rooted in his heart. Even while actually experiencing that kind of hardship, still he felt compassion. It was important for his own sake."

Revenge, retaliation, retribution, and reprisals never work. This never gets us what we want. Acts of kindness, however, can go a long way in healing ourselves, healing others, and extending healing to our global family. The Dalai Lama stated succinctly, "My religion is simple, my religion is kindness."

Grieving: The Doorway to Deep Compassion

A few days after the devastating 2005 Hurricane Katrina struck the Gulf Coast, I awoke one morning at approximately 4 a.m. and couldn't get back to sleep. I lay awake pondering the plight of countless numbers of human beings that had been inundated in the wake of such a dramatically destructive force. I found myself contemplating the horrific images of the mass devastation that claimed so many lives and left behind thousands of injured and homeless evacuees. I had heard people refer to this disaster as being of epic proportion or of biblical significance; a disaster unlike any that this nation has ever experienced before. It certainly did seem to force us to confront the stark reality of the times that we live in.

I got out of bed at 6:30, turned on the TV and watched a newsman interview a man by the name of Hardy Jackson. Jackson's story moved me to tears. He told the journalist how he'd tried to hold onto his wife with one hand while attempting to cling to his children with his other arm. The water level was high and the current was strong. As he spoke, he couldn't contain his deep pain any longer. A well of emotion surged up and overflowed. He sobbed as he described how his wife had pleaded with him to let her go and to save the children. She knew he couldn't hold on to all of them much longer. The situation reminded me of the stunning scene from the movie *Sophie's Choice* when a mother is forced to choose which of her two children would live and which would die. Hardy told the reporter that, as he'd reluctantly released his wife to her death, he'd made a promise to her soul and to God that he would take care of his surviving children. He wept, saying he had nowhere to go; he had lost all of his material possessions. The reporter began to cry, and my wife and I cried along with them.

That same week, 900 Iraqis were killed when they attempted to escape a suicide bomber. The bridge that they were traversing collapsed. It was later noted that the threat posed by the suicide bomber was not real. We seem to be experiencing a series of raptures, including the Indonesian tsunami and the earthquake, followed by the tsunami devastating Japan, in which thousands of people lost their lives. In the blink of an eye, countless numbers of people are plucked from their fragile lives on Earth.

Crises seem to bring out the best in people and the worst as well. There are those who are a part of the solution, being of service and giving of themselves selflessly while there are those who are part of the problem. The looters, rapists, and murderers who take advantage of the chaos as they act out their evil agendas, could make you despair about humanity and the crises confronting our civilization. Thank God for those who put their needs aside to care for the needs of others; the kind and compassionate ones...the Spiritual Warriors who step up to answer the call.

The Eye of the Storm: Being Centered in Compassion

Spiritual Warriors actively cultivate and nurture their capacity for being understanding, forgiving, kind, caring, empathetic, and compassionate. They don't see this practice as a sign of weakness or as being less manly. They have learned to resolve conflict and communicate effectively and lovingly. Spiritual Warriors care about how some people can become disconnected from their compassionate natures and behave violently toward others, while others can remain compassionate even in the most challenging of circumstances. It is a powerful spiritual practice to see one's self as the eye of the storm. When the storm is raging around you, if you can remain centered in compassion, then you will be less likely to react inappropriately. You will find yourself much more endowed with the capacity for right responsiveness.

Practicing and modeling compassion for our children is perhaps the greatest gift of love that we can present to them. Equipping them with certain moral competencies prepares them for dealing with the challenges that they will face as they leave home and go out into the world on their own. In *The Good Son*, Michael Gurian states that the ultimate goal of a young man's development is the successful learning of ten universally accepted moral competencies: Decency, fairness, empathy, self-sacrifice, respect, loyalty, service, responsibility, honesty, and honor. Gurian states that, "These are the values that measure a good son, and they are the bedrock of compassion.

Possession or lack of them makes or breaks a man. Ensuring that our sons develop them is one of the most important duties of not only an individual family, but of our civilization...Today more than ever, few things are more important to all of us than to live with, produce, nurture, and enjoy good men."

Chapter 12

Joy

Whoever possesses abundant joy must be a good man.

—Friedrich Nietzsche (1844 - 1900)

JOY IS THE SIXTH AND ultimate challenge—for a reason. As young children we spontaneously expressed joy. We played, laughed, and loved unconditionally. We simply radiated happiness and joy. However, as we age we begin to lose our capacity for expressing ourselves as freely. We replace joy with hesitancy, reticence, even fear. We begin to focus more on happiness as a commodity. We begin to believe that we need something outside of ourselves in order to be happy.

Our innate capacity for accessing our joy is soon forgotten and replaced by an outward quest for something or someone that will provide our happiness for us. We are hardwired to avoid pain and seek pleasure. It is therefore easy for us to find ourselves indoctrinated into a belief system that informs us that if we look outside of ourselves, we will find something that is guaranteed to relieve our suffering and make us happy. However, externally based happiness is always fleeting and transient. It eventually wears out, breaks down, rejects us, vanishes, or dies, leaving us empty and bereft.

Living a life in which we have high expectations of something outside of ourselves fulfilling our needs only seems to set up unrealistic expectations that eventually leave us feeling bitter disappointment. Nothing outside of us can fulfill the longing that we have for feeling connected to our joy. This was our natural state of being when life was simpler, and we were more intimately connected to our inner state of wholeness and goodness. Jesus reminded us, "Be ye simple like little children."

When we get in touch with what's really within us, which is God-centered and therefore good, we tap into the wellspring of joy. The easiest and most direct route to accessing the quality of joy is to be clear that no matter whom we think we are or what we think we are here to do, we are fundamentally here to be of service. It is to be endowed with a desire to express the higher spiritual good. When we realize this basic fact, our life takes on new meaning, and our path becomes clearer and more assured. We get to show up each day, not just to do a job, but also to fulfill our divinely inspired vocational contract, which is to represent God in human form. We are essentially here to give our gifts to the life that we have chosen to live. Therefore, each task we take on or that is assigned to us gives us the opportunity to fulfill our destiny in the universe by serving God.

Real Life Heroes

One of the men in our community, Phil Gross, is an educator and executive coach by profession. I have been impressed by how he has modeled, in his own life, the importance of an integrated approach to the six Spiritual Warrior Challenges in addition to holding them out to his students and clients as attributes to attain.

One day, Phil quietly asked if he could share something with me, something personal that was close to completion. He had befriended another man in his networking group who, as he had come to realize, was suffering from a kidney ailment that would prove fatal if he were not to receive a kidney transplant. Nick had already been waiting for a kidney for four years, and time was running out—he couldn't last more than a year. Phil's heart opened to this man's story, and he offered to help if he could. As it turned out, tests revealed that he was a match. This would allow Phil to successfully donate one of his own kidneys to his friend. Phil was understated about this very compassionate gesture. It's not uncommon for real life heroes to be quiet about their accomplishments.

In fact, Phil really did not consider this a heroic gesture at all. He considered it to be a normal act of love and caring that anyone would do for a friend, even though he confesses that he is aware that there are those who would not be moved to perform this act of caring for another. But for him, it was an automatic gesture of loving-kindness, and he viewed it as a great honor and privilege to be able to be of service.

The time came when Phil entered the hospital for the surgery that would remove one of his kidneys and allow it to be transplanted into Nick's body. Phil was like a little kid. He was so excited and joyous that the day finally had arrived when he could share this compassionate and selfless gift of life for another. Nick, the recipient, expressed that he felt infused with the qualities of a good man when Phil gifted one of his kidneys to him. He promised that it would be the gift that keeps on giving. He often reminds us that he's walking around, energized by the kidney and love of the man who became his best friend. Nick joined our Sacred Path Community, attending and teaching parenting at our retreats. He now serves on the Wisdom Council.

Be Not Afraid

Pope John Paul II died in 2005 at the age of eighty-four. When he became pope he was fifty-eight years of age. He always reminded me of my father, who was also Polish, had been an actor, was a powerful, dynamic, rugged individualist, and who also passed away at age eighty-four. The Holy Father's remarkable twenty-six-year papacy was the third longest in history. He was a controversial figure who will be remembered for many things. One, surely, was his style of teaching. "He's taught us how to live; he's taught us how to suffer." Jim Mulligan, a Missouri deacon studying in Rome, told *Newsday* Magazine, "And now he's teaching us how to die." As one of John Paul II's biographers, theologian George Weigel wrote the pontiff's struggle during the last month was his way of "bearing witness to the truth that suffering embraced with obedience and love can be redemptive." He reminded us to "Be not afraid."

Of his many accomplishments, I was impressed with how John Paul II devoted his energy to travel and diplomacy and to teaching and praying for his flock. "He saw himself as a pastor to the world," remarked the Reverend Peter Hans Kolvenbach, head of the Jesuit order and a member of the Roman Curia. That mixture of devoted ministry and diplomacy set a pattern in which John Paul II visited more than 135 nations—some of them many times—and journeyed the equivalent of three times the distance to the moon.

He also used his foreign trips to advance ecumenical and interfaith relations. He sat shoulder to shoulder with Hindu Holy Men, Buddhist Monks, and clerics representing a vast array of religious and philosophical beliefs. He was the first pope to visit a mosque and a synagogue. During a trip to Israel, he lit an eternal flame in remembrance of Holocaust victims, taking the opportunity to condemn anti-Semitism, and he publicly apologized for Catholic offenses at times throughout history. He forgave Mehmet Ali Agca, the man who attempted to assassinate him, and declared a Holy Year of Redemption in 1981. He preached forgiveness and compassion worldwide, and during his own illness, he communicated strong and moving messages about the value of life. He delighted youthful audiences with his joy-filled laughter, joking, and singing with them but also implored them to "Look to Christ, who gives you the meaning of life."

On the night that he made his transition, the Holy Father, according to an eyewitness, heard the end of a prayer at a Mass being recited in St. Peter's Square below. He said, "Amen," then drew his last breath. I will remember John Paul II as a man of peace, a man of principal, a man of prayer—a genuinely good man.

Be of Good Cheer

> *Spread love everywhere you go. Let no one ever come to you without leaving better and happier. Be the living expression of God's Kindness: Kindness in your face, kindness in your eyes, kindness in your smile, kindness in your warm greeting.*
>
> —Mother Teresa (1910 – 1997)

In conclusion, the payoff for living the preceding six characteristics and rising up to the challenge of being a Spiritual Warrior is to experience the radiant presence of joy in your life. Each one of us has the opportunity to express our God-Self and make this world a better place. In learning about and practicing the attributes of a Spiritual Warrior, we get to experience the power of Spirit working in our lives, centering us in peace, love, and joy. My Great Uncle Howard, who lived to 103, was a Quaker, and he loved to remind people to "Be of good cheer."

Part III

SPIRITUAL WARRIORS IN THE WORLD

Chapter 13

Finding and Renewing Your True Love

Love one another, but make not a bond of love:
Let it rather be a moving sea between the shores of your souls.

—Khalil Gibran, *Love Letters in the Sand: The Love Poems of Khalil Gibran*

THE LONG SHADOW OF the Father Gap can spread over love, marriage, and parenthood without a man even realizing it. A romantic relationship can unexpectedly cause him to re-experience a lot of earlier losses in his life (such as the loss of his father—or his father's attention). It can trigger sadness and depression. In older men, new situations can trigger grief over the slipping away of youthfulness. One trigger can be the act of becoming a parent, leading some men to start looking elsewhere for attention—to a new girlfriend, perhaps.

Whatever the timing and whatever the trigger, men too often feel estranged from their partners. I hear this same lament from men over and over: "I wish my wife were nicer to me. She's just not as sweet or feminine as she used to be." Women, on the other hand, tell me that if their husbands were more present and responsive, they would be sweeter and more responsive to them. They want their men to be good husbands and fathers.

Marriage Problems Begin Before Marriage

Typically, a woman marries a man she believes shows promise, taking him on as a viable project. A man, on the other hand, meets a woman and decides that he likes her just the way she is—and hopes that she'll stay that way. In other words, women meet men and want to change them; men meet women and don't want them to change. Herein lies the fertile ground for disappointment—when maidens become matrons and princes don't become kings.

For better or for worse, straight men are genetically predisposed to be attracted to maidens, or to the maiden element in non-maiden women. Men, as discussed earlier, perceive such women as having a lot of nectar, being succulent and sweet. But after a man marries a woman and she becomes a mother, he witnesses that nectar being given to his children, and as a result, he can feel dejected, even betrayed. It's as though he's lost his girlfriend. Having children often exacerbates the distance between husband and wife, resulting in *triangulation trauma*. The children become the hub of the wheel, with wives (including mothers who work full time) devoting the bulk of their emotional energy to child care while their husbands continue to focus on their careers. Parents become the marginalized spokes on the wheel, extending outward from each other in opposite directions.

One day during a painful therapy session, a client drew a picture for me. It was a triangle in which he had placed the children at the top and he and his wife at opposite sides at the bottom. He was dismayed to realize that he and his wife had been displaced from the top of the pyramid and were now estranged at opposite points on the bottom. "Our relationship has become an extension of the kids, who command most of my wife's attention," he said. "Even the dog and the bird come before me."

Male Provider Syndrome

Often men experience what I call the Male Provider Syndrome, lying awake at night worrying about how they're going to be able to handle all of the expenses required to keep the family boat afloat. Even in two-income homes, men feel they carry the burden of providing for the family squarely on their own shoulders. A man can also feel like a success object, appreciated only for his income. "Around my wife and kids I feel like all I am is an ATM," one man complained. Beyond their resentment, men feel grief about this that can foment into grievance.

Many couples don't even have the luxury of fretting over gender roles or syndromes. Much as a man might like to play "protector/provider" to his woman's "nurturing maiden," the reality is that the bills have to be paid, which costs a lot in terms of energy and time as well as cash. The protector ends up not being home enough to protect anything, and the provider (be it the man or the woman) can't do the job without the help of the other.

The cost of living is a huge economic reality that today's families have been slow to face, but tough economic times have brought families face to face with unremitting challenges and daunting crisis. Many of us grew up with the old yardstick that one's rent or mortgage should cost about a quarter of one's monthly income, but today it's more like half or three quarters of one's income. This has a tremendous impact on the choices couples make. After living expenses, childcare, housework, errands, and all the other costs and duties it takes to run a family, most find they are unable to save for their children's college or put money in the bank for their retirement or to cushion against the lean times. What most couples end up doing is not looking for the *best* solution but looking for the *least worst* solution.

But grievance can give way to renewal. As we've seen, a man wants to feel honored by his wife, and his wife wants to be cherished by her husband, so when a man makes cherishing gestures, it will augment the very sweetness that he seeks in his mate. A man should treat her like the woman he wants her to be. In short, he can't ask his woman for what he's unwilling to give himself.

When a man can face these issues, he has a chance to redefine himself as father, as faithful companion to his partner, as friend, as mentor, and finally as citizen of the world. Men can reconnect with women through renewing the courting behavior that brought them together in the first place. When women describe what it means to feel cherished, it's often the simple things men can do that will do the trick—asking a question about her activities during the day, actually listening to her answer, or simply exhibiting good manners, such as opening a door, allowing a woman ahead of him in a checkout line, giving her a compliment, or carrying a package to the car. It's amazing how good manners have been dropped, perhaps out of fear that it will be interpreted as "sexist." But these seemingly small things can turn the tide in a relationship. It turns out it's not that complicated. It's showing respect, and respect is powerful.

"He Doesn't Communicate"

Linguist Deborah Tannen, Ph.D., in her book *You Just Don't Understand: Women and Men in Conversation* (1990), presented ground-breaking research confirming what we suspected all along, which is that men and women have innately different communication styles. Her thesis is that men engage the world as individuals in a hierarchical social order in which they are either one-up or one-down. "In this world, conversations are negotiations in which people try to achieve and maintain the upper hand if they can and protect themselves from attempts by others to put them down and push them around," Dr. Tannen states. "Life, then, is a contest, a struggle to preserve independence and avoid failure."

If we trace male behavior back 40,000 years, when the masculine societal role was more clear-cut, men were hardwired to be warriors and hunters. Their communication styles needed to be quick, to-the-point, and decisive. Self-preservation and basic survival demanded that men cut off their emotions and think, plan, strategize, and take action. Men needed to be wily and cunning and intimately connected to their animal instinct.

Since a man is genetically driven by his provider-protector mode, he tends to be non-emotional. He does this so that he can focus on the problem, determine what's wrong, figure out if it's a threat that has to be dealt with, and then find a way to deal with it. He doesn't want to be caught with his back to the door. He wants to stay free and have a clear view, so he can determine what moves he has to make. His sense of personal independence, therefore, is held in the highest regard.

Tannen contrasts the masculine scenario with information that suggests that women tend to approach the world as individuals in a network of connections. "In this world," she says, "conversations are negotiations for closeness in which people try to seek and give confirmation and support and to reach consensus. They try to protect themselves from others' attempts to push them away. Life, then, is a community, a struggle to preserve intimacy and avoid isolation. Though there are hierarchies in this world too, they are hierarchies more of friendship than of power and accomplishment."

Mars and Venus in the Cave

Historically, women's roles have been based on their capacity for giving birth, raising children, and homemaking. Their primal instinct is to sit on the nest while men's primal instinct is to circle the nest. The nesting instinct, combined with the capacity for child rearing, sets women up to be natural face-to-face communicators. The satisfaction of basic needs is more readily attained through intimate exchange. Men tend to be programmed to survey and surmise from a distance. Their natural inclination is to follow objects moving through space, and that includes the male pastime of scanning for attractive women. Men make solitary and often crucial decisions regarding what they see. Their communication process with others is a more shoulder-to-shoulder approach as they scan the horizon and assess the situation. Women are therefore predisposed for interdependent, collaborative relating, and men are geared-up for independent, isolated decision-making.

Communication between men and women is a continual balancing act, juggling the conflicting needs for intimacy and independence. If women need to speak and hear a language of connection and intimacy while men need to speak and hear a language of status and independence, then it can truly seem as though they are speaking different languages, as was suggested by author John Gray in his book, *Men are from Mars and Women are from Venus* (HarperCollins, 1992).

Building a Bridge

In our contemporary culture the demands of survival have shifted, requiring men and women to adapt to an ever-changing role structure. More and more women are working outside the home, sharing the provider responsibilities with men, while more men are improving their parenting skills and sharing the duties of homemaking. This raises the expectations that, through shared experiences, men and women will begin to have an easier time communicating. However, it has been my observation that the only thing that has been raised is the stakes.

The external stresses on both men and women have only increased, while good communication hasn't, judging from the high divorce rate and numbers of couples coming into my office who are dissatisfied with the quality of their relationship. I find myself having to help them comprehend and accept their different communication styles and realize that, just because they have unique ways of conversing, it doesn't mean that they are incompatible. My job is to try to help couples build a bridge to span their different emotional languages. It's a bridge that allows them to cross from their own ends, at different rates, and meet somewhere over the chasm that separates them.

When I evaluate a couple's capacity for communication, the first thing that I assess is the degree of *safety* that exists between them. If they can feel safe with each other, then they can also be vulnerable with each other. Vulnerability essentially means being capable of being wounded. Each individual needs to feel it's safe to be open, trusting that the other will not wound him or her. This sets the stage for intimate contact—a couple's ability to be authentically honest and vulnerable with each other in a safe environment.

The language of intimacy expresses *we're close and the same*. The essential element providing connection here is symmetry. The symmetry of connection is what creates the presence of community or the feeling that *we are in this together, struggling for the same thing—closeness*. This understanding allows us to relax into the realization that, *even though we are different and have unique ways of expressing ourselves, we want the same thing*. This shared awareness reinforces the feeling of mutuality, which is the basis or foundation for satisfying and mindful communication.

Bruce Derman, Ph.D. in his book, *We'd Have a Great Relationship, If it weren't for You* (Mutual Connection Press, 1994), believes that "Any couple who are genuinely involved have the same capacity for intimacy, as reflected by their mutual fears, or they wouldn't be together. The moment that a man can recognize their sameness and maintain the equality, he can experience the love that is inherent in his relationship and will not be as prone to divorcing, unnecessarily."

Derman further believes that "Men are underrated as relational beings and woman are over rated, and the professionals who get caught up with the differences between the sexes fail to support the mutuality that exists."

Mindfulness and Neural Science

Mindfulness can be characterized as purposeful attention to *what's so* in the present moment with relaxed presence and focused awareness, devoid of critical judgment as in condemnation, but rather utilizing wise judgment as in discernment.

Current research shows that we can influence the minds of others in meaningful and measurable ways, especially if we have visual and auditory contact with each other. There's a term for this—*Neural Resonance*—and it supports the metaphysical Law of Attraction. A thought atmosphere surrounds every person. This is the direct result of conscious and unconscious thought, which influences what comes into one's life. Through this power we are either attracting or repelling. Negative emotions easily undermine our positive intentions and goals. It's important not to give in to them. Acknowledge them, understand them, and then ask yourself two simple questions: How do they make me feel? And how do they affect the people with whom I engage?

The brain gives far more attention to negative feelings and thoughts than it does positive ones because it reacts to them as if they were a threat to your survival. There is a vast amount of evidence indicating that meditation, contemplative prayer, and positive thinking help us to function better, internally, and externally. Optimism can add several years to our lives, and we have to practice regularly to keep the brain's reptilian limbic system calm.

Meditating can change the structure and functioning of the brain in ways that generate empathy, compassion, and inner peacefulness. This in turn lowers neurological fear and frustration. Through neuroplasticity, you actually can build and strengthen neural circuits that help you succeed in creating positive, meaningful relationships. Couples that meditate together generate an inner calmness, serenity, and equanimity that allows for greater harmony.

While it's often true that opposites attract, that's not always the best recipe for relationship survival. In reality, we need to attract people who share similar values, keeping in mind that the ideal relationship is not an illusion, but a reality. You can aspire to attract and recognize your perfect mate by listing the top ten qualities of a sacred companion or soul mate and meditating on the visualization of the person that you wish to invite into your life.

Hearts and Minds

In *intimate* relationships we need to partner with people who share similar values about love, parenting, and other significant issues. When you observe another person's face and body language and listen to the tone of voice, your brain begins to mirror the neural activity of his or her brain. This is called empathy. Neural chemicals that stimulate bonds of friendship and intimacy are released and we become more socially cooperative, compassionate, and fair. In the field of neuro-economics, this is known as *reciprocal Altruism*. The moment your face or tone expresses anger or suspicion, the other person's brain triggers a fight or flight response. *Neural dissonance* then occurs, causing us to react unconsciously with selfish and often punitive behavior.

Changes in the body's internal chemistry have demonstrated a variety of results. As levels of cortisol, the stress hormone, decrease, and the interplay of hormones and neurotransmitters increases, a condition of internal well-being and harmony grows. Four compounds—dopamine, norepinephrine, oxytocin, and serotonin are particularly critical in inducing the state we call *love*. When any of these bio-chemicals is low or depleted, it can cause the less loving state of anxiety and/or depression.

Research is being conducted at the HeartMath Institute in the Santa Cruz mountains of California on the emerging understanding of the importance of the heart as a pathway into decreased stress, increased well-being, and higher levels of creativity and consciousness. The research has illuminated that the heart plays a particularly important role in creating coherence, a state of efficiency in which everything works together in an orderly and synergistic manner.

Our thoughts and emotional states can be considered "coherent" or "incoherent." Positive emotions, such as love or appreciation, can be described as coherent states, whereas negative feelings, such as anger, anxiety, or frustration, are examples of incoherent states. HeartMath studies have shown that people can increase coherence and achieve physiological and behavioral changes that last. Focusing on the heart and recalling positive feelings creates a state of flow and ease rather than stress, depletion, and disease. A kind, loving, peaceful, compassionate, and generous demeanor can attract wonderful people into your life, people who will have the desire to help you reach your highest goals and dreams.

Weathering Relationship Perils

Most people would tend to agree that to have a productive, satisfying, and sustaining relationship requires tremendous intention and commitment. Relationships command a lot of maintenance in order to get through the trying times and go the distance. It is estimated that the average length of new relationships is somewhere between four and seven years, and even less for those who don't legally tie the knot. With one out of two marriages ending in divorce, there are obviously significant pressures on couples pushing them toward separation these days unless they take actions to keep that from happening.

How to weather the storms that put relationships in peril and how to survive the ups and downs has been the concerned focus of relationship counselors for years. Most couples enter counseling when it's too late. Rather than nurturing the relationship during the early stages—when there's the open spirit of love and enthusiasm—many people tend to get hopelessly locked into a power struggle and wind up irrevocably closing the door to the future.

Successful relationships are an extension of the individuals who comprise them. To the extent that each individual manifests a healthy and functional lifestyle, the relationship itself will serve as a mirror reflecting how the couple expresses internal harmony and balance. An intimate relationship can be a *crucible* or strong container capable of supporting the partners as they both make their way toward spiritual awareness and development. The relationship container holds the potential for revealing the lessons that each individual needs to learn for the evolution of the soul's growth as it expands into greater realms of consciousness.

When people feel that their relationship has broken down and it's time to check out and to find a replacement, the individuals are typically up against their toughest personal lessons. With the right kind of help and guidance, couples can usually see what their roadblocks are and open up their communication to explore the concealed truths that are inherent in their process.

It's important for couples to learn that there are two pure emotions, one of love and the other of fear. Pain, anger, frustration, and boredom arise from fear, which can cause us to self-protect and express unloving behavior. The path of love, on the other hand, fosters an open and safe atmosphere where learning can be fun and joyful. Moving through fear and practicing loving behavior is the ongoing challenge for all who participate in the relationship game.

Five Relationship Stages

Lasting relationships tend to go through distinct stages. It is important to note, however, that as couples move through the five stages, elements of each of the other stages are present within each stage. It is common for good times to be present as well as growing pains. No relationship exists without problems—but problems can be viewed as important opportunities to learn and grow.

Stage One—Romance and Attraction

It's the honeymoon phase during which individuals hold a common vision of what's possible and what could be. It's a time of great hope, excitement, and expectation, where fantasy plays a key role in creating the tendency to see your partner in the best possible light. This stage is typically loaded with projections and introjections, where the partners strive to live up to each other's ideal image. It can look like a state of temporary insanity because, in the long run, it fails to deal with the real world issues that are consistent with real, down-to-earth people.

Stage Two—The Power Struggle

In the power struggle stage one moves from the romantic vision of oneness to the *di*-vision that you are different than I thought you were—we are both different than we thought. Romantic illusion of unity becomes *dis*-illusionment of separateness. Here we try to get our partner to conform to our expectations, which causes us to attempt to control the other. This is where co-dependency (symbiotic enmeshment) and counter-dependency (estrangement) issues arise and where most relationships break down or lock into dysfunctional longevity.

Stage Three—Stability

The power struggle stage comes to an end when we have the courage and wisdom to accept life and our partner *as they really are.* We stop trying to change them and instead change the way we deal with them. We stop blaming and start supporting. We stop focusing on "what isn't" and focus on "what is." The ideal vision that came to be experienced as *di*-vision is now experienced as *re*-vision—a revised way of perceiving each other.

Stage Four—Commitment

In this stage, we make a clear decision to work things out, to stay rather than to leave. We let go of our attachment to our fantasy of the way it is *supposed* to be and begin to accept and appreciate the way it really is. We now perceive our partner as basically trustworthy and feel safe to be our true self without fear of punishment or blame. Differences are dealt with from clear communication, the spirit of cooperation, the willingness to compromise, and the desire to negotiate. It is through the mutual intention to stay together during good times and bad times that allows committed relationships to endure over time.

Stage Five—Co-Creativity

This stage is marked by interdependent reliance. As couples experience collaborative thinking and joint decision-making, they manifest the conditions for the co-creative stage of the relationship journey. The "yours" and "mine" mentality emerges as a collective synthesis of "us," which forms the partnership state. Here, the couple experiences mutual support for their goals and realize that they can produce more by working collaboratively than by working solo. Statistically, the union of the two people working in co-creative alliance produces *four* times the amount of creative energy than one person working alone.

The couple gives meaning to their individual lives in the larger context, beyond the pair. They have a natural urge to co-create together through consciously raising a child, a joint artistic expression, or working together in community service. They apply the tools and skills of their relationship to include the world around them. These couples have transmuted any tendency to be neurotically needy into a mature trust that each is accountable and can depend on the other. They have grown to a collective maturity to include the needs of others and a desire to make a difference in the world.

All five stages are potentially present all the time in each to different degrees, so try to flow with the ups and downs and hang in there for the bumpy parts. You'll reap the rewards as the road smoothes out.

When Love Gets Misplaced Again

But what do you do when you've been through all these stages, and then get to a point where you feel as though, while you still love your partner, you're not *in love* with your partner?

Of course, couples heading into marriage want their relationships to be full of joy, passion, and great sex forever. They want their relationship to remain the way it was when they first met, began courting, and fell in love.

That would indeed be nice. The trouble is people do change, and relationships change as well. Over time, some couples deepen their love, and their relationship flourishes. Sadly, other couples gradually lose their love and enthusiasm for one another, sexually as well as in other ways. When Oprah Winfrey still had her TV show, she dedicated an entire episode to the epidemic of loveless, sexless relationships.

Why do some relationships make it, while others don't? Why does the intimacy in some relationships flourish, while getting buried in others? Is the love lost forever or just temporarily misplaced? What are the secrets of a happy, fulfilling, and durable relationship?

Three Leading Reasons for Divorce

Infidelity, psychological abuse, and physical violence are the three leading reasons that one out of every two marriages ends in divorce. It has been reported that over 75% of men and approximately 35% of women have been unfaithful at some time during a monogamous marriage. Current statistics reveal that the percentage of unfaithful women is climbing and some have it at over 50%.

When relationships end in divorce, the impact on children can be severe, as a segment of the *20/20* TV show pointed out. Longitudinal studies on divorce reveal that children are affected far more drastically than was formerly believed. It may be said that there is one thing worse than divorce, and that's a really bad marriage.

Psychological abuse and physical violence are frequently tied in with infidelity and/or addiction. The lying, cheating, denial, deception, and betrayal are all destructive to an intimate relationship. There has been so much information in the form of feelings and thoughts that has been withheld from each other that the very life breath of the relationship gets snuffed out.

Survival Through Self-Expansion

As bad as all this gets, many couples can still recover from the destructive impact of infidelity, addiction, dysfunction, and abuse and actually resurrect their relationship, regaining stability, recommitment, and lasting love. They can divert divorce.

Even when there has been deep hurt from infidelity, long-term monogamy is once again doable if couples have good communication skills. Healthy communication can rekindle passion and dynamic sex. Just start somewhere. How about, *"Honey, I've been missing the intimate time that we used to have just for us and would like to find a way to put it back into our relationship."* Her response might be: *"Do you think we can take some time to come home for lunch at some point during the week? In fact, how about a 'nooner' this Friday?"*

Current research has been focusing on modern relationships. Modern couples seem to be looking for "interesting" partnerships. They want partners who *enhance* their lives, partners that they can grow with over time.

Caryl Rusbult, a researcher at Vrije University in Amsterdam, coined the term the "Michelangelo effect," referring to the manner in which close partners "sculpt" each other in ways that help each of them attain valued goals.

Gary W. Lewandowski Jr., associate psychology professor at Monmouth University in New Jersey, has studied how individuals use a relationship to accumulate knowledge and experiences, a process called "self-expansion." The research reveals that the more self-expansion people experience from their partners, the more committed and satisfied they seem to be in the relationship. Dr. Lewandowski discovered that, "People have a fundamental motivation to improve the self and add to who they are as a person. If your partner is helping you become a better person, you become happier and more satisfied in the relationship."

In expansive partnerships, couples do not lose themselves in the marriage. Instead, they grow in it. Behaviors and character traits that had previously not been a part of their identity become essential to how they experience life. Research was conducted at UCLA's Family Studies Center on fifteen hundred couples that had been together for five or more years and acknowledged having a strong, close, deeply committed bond. Their relationships had six characteristics in common:

1. There was a physical attraction between them;
2. They were in the relationship out of clear choice rather than out of obligation or fear of being alone;
3. They shared fundamental values, beliefs, interests, and goals;
4. They were able to express anger clearly and directly, and they resolved differences through communication and compromise;
5. They experienced laughter, fun, pleasure, and play.
6. They were able to express support for each other and support each other's activities, interests, and careers.

Most relationship experts understand that good, lasting relationships mean that each individual must be willing to make the relationship a priority, giving it time, energy, and nurturing. The partners constantly *re-choose* each other. The danger—and what I so often see happening—is that after six or seven years, especially where there are children involved, couples get tired and feel on the verge of burnout. That's when those traits inherent in true friendship and close companionship take on greater importance. The partners must constantly re-choose each other and feed positive energy to the relationship even when they want to pull away. They double down on their effort to make their mate their priority again, each one knowing the other has their back and is looking out for their best interests. They stand by each other through the ups and down times. It can be hard.

A Therapist's View

Forty years of practice as a marriage and family therapist have taught me that men and women essentially want the same things from each other. In the intimacy of the therapy room, I hear men say they want to feel respected and admired by their partners, and I hear women say they want to be nurtured and desired by their partners. Both need to feel appreciated. Men tell me that their partner's sweetness helps them to keep their hearts open. Women tell me that a man's self-confidence is sexy. Women want to be cherished, and men want to be honored. Men become fearful and resentful when their partners lose the sweetness and become brittle, bitter, and "bitchy." Women fear and resent it when their partners become disenchanted, disengaged, and passive, or controlling and domineering.

For a woman, remaining vulnerable and open to her partner and able to exude that attractive energy is what keeps him turned on. For a man, feeling secure and special is what keeps her turned on. If she gets any messages that she's not the number-one person in his life, she will start to close up, and then after a while the mutual attraction will wane.

Understanding is the bridge to compassion, and compassion can be the spark that reignites the passion.

Don't take each other for granted, but rather recall how it felt when you were first discovering each other and were falling deeply and madly in love. It is possible to fall in love all over again!

Chapter 14

Your Work that Works

Choose a job you love, and you will never have to work a day in your life.
—Confucius (551 - 479 BC)

WORK IS A DEFINING force in a man's life. A man's ego is grafted to his perception of whether or not he is successful. Yet, many men can't stand their jobs, and others can't find a job to even determine if they like it or not. Many feel that they are prisoners of their work that gives them little satisfaction and provides them with few tangible rewards, while others feel locked out of work that they desperately need. In either case, it's pure drudgery to them and stands in the way of fulfilling any sense of destiny. A man's self-esteem is vulnerable to his interpretation of how productive and valued he is as a good worker and provider.

Studies show that the level of worker disengagement is at an all-time high in this country. It's up to about 75%. People don't seem to care about their jobs, and no longer give anything extra. Statistics reveal how work is changing in the lives of men. Men are complaining more, withdrawing more, are more exhausted, and are feeling more used and abused. For many, the whole process of seeking work is an unrewarding task, given the lack of jobs due to out-sourcing and the downturn in the economy.

Men today are working about 160 hours more per year than their fathers. That is the equivalent of one whole month of forty-hour weeks. When workers are asked, "When does your work week end?" they can't define it because they're dealing with unlimited e-mails and the constant demands of having a cell phone with them 24/7.

America is suffering from burnout. This puts us at risk of losing the great imagination, creativity, craftsmanship, and the I-can-do-it attitude that has characterized American men since the country was founded on the work ethic of the Masons.

When today's males were boys, they felt that their father's work was more important to them than being fathers. Now that men are working longer hours, how do you suppose their children feel today about their relationships with fathers who are so consumed by work and the need to earn enough money? Men are perpetually driven by the need to keep up so that they don't fall down and out.

This is impacting the younger generation of men in their twenties who are resisting participating in the work force in the ways that their middle-aged fathers have been doing. And at the same time, jobs are scarce, and young men fear that they cannot even enter the workforce, let alone progress in it. Aware of the dissatisfaction they see in their fathers, combined with the absence of career opportunities, they are finding other ways to devote their time and attention.

Demise of the American Dream

Due to the widespread belief that the Great American Dream is now out of reach and probably a phenomenon of the past, there seems to be a budding trend among the younger males to create a work/life balance with real time off from work. Killing oneself through overwork won't bring the rewards that their parent's generation garnered anyway. However, their fathers are prone to question the work ethic of their sons.

Workers in America at one time had strong cultural and family traditions. We worked an eight-hour day and took the weekend off for other activities. Families tended to eat breakfast and dinner together. Husbands often came home for lunch as well. Americans looked forward to an affordable family summer vacation each year.

There is growing evidence that values concerning work are dramatically changing and impacting the traditions that were once heralded as the backbone of the American culture. The economic downturn here and abroad is wreaking havoc with one's ability to maintain balance between work, recreation, relaxation, and the bond that once stabilized the family structure.

There are factions within this country that are quite divergent. One faction is attempting to find work and to earn enough to be able to make ends meet. Another faction, identified as the 1%, is caught up in a quest for material satisfaction. The middle class is diminishing and being absorbed into the haves and have-nots. Those that endeavor to find viable work and those that turn to wealth and possessions for meaning and don't find it share a common outcome, a sense of existential meaninglessness. In the face of such uncertainty and chaos we experience much more alienation and estrangement, leading to more family dysfunction and personal dissatisfaction.

We often embrace our roles as husband, father, and provider with a daunting understanding of their significance in the lives of our mates and children. We feel stretched thin to balance these roles and to also have a life. We feel constrained to keep up with the financial demands of providing a lifestyle for family members that is driven by societal values that have run amuck.

The Price of Passion

Consider the role of passion in your life and in the world of your work. Passion is an emotion, and emotion and work are usually considered incongruent. However, if you think about it, you'll find that passion is at the root of creative genius, personal transformation, and notable events. Passion is emotional energy. It stimulates life and energizes individuals to work toward goals, new products, inspired ideas, and creative ways to deliver services to the public. Inventions and scientific discoveries are produced because someone or some organization is passionate. Consider that if Steve Jobs had not been driven by his passion, Apple would not have risen to the top of the ladder of successful businesses, and he would not have made his mark and changed the world forever. Passion seems to be consistent with what we're striving to accomplish in employment organizations today.

While it's critical for a man's sense of his Male Net Worth to get in touch with his passion, once he does so he has to deal with some of the "new realities" of the modern workplace—because following one's passion can be a very expensive undertaking. Especially if he's in a marriage or committed relationship, he'll need to be prepared to make some compromises.

A typical case is Marshall, who works in the movie industry as an animator. He's very clear about his *dream*: He wants to be a director of full-length animated films, and he's got the talent. When he gets work, it pays well, but it can be months between jobs, and he gets no insurance. His wife, Alicia, works as a producer's assistant and earns a steady salary. She has been on the job ten years and gets insurance coverage for the family. They have two young sons, and Alicia would like to stay home but cannot if she wants insurance. She's always exhausted and frequently on edge. They have a nanny whose salary eats up a big portion of their income.

Like so many women, Alicia has moments when she blames her husband for not being willing to give up his dream and go to work at the corner gas station (and then she *hates* herself for feeling that way). More often, she blames herself for "wanting it all and not handling it well" instead of looking at some of the real economic conditions in the world outside her front door.

When Your Work and Her Work Clash

Today one in three married women out-earn their husbands (a Bureau of Labor Statistics figure). Old male-female work roles are pretty hardwired into us, going back to the cave, and attitudes at depth don't change as fast as we'd like them to. Elicit a candid response from a woman who is one of these "high-earners" with a stay-at-home husband, and you're likely to find a woman who may *talk* a good game, but at a gut-level (which she may not even be aware of) she resents it—even worse, she feels contempt for the man who isn't pulling his own weight. As one such wife put it, "I've had moments where I felt, 'Why do I have to be the man in this relationship.'" Worse, some of the men feel exactly the same way because of their own hardwiring. If couples aren't honest with themselves about how they really feel instead of trying to be trendy, it can be destructive.

One thing I've noticed working with such couples in my practice is that many women are actually sympathetic to their man's dream and want him to go for it—just as she wants him to encourage *her* dream—but there's a limit on the sacrifices she's willing to make and for how long. A deep mutual understanding of what the other experiences on a daily basis is an important step in dealing with all this.

Men need to know that no matter what women say aloud, most working mothers experience guilt about working outside the home, especially when they have younger kids. Any comment from their man, such as, "We're out of orange juice," or "I thought you said you'd be home at six," can trigger a defensive response. Men can help a lot by saying instead such things as, "Don't worry about dinner, I'll pick up take out," or "I truly appreciate what you're contributing," or "I want you to have your dream." She'll breathe a sigh of relief and *want* to do something nice for the man in return.

Raising Men's Sense of "Male Net Worth"

As discussed in the earlier section on Male Provider Syndrome, many men lie awake at night worrying about work and its impact on their roles as provider for their families. Symptoms of anxiety, depression, and despair can cause a man to feel he is being swallowed up. However, a man can reassess his lifestyle to make the necessary adjustments to live within his means and can reduce the stressful symptoms that are plaguing him and instead help him raise his sense of "net worth."

Part of my work as a therapist is to help men assess their assets, reevaluating and recasting their ideas of success and what "good work" is for them. Too many men get addicted to winning the game of success, which is different and ultimately far less rewarding than being truly successful. Some men enter therapy awash in material success but bankrupt in authentic manly value. They've invested in a kind of false masculinity, measuring manliness by their material muscle. I endeavor to help them map a new pathway that can keep them financially secure and help them raise their Male Net Worth by leading them to examine their belief systems to see what is keeping them from genuine achievement and real satisfaction.

A former patient, Gordon, was able to raise his "Male Net Worth" and even his financial net worth once he was able to believe in himself and what he was doing. Faced with a raging cocaine addiction and an unfulfilling professional life, Gordon began to realize that unless he came to terms with his self-destructive behavior he would wind up in prison or dead. He had a curiosity and passion for spiritual pursuits, and I could tell that it troubled him that he was not living in accord with what he knew to be his true values and aspirations.

Gordon was able to turn a corner, get sober, and establish a loving relationship with a good woman. By raising his self-esteem, he was able to bring his "Male Net Worth" in balance with his innate entrepreneurial talents. Today, his greatest joy comes from his ability to be of help to others. He turned his life around, creating and then becoming the CEO of a four billion dollar recreation-oriented resort—an enterprise that made his life more balanced, more loving, and more fun.

Years after we had worked together, I received a letter from Gordon in which he expressed, "It has actually been five years since we last met in person; however, the influence of knowing you still lives on in my life. I am a sober professional with a successful and productive home life that is the envy of all within my personal circle; it may surprise you to learn that within my circle, people actually approach me for counsel in hopes of being able to achieve the spiritually peaceful disposition that I exhibit every day."

Gordon went on to say, "My definition of peace is serenity in the face of turmoil. With or without the use of those exact words, my ability to maintain 'peace' regardless of the circumstance stems directly from what I had learned from you and my exposure to you as my then example of 'A Man.' It warms my heart to personally share with you the results of the impact your influence has had on my life."

Giving Boys Important Work

In his book, *The Wonder of Boys: What Parents, Mentors and Educators Can Do to Shape Boys into Exceptional Men* (Tarcher/Putnam, 1997) Michael Gurian states,

"An essential element of happy boyhood and happy manhood is the love of work—not all work but especially those few and important tasks through which boys and men learn intimacy with others, physical and mental maturity, self-confidence, and the ways of the world. Males are both hard- and soft-wired to work at tasks, achieve definable objectives in the tasks, and gain self-image from working at the tasks. Without constructive work, men often feel terribly lost. That the same can be said of girls and women in their way takes nothing away from the fact that for so many boys and men, working often feels as important as breathing."

Gurian goes on to say,

"Boys don't just need work, they need important work. That means they need us to be involved with them in that part of work where we can give wisdom and blessing. They need us to show them how the work is a vehicle for experiencing deep joys and sympathies other than the work itself. They need us to explain the importance of the work to them, putting it in a context of importance to themselves, their family, their community, and their society. They need us to show them how essential it is in their husbanding and their sacred roles. When the work is drudgery, we must help them find meaning in it. Somehow, we must help the boy find the piece of the job that is sacred."

In conclusion Michael encourages,

"As boys are led by parents, mentors, and educators into a rich life of work and play they need a language too for 'inner work.' From very early on in a boy's life, we need to show the boy that his managing and soothing of his own fears, pains, griefs, and angers are 'the work of being human, the internal work of being a boy, then a man, a lover, then a husband.' How wonderful it is for a boy when the adults around him ask, 'What are you learning about yourself, your friends, and your community as you do such and such work?' For a boy's work to be important, it needs the dialogue of elders constantly around it."

Finding and Fulfilling Your Destiny

"One of the hallmarks of honorable men is they do their jobs and earn their way. Millions of ordinary guys no one has ever heard of spend their lives going to work every day and putting in a solid eight (or ten) hours routinely without goofing off, sleeping on the job, or avoiding the responsibilities of their positions. They aren't necessarily geniuses or rock stars. But they show up on time and give their employers a full day's work for a day's pay.

The world counts on these quiet heroes. They keep the trains running and the phones working. They come home tired at the end of the day, knowing they've earned their way."

— *The Men's Code of Honor: 66 Principles that Make a Man*
by Dan Stradford, Whisper Canyon Publishing, 2112

Brad Zervas, Executive Director of The Boys Club of New York, transformed his life from working at a high-risk job to a position that he feels is "living his destiny." He had been working in the prison system, enduring periodic lockdowns when prisoners would become agitated, creating the threat of rioting. Brad's wife was concerned for his safety and encouraged him to find another job. He took a position in a New England Prep School in which he met some boys that had been assisted by The Boys Club of New York to stay in school, work hard, and aspire to higher education. This inspired Brad to get involved with the Boys Club and eventually move into the position of executive director.

Another example of a man who found new meaning in his life is tobacco heir Patrick Reynolds, grandson of R. J. Reynolds. Patrick came of age without the male guidance that he needed to teach him what it meant to be a man and how to work with his inheritance. After an attempt at an acting career and having blown through his inheritance, he was inspired to become an anti-smoking activist and formed a non-profit foundation to support his cause.

Infusion of the Sacred

> *Businesses based on money motivation tend to fail while those centered on what one loves to do tend to succeed.*
>
> —Leonard Orr, prosperity consultant

In surveys asking people why they work and what they value about their workplace, being in good relationships with their colleagues is always at the top of the list. Productivity and satisfaction result from a good collegial atmosphere. People also indicate that replacing values centered on personal consumption and greed with values that are spiritually centered on love and kindness makes for a healthy work culture.

A healthy infusion of the Sacred into the mix, along with the other material ingredients comprising your work in the world, will allow you to experience more personal satisfaction on a day-to-day basis. Balancing material and spiritual pursuits is the key to a successful lifestyle.

Prosperity consultant, Leonard Orr teaches that there are four metaphysical laws of wealth:

1. *Earning*: All wealth is ultimately created by the human mind. Thought is creative, and energy flows in the direction of our thoughts. He suggests that a good

affirmation to meditate on is: "I deserve to be wealthy. My job is the pipeline through which I tap the world economy for my prosperity."

2. *Spending* and *Exchange:* The purpose of money is to create exchange. He encourages us to produce enough to provide for others and gives us the following affirmation to contemplate: *"The more willing I am to spend my money with other people, the more willing they are to spend their money with me."* Here are a couple of others to work with: *"My income now exceeds my expenses," and, "Every dollar I spend comes back to me multiplied."*
3. *Savings*: It's wise to set aside a portion of your present production in order to provide for your future. Suggested affirmations to contemplate are: *"A part of all I earn is mine to keep,"* and *"My income increases every day whether I'm working, sleeping, or playing."*
4. *Investing*: This is a way to increase future savings and to enhance future production. A couple of thoughts to affirm and apply are: *"All my investments are profitable,"* and *"Part of all my profits goes into permanent wealth, current expenses, capital, and reserves."*

It can be helpful to write your affirmations ten times a day and to observe your mind to see if any thoughts arise that are counter to the truth that you're aspiring to manifest into results. You might write the affirmations on small cards that can be placed in locations where you can see them, like on your mirror so that it's apparent while you're shaving, or on your checkbook or computer screen. Contemplating high-powered thoughts that you want to affirm is a great way to recondition your mind to expect successful results and raise your "Male NetWorth."

Chapter 15

Mindful Manhood

Look at every path closely and deliberately.
Try it as many times as you think necessary.
Then ask yourself, and yourself alone...
Does this path have heart? If it does, the
Path is good. If it doesn't, it is of no use.
— Carlos Castaneda (1925 – 1998)

THERE IS A COMMON BELIEF that meditation is strictly a practice in which you free your mind of all thoughts so that you can have an absolutely blank screen. Therein lies the rub. Men don't easily surrender to "nothing." We are wired to move from something to something else. When I ask men if they meditate, I often hear something like, "I've tried it, but I can't quiet my mind enough to get any benefit from it. I just feel more frustration," or, "My brain just won't shut off. I'm bombarded with so many random thoughts, so trying to meditate is just a bust." Men often tend to resist meditating because they believe it is a passive activity that is virtually impossible to accomplish, let alone to master.

Meditation, in actuality, is an *active* process. It can be done with eyes open, in a noisy, busy location, and even on the run. You don't have to shut out the world or have a quiet and darkened place in which to sit in a particular pose. Mindfulness meditation is quite interactive because we are engaged in the world with the intention of finding peaceful balance, internally and externally. Mindfulness can be characterized as purposeful attention to what's so in the present moment with relaxed presence and focused awareness, devoid of critical judgment (as in condemnation) while utilizing wise judgment (as in discernment).

A longtime friend and colleague, Ron Alexander, Ph.D., published a book on mindfulness titled *Wise Mind, Open Mind: Finding Purpose and Meaning in Times of Crisis, Loss, and Change* (New Harbinger, 2009) He explains that,

> "In Buddhism, wise mind is a state of consciousness that allows you to observe your thoughts without becoming emotionally invested in them. In wise mind you stop running with your thoughts wherever they take you and find yourself sitting with a sense of serenity and clarity, observing what your mind churns up and easily discerning its qualities, setting aside what's unwholesome and taking delight in what's wholesome." Wise mind results from building *mindstrength*, the ability to use mindfulness to master thoughts, beliefs, and emotions, and tap into the core creativity that empowers you to take positive and wise action."

Over the course of a full year, I facilitated a series of six *practicums* for men on mindfulness. A practicum is essentially an experiential workshop in which you get to experiment with the process of learning skillful actions or practical tools for accomplishing intended goals. The overall purpose of the training was to investigate and understand how mind, brain, and body work together in ways that enhance personal growth and development through engaging in the practices of meditation and conscious connected breathing.

The willingness to become intimate with the mystical nature of our souls, in contrast with the mind's tendency for attachment to the conceptual illusions about the world, allows you to more fully comprehend the distinction between self and selflessness. Our challenge today is how to find interior peace, compassion, and wisdom within our hearts in the midst of a world of turbulent change. We are challenged to engage with the exterior world while walking a path of enlightenment, guiding us to become the Spiritual Warriors that we are destined to be.

In training yourself to live in a heightened state of mindfulness, it is helpful to engage in certain practices that concretize the experience, making it real and vital for you. It's well worth taking the time to learn how to incorporate this useful tool into your life. Having the right tools for the task at hand can be most helpful. Practices, like tools, are practical instruments for use in dealing with life's challenges. We may not be able to control what lesson life has dealt us, but with the right practices at hand, we have a better opportunity to control how we respond to the challenge.

Let's consider seven of the many practices that can expand your state of mindfulness—the practices of non-resistance, refraining, patience, stillness, solitude, discernment, and light-heartedness.

The Practice of Non-Resistance

How often do you feel truly at ease within yourself? On the level of your thinking mind, do you find a great deal of resistance in the form of judgment, discontent, and mental projections? On the emotional level, do you notice an undercurrent of unease, tension, boredom, or nervousness? Both are aspects of the mind in its habitual resistance mode.

Let's consider the condition of resistance and the *practice of non-resistance.* For a moment, place both of your hands in prayer position, palm against palm. Simply feel the touch of your flesh and the warmth of your body heat. Now apply some gentle pressure, one hand pushing gently against the other. Just feel the subtle tension that has been created by this act. Increase the pressure slightly and notice how it feels. Notice how the resistance translates through your hands and into your arms and up into your shoulders. Increase the pressure even more and notice how the tension can be felt in your chest and upper back. Become aware of how far the pressure has radiated from the source of the tension in your hands into other parts of your body.

You are now practicing mindfulness. You are focusing your attention on the awareness of how resistance affects your physical body. Perhaps, you are also aware of how this process is affecting your thoughts and maybe even your emotions. Now release the tension and notice what it feels like to be free of its effects. You have just *let go* and in a way have surrendered. There's no more fight. You are non-resistant—at least for the moment. Most people, maybe even you, are typically unconscious of the resistance that exists in their lives on a day-to-day basis, but it is present nonetheless, doing whatever it's doing.

Take a few minutes now to contemplate this question, "Where else could resistance reside within me, and how am I dealing with the stress that is impacting me from the outside?" How do you hold on or hold back? What are you resisting in your life today that you might choose to let go of and free yourself from, creating more space and spaciousness around and within you? What fills your mind with thoughts that plague you? Do you tend to obsess on thoughts that just cause worry, nervousness, and anxiety? What would it be like to free your mind from ego-driven chatter and experience the peace that passes all understanding and accentuates through stillness and silence?

A man in one of the weekly groups that I facilitate stated that he didn't quite understand why resistance was not called for under certain conditions. His concern was that if he didn't resist some of what people within his family and work life were trying to impose on him, he'd just be swept away by their influence and would lose himself under their control. He asked, "Shouldn't we resist giving in to people who don't have our best interests in mind or might be harmful to us or wrong for us in some way?"

This is a reasonable question that brings up the idea that perhaps we should avoid an external condition that we don't want by not giving into it. The answer, I think, is the same, no matter if we are dealing with an internal or an external condition. Resistance breeds persistence. In other words, the very thing that we resist often lasts longer or gets stronger when we feed energy to it by resisting it. When we resist something, we attempt to *not* be taken over by it. Those who practice the martial arts tell us to give in to it without giving up, and find the solution from within rather than from without. We neutralize the energy of something that we would have resisted by softening and merging with the energy, then transforming it from the inside.

In her book, *One Day My Soul Just Opened Up* (Fireside Books, 1998), science of mind practitioner Iyanla Vanzant states,

> "Resistance to doing what we know must be done is a derivative of fear. Fear is a tool of the ego. Fear, cleverly disguised as resistance, supports unwillingness. We are unwilling to be wrong, to look or sound stupid, to be challenged or defeated. The more entrenched we become in resistance, the further we move away from a state of willingness. The divine does not remember our errors or calculate our perceived defeats. Nor does the divine energy of life judge our methods or choices. The divine merely asks us to be willing to do whatever is necessary to move into our own state of divinity, which means that we must develop wisdom, judgment, and courage through willingness."

Eckhart Tolle states in his breakthrough book, *The Power of Now*,

> "In ordinary unconsciousness, habitual resistance to or

denial of what *is* creates the unease and discontent that most people accept as normal living. When this resistance becomes intensified through some challenge or threat to the ego, it brings up intense negativity such as anger, acute fear, aggression, depression, and so on...The best indicator of your level of consciousness is how you deal with life's challenges when they come. Through those challenges, an already unconscious person tends to become more deeply unconscious and a conscious person more intensely conscious. You can use a challenge to awaken you, or you can allow it to pull you into even deeper sleep."

Eckhart's message is meant to awaken us to the fact that it is essential for us to bring more consciousness into our lives and to grow in our awareness and presence; essentially, to be more mindful. This generates an energy field within us that creates a high vibrational frequency. He tells us that when every cell of our body is so present that it feels vibrant with life, and when we can *feel* that life in every moment as the pure joy of being, then it can be said that we are resonating in a state of mindfulness.

In addition to meditation, conscious connected energy breathing, a dynamic breathing practice also known as rebirthing, accelerates this process. The term rebirthing was coined by Leonard Orr in the late 1960s. He discovered that connecting your inhale to the exhale in a relaxed continuous rhythm is a safe and powerful method for healing any damage done to the breathing mechanism during or after birth. Leonard recommends that ten simple coached intuitive breathing lessons restore full power of the breath to revitalize and energize body, mind, and spirit. Rebirthing can release restrictions in breathing and resistance held throughout the body due to past traumas. Those experiencing the practice can learn to breathe energy as well as air and can clean and balance their energy bodies. The secret to deep relaxation and ability to release tension and restore equanimity is through transforming negatively-held beliefs and core laws into positively-charged affirmations.

In a talk called "Grief and Fear: Touching No Birth and No Death," given at the San Diego Civic Center in 2002, renowned Buddhist monk Thich Nhat Hanh said, "To live mindfully means to be able to breathe in the here and now and to look deeply into our feelings and our perceptions."

These practices can be helpful tools on your journey to a more mindful state of being, so prepare yourself to slow down and learn to relax and experience the true meaning of rest. Find a comfortable place to just *be* for a little while and take a few deep breaths or even twenty connected breaths as you consider where you want to go with your life and what transformation may be required to allow you to be more fully present in the *now* on your personal spiritual path to enlightenment.

Let's continue by considering the *practice of refraining*.

The Practice of Refraining

Many years ago, when Buddhist teacher and psychologist Jack Kornfield was about to leave Thailand after an intense learning experience, his teacher, Ajahn Chah Master Chah, encouraged his student to return to the states and "teach people the practices of compassion and loving kindness so that they discover it; that it's possible for them. Teach people the practices of letting go of fear and confusion and grasping and anger so that their hearts can be free."

How do you quiet the mind? How do you open the heart? How do you release the small sense of self, that's referred to as the "body of fear" or the "pain body?" How do you let go of the confusions that we get lost in throughout our day and come to a place of trust and release that has wisdom, that's not foolish, that can see clearly, and that meets the world with respect and courage rather than with confusion or fear?

Kornfield learned that the direct practices of quieting the mind, opening the heart through mindful attention, the cultivation of compassion and loving kindness, and steadying oneself though the practice of refraining in the midst of the ways of the world, are useful to everybody.

"Be still, and know that I am God" (Psalm 46:10). This scripture asks us to stop what we're doing and be in a place of non-activity in order to sense, feel, and know the presence and power of God where we are. We have to be still and refrain from activities that divert our focus from what's truly important and significant. There are times that we can get so distracted by the mundane activities of life that we lose our sense of oneness and connectedness to our source.

Have you noticed those times when a tiny negative thought crosses your mind and, like a magnet, starts to attract other frustrations and irritations? Picking up speed, your mind becomes a whirlwind of chaos and ascends to a maelstrom of fear, fury, or depression. Anxiety and physical complaints jump on board for the quick ride to unhappiness and hopelessness. Your ego begins to play the victim, groveling in misery. Fortunately, there is a way to stop this emotional churning.

The antidote comes in the form of a reminder to, "*Let go, let God*," which is immediate and calming. In changing your perception, you release the problem and surrender all attempts to control the external world. Turning within, you notice that God or universal intelligence or the divine creative source has the answer and is available to guide and comfort you. Returning to peace, you relax and remember that there is a divine order in the universe.

Buddhist Nun Pema Chodron teaches that,

> "Refraining is very much the method of becoming a Dharmic person. It's the quality of not grabbing for entertainment the minute we feel a slight edge of boredom coming on. It's the practice of not immediately filling up space just because there's a gap."

She suggests that,

> "An interesting practice that combines mindfulness and refraining is just to notice your physical movements when you feel uncomfortable. When we feel like we're losing ground, we make all kinds of little jumpy, jittery movements. You might notice that when you feel uncomfortable you do things like pull your ear, scratch something even though it doesn't itch, or straighten your collar. When you notice what you do, don't try to change it. Don't criticize yourself for whatever it is you're doing. Just notice what it is."

Chodron continues,

> "Refraining, or not habitually acting out impulsively, has something to do with giving up the entertainment mentality. Through refraining, we see that there's something between the arising of the craving—or the aggression or the loneliness or whatever it might be—and whatever action we take as a result. There's something within us that we don't want to experience, and we never do experience, because we're so quick to act. The practice of refraining is a way to get in touch with basic groundlessness —by noticing how we try to avoid it (*Comfortable with Uncertainty: 108 Teachings on Cultivating Fearlessness and Compassion,* Shambhala Publications, 2002)."

Numerous different scientific studies have been done in the last ten years showing the effectiveness of training our attention. Now neuroscientists recognize that the neuro-plasticity of our brain lasts until the very end of life; that it's never too late to train the mind and change yourself; that where you put your attention actually changes your nervous system in measurable ways, so that if you practice anger, after a while those neural pathways get reinforced. If you practice equanimity or love or compassion, those neurological pathways become transformed in a measurable way.

Jon Kabat-Zinn pioneered trainings in the west on Mindfulness-Based Stress Reduction and Mindfulness-Based Cognitive Therapy. Kabat-Zinn is the founder and former executive director of the Center for Mindfulness in Medicine, Health Care, and Society at the University of Massachusetts Medical School. He is also the founder (1979) and former director of its renowned stress reduction clinic and professor of medicine emeritus at the University of Massachusetts Medical School.

Mindfulness-Based Stress Reduction is an eight-week course that combines meditation and Hatha yoga to help patients cope with stress, pain, and illness by using moment-to-moment awareness. Kabat-Zinn and colleagues have studied the effects of practicing moment-to-moment awareness on the brain and how it processes emotions, particularly under stress, and on the immune system. Over 200 medical centers and clinics in the US and elsewhere now utilize the Mindfulness-Based Stress Reduction (MBSR) model.

There are many beautiful practices for embodying inner well-being in your life. For instance, the practice of *wise speech* is about speaking words that are true and useful, that are timely and to the benefit of everyone concerned. When you're in conflict or in a situation where there could be problems or harm in what you're saying, incorporating the practice of refraining trains you to take a deep breath, quiet yourself, and get in touch with, or listen for, your deepest intention. The intention behind the words is more important even than the words that are said. You allow yourself to suspend what you *might* have blurted out and hold it up in your mind to see the intention behind the thought and ask yourself if the expression of it is 1. good for you, 2. good for the recipient, and 3. will it hurt anyone?

I was working with a man recently who was attempting to discern whether or not to remain in a relationship with the woman he had been living with for eight months. Their communication had degraded into arguments fraught with bickering and quarrels where mutual respect was lacking. He was having trouble interrupting the pattern and being able to maintain harmony in the face of disagreements. Though they had discussed marriage, he was now feeling the need to leave the relationship in order to restore peace and equanimity in his life. I asked him to state his highest intention for the relationship so that he was aware of what he wanted. I then worked with him to find the words to convey it to his partner.

He practiced taking some deep breaths to relax and center himself, and then he expressed his intention of refraining from conflict in order to transform their communications into something more loving. He wanted to have a safer environment so that they could both be more vulnerable, and therefore more intimate. I suggested that the two of them sit together and breathe to get centered before actually conversing.

When the moment came, he found the words within to comfortably express himself: "My highest intention is that we go forward and improve upon our friendship, staying connected and continuing our relationship with respect. I love you and don't want to argue with you. Let's find a better way to resolve our disagreements so that we can feel that our mutual needs are being met." They discovered that the points they wanted to make could be expressed with respect for the other's point of view. Their listening and their words conveyed greater compassion and care.

Another aspect within the practice of refraining is that of *letting go*, knowing when to refrain and when to let go. This is the teaching about not grasping and holding on and trying to control people.

You will notice the distinction between refraining and the actions of oppressing, suppressing, and repressing that lead to very different outcomes. Oppression is when you control another by holding him back or putting him down. Suppression is when your conscious mind decides to not deal with something and pushes it aside. Repression is when your unconscious mind makes a decision not to deal with something and not to allow it to even intrude upon your consciousness. All three of these dynamics tend to lead to the feeling of depression because they are the opposite of expression. And the by-products of this are harbored resentments, loss of energy and vitality, and a lack of joy.

With the practice of refraining, one learns to suspend a thought or action long enough to set up the process of mindful discernment in which you present yourself with the opportunity to decide what is the best course of action to take. The evolution of this process takes you from: 1. refraining to 2. suspending to 3. discerning to 4. deciding to 5. taking skillful action.

Now let's take up the *practice of patience.*

The Practice of Patience

What is your relationship with patience? Are you a patient person? Patience is one of the cornerstones of mindfulness practice. When we practice patience, we allow grace to flow into our lives; we open up to something bigger than ourselves. And it is only through grace that universal intelligence can provide us with miraculous outcomes much greater than we may have requested or even envisioned.

Most people are in a big hurry today. We're over-busy and lack enough time to get our tasks done, let alone slow down in order to rest, relax, and recreate. We find it difficult to wait and allow things to come to us and unfold in their own time. We're in such a rush to see the bloom that we risk breaking off the bud trying to get it to unfold for us in *this* moment rather than allowing it to unfold in its own perfect time.

Psychiatrist, Edward Hallowell, M.D., has authored many books on various psychological topics, including problems with attention, focus, stress, and worry. His national best-sellers, *Driven to Distraction* (Pantheon, 1994) and *Answers to Distraction* (Pantheon,

1995), discuss attention deficit disorder in children and in adults.

He wrote a book called *Crazy Busy* (Random House, 2007) about this growing phenomenon after being on vacation with his family in a cabin on a lake and having to use an older model rotary dial telephone. He found that he felt impatient with the rotary dial. He had become so accustomed to the rapid response of his cell phone that waiting for the dial to return so that he could dial the next number caused an irritating reaction.

The new technology can be helpful, but when it fails, it can leave us feeling adrift and uncomfortably helpless. We've become dependent on a need for our lives to function consistently, efficiently, and now rapidly in order to keep up. Ask yourself, Where do I find myself being impatient? Is it when I'm trying to get to an appointment and find myself stalled in congested traffic? What causes me to become impatient with myself or with others? Can I wait comfortably for my meal when the restaurant is crowded, and my waiter is tending to many other patrons as well? Am I okay if my cell phone is on the blink or if my car or my computer is in for repair?

Things can only come to us when we are ready. In the process of our expansion and attraction, there are some vital stages that cannot be skipped—they are nurturing, deepening, aligning, and, yes, waiting. And all of these mean cultivating patience.

In practicing patience to its fullest, we also have to learn to identify our dreams and aspirations. This process entails finding out what we want and then holding that truth deep within our hearts, allowing it to guide us from within so that we respond to each present moment authentically and in alignment with our heart's desire. In cultivating our dreams, we nurture them into existence, allowing them to develop in their own time. The secret is to stay focused on the now and not worry about the future because the future, in fact, is just a series of incremental "nows."

A helpful mindfulness meditation practice is to sit comfortably and place both hands palms open, facing up, resting on your thighs, and just feel the breath as you inhale and exhale. Observe your mind by silently saying the word "thinking" every time a thought passes by, and then bring your attention back to your breath and the space between your thoughts. As you center yourself, you might begin to connect with some deeper spiritual truths and contemplate some questions. What are you really feeling about your current situation? What do you love, and what no longer rings true? What's missing, and how can you become fulfilled? And most importantly, what is your next frontier of growth? What do you need to experience in your next cycle of evolution? Once you have a clear sense of your goal, nurture it by holding it deep in your heart and focusing on what you can do in the "now" each day to move toward it.

When we can attune ourselves to the voice of our higher power or expanded consciousness, we develop faith, which is comprised of courage, determination, and trust. We learn to pace ourselves and discover the art of divine timing. It can be quite helpful when you are feeling impatient in the moment to take some deep breaths and utilize the mindfulness meditation mantra as you inhale, *I am patient*, and on the exhale, *I can wait*. Performing this meditation for a few minutes can have the effect of making the wait seem shorter and less irritating, perhaps even pleasant.

To strengthen your inner connection to faith, you start by developing a robust relationship with your higher power. This means communicating with it as if it's your best friend—an awareness or presence that is constantly with you everywhere, in every situation.

The next step to reaching for your ultimate destiny is to align with who you need to become to achieve it. If we don't prepare ourselves for success, it can very easily make us uncomfortable, and we will sabotage it to return to our small, familiar selves. One of the marks of a Spiritual Warrior is to not play small but to allow your light to shine brightly as you expand your awareness and allow your radiant consciousness to grow and develop.

How can you constructively spend your time waiting for your vision to manifest? What beliefs do you have that might prevent you from being able to hold and enjoy the experience? You can start to dissolve them by tracing them back to their source, to the first time you ever took them on. Take a soul-level look at the time and ask yourself what were the lessons and gifts in that situation? Which of your strengths was it meant to develop, and how would you deal with it differently now? And what will it take for you to become more aligned with your imminent success?

An essential quality of the practice of patience is gratitude. While you're waiting for your desired outcome, focus on the gifts of life that you currently enjoy. If you don't have riches, do you have health? If you don't have a relationship with a partner, do you have family? If you don't have peace or fulfillment, do you have hope? This not only helps you feel less incomplete but it also prepares you to hold on to your dreams when they materialize.

In practicing the art of gratitude, you will develop a much greater capacity to appreciate your dreams when they come true. In waiting, we allow a greater truth to emerge from within us. If we stay mindful and cultivate patience, we begin to see the bigger picture of our desires, we hear our inner voice telling us a deeper truth, and we experience life more keenly. Waiting deepens and enriches us. You might consider that you're living the unfolding of God's perfect plan for you.

The Practice of Stillness

The reason why stillness is crucial to mastering the path of mindfulness is because only when you are able to quiet the noise of your ego-thinking-mind will you be prepared to hear the still quiet voice of your intuitive soul. You might also consider it to be your true inner knowing that speaks through the voice of your enlightened-natural-self. Through this preparation you will be able to incorporate one of the most important of the six practices.

Eckhart Tolle, in his book, *Stillness Speaks* (Namaste Publishing, 2003), states that,

> "When you lose touch with inner stillness, you lose touch with yourself. When you lose touch with yourself, you lose yourself in the world. Your innermost sense of self, of who you are, is inseparable from stillness. This is the *I Am* that is deeper than name and form."

By letting go into stillness, you have permission to slow down and give your nervous system a rest. When you allow yourself to surrender to this extraordinary state of calmness you create the precious opportunity to de-stress yourself and return to balance.

When we enter the dimension of stillness, we touch the deeper sense of awareness that allows us to truly know. In "Discourse 40" from Paramahansa Yogananda's extraordinary two-volume Darshans on *The Second Coming of Christ: The Resurrection of the Christ Within You* (Self Realization Fellowship, 2004), he states, "When bodily motions cease and thoughts become quiet, God begins to appear as the blessedness of stillness and divine bliss on the altar of peace and changelessness."

On the back cover of Tolle's book, he states that,

> "Stillness is also inner peace, and that stillness and peace is the essence of your being. It is the stillness that will save and transform the world." In *The Power of Now* (New World Library, 1999), Eckhart encourages us to, "Pay more attention to the silence than to the sounds. Paying attention to outer silence creates inner silence: the mind becomes still. A portal is opening up. Every sound is born out of silence, dies back into silence, and during its life span is surrounded by silence...You cannot pay attention to silence without simul-

taneously becoming still within. Silence without; stillness within. You have entered the Unmanifested."

Eckhart recommends that,

"One way to approach silence as a spiritual practice is to remain in a listening mode during your silent time. The still, small voice within might not arise in the form of words—it may come in an idea you had never thought of before, or in the image of something or someone. It may not even come to you during the silence but perhaps afterwards and when you least expect it. One of the most powerful spiritual practices you can adopt may also be one of the easiest to do after you have mastered it."

Allow yourself today to sink deeply into the stillness that makes it possible for you to completely surrender to whatever you may encounter on your way to ultimately becoming the bliss of Samadhi. It begins with you.

The following can be helpful in learning how to practice an hour of silence: Endeavor to schedule your hour of silence at a particular time. Work up to an hour in increments of ten minutes. During that hour, turn off the phone, TV, radio, computer, and all other appliances and communication devices. Set aside all books and other reading material. Light a candle to be a witness to your hour of silence. Burn some incense if you wish. Sit quietly and rest in meditation—follow your breath, gaze attentively at a natural object like a candle flame or a flower, engage in work that does not require you to hear, see, or express words.

Effortless housekeeping, gardening, or a long walk in nature can be excellent activities of silence. Listen to the silence, all the time enjoying this hour-long respite from thinking, reviewing, planning, and imagining. Just stay in the present moment. Breathe deeply and mindfully, bringing in the silence, expelling mental noise. At the end of your hour of silence, let your first word be an expression of gratitude or love, then go about your business.

The Practice of Solitude

It seems that we've become a society that values activity over action, distraction over focused attention, distance over presence, and denial over conscious awareness. The widespread symptoms of depression, anxiety, and ADD/ADHD may be symptoms of a culture that doesn't allow itself the time to be quiet and to rest. Feeling the need to be constantly busy is an easy distraction from the task of turning inward and dealing with what's truly going on inside. Activity isn't necessarily wrong, but many of us are out of balance, and the need to be active arises more out of a defense against what might surface during a period of silence and stillness.

I have found that many men have a lot of trouble just being alone. They tell me that they feel lonely, and that causes anxiety and depression. I explain to them that solitude offers an opportunity to explore the sense of loneliness and alienation that they feel and to realize that being alone need not doom them to the negative side of aloneness.

There are two sides to aloneness. One is lonely. That's when you feel a victim of being alone. The other is solitude. That arrives when you have mastered the antidote to aloneness by sitting in your loneliness and learning from it. You have to be brave and face your fears. Most of the time loneliness comes not so much from the act of just being alone but more from your not feeling safe and comfortable just being alone with yourself. You can also feel lonesome, and that's when you feel depressed or sad because of the lack of friends and companionship. There is a time to be alone and a time to connect and engage with others.

If you can't comfortably be with yourself then you'll find it hard, if not excruciating, to intimately be with another. This usually leads to isolation and estrangement. The answer is that you have to be alone with yourself until you unravel what's at the root of your loneliness.

What happens when one enters stillness and is silent for a long period of time? Eckhart Tolle's teachings provide the answer.

> "The outer noise goes first, and then the inner noise starts to evaporate. Soon, quiet reigns everywhere, it seems. Time slows to a crawl. Sound becomes a curiosity—natural sounds, especially, like the flow of water or the rustle and sway of tall grass, become occasions for deeper listening and lead to a most profound inner calm."

Tolle suggests,

> "That in such moments as these, we sense the presence of something deep and true. We enter into our own fullness. Somehow the worry and burdens of life drop away. We are summoned to be more truly alive. It is the call to spiritual solitude, the call to be intimately with oneself, to simply be."

Solitude summons us to personal reflection and introspective healing. It calls to us as a sacred time of rejuvenation in which balance and wholeness are nurtured. Quiet, contemplative time alone fosters in us an opportunity for expanded awareness of our true essence. In this spaciousness of inward reflection, we pause from recounting our story over and over and discover the freedom to live fully in the now, in the space of the present moment.

Solitude can open a doorway in us to awakening, guiding us to an awareness of our own true nature and offering us a way to connect profoundly with our own true being. Marsha Sinetar, Ph.D., is an organizational psychologist, mediator, and writer who for the past several years has been increasingly immersed in the study of self-actualizing adults. In her book, *Ordinary People as Monks and Mystics* (Paulist Press, 2007), Sinetar states,

> "Spiritual solitude is a deep call or summons to turn our attention toward God. This summons is often a hallmark of wholeness. It is a hallmark of wholeness in the sense that the person who is growing spiritually whole in a maturing way makes a radical turn toward something true within."

She goes on to say,

"Something in our soul moves us to lean into God from our deepest, hidden springs of being. There is a subtle, awakened state that involves the soul's unending communion with God. To hear that summons and to attend to it, one needs a bit of time alone, but this is not the same as isolation. What I'm talking about with regard to wholesome solitude is not about form. We don't approach our solitude in any kind of formulaic way. It's not a drama; it's not isolation. It's really a full recovery of our humanity."

In Sinetar's research and observations, she discovered that people who take time out from their busy lives to be alone tend to be self-governing. They have a tendency to look within for their guiding values, the rules by which to live. Those that heed the call to solitude are true contemplatives and tend to embrace a state of Christ-like or God consciousness. That consciousness doesn't develop by being too much in the world. We're in the world, but we're not *of* it, as Jesus proclaimed. We're no longer struggling to find God. At this advanced spiritual juncture we are feeling deeply connected and are turning within and listening. We are growing into what we are meant to be and expressing more of what we already are.

So when one turns away from the world of material distractions and diversions and turns within to contact the inmost purity that beckons, "Follow Me," as in the story of Jesus, who says, "Leave everything and follow Me," you enter a spiritually maturing process in which you turn to your higher self for guidance. Sinetar states, "When we are summoned to a spiritually maturing solitude and answer that call in wholesome ways, we are led into a larger life. We expand into our spiritual wholeness."

We're now ready to turn our attention to the *practice of discernment*.

The Practice of Discernment

The other day I was reviewing my notes from a retreat I attended a number of years ago called The Heart of Meditation Retreat. The retreat was conducted by a married couple, devotees of the deceased spiritual master Osho (aka Bhagwan Shree Rajneesh). During an evening Darshan (enlightened lecture) we watched a video of one of Osho's discourses. It commenced with one of his followers speaking to him about her frustration with her process. She said, "Beloved Osho…there is a confusion in me that keeps coming again and again. The message I have gotten from you more and more is to relax with myself, to watch and wait, but I also feel this urgency to wake up now, and then another part screams, 'But how?' What do I need to do? Do I need to push myself through this wall? Could you make this clear to me?"

Osho's response to this woman was clear and concise. He said,

> "The mind is confusion; it is not that you are in confusion. And there is no way for the mind to be not in confusion. Mind's whole structure is based on confusion. Mind is duality; it is always split. There is no single point on which the mind agrees in totality. Half of the mind will agree, and half of the mind will disagree, and whatever you choose you are choosing only the half. The remaining half is going to take revenge. The unchosen part, the leftover, will wait for its chance to show you that whatever you have chosen is wrong. But it does not matter which part you choose. Choice itself is wrong."

Osho went on to explain,

> "So the first thing to be understood is that there is no mind which has ever been without confusion. Have you ever considered that peace of mind has never existed? Peace of mind is intrinsically impossible. Peace happens only when mind is not. It is not peace of mind; it is peace beyond mind."

He offered an illustration,

"It is almost like a lotus flower; it grows in mud and water; it is a miracle of nature that out of dirty mud and water it brings out one of the most beautiful flowers in existence. But mud and water are not the lotus flower. The lotus flower blossoms only when the lotus plant has gone beyond the mud, beyond the water, has transcended both—then it opens up to the sun, to the sky, and releases its fragrance to the wind. Although it comes from the mud, it is not mud anymore."

He went on to say,

"The same is true about peace. Mind is muddy; all kinds of relevant and irrelevant thoughts are jumbled there. It is a crowd, with so many fragments fighting with each other that you can call it a battleground. Mind cannot be at peace. But you can go beyond mind because you are not the mind. You can transcend and become a lotus flower. And then there is peace, there is beauty, there is bliss, and all that you have always dreamt about but have had no experience of."

Osho's message to this student and to all those that followed his teachings was to relax, watch, and wait. He said,

"The message remains the same because that is the only way to transcend the mind. The watcher is always above the mind. The watcher is never part of the mind. The mind is just like a TV screen on which thoughts, dreams, imaginations, projections, desires, and a thousand and one things go on passing. The watcher is not on the screen; he is sitting in the movie hall. But the problem arises when the watcher becomes identified with something on the movie screen."

In order to not become triggered by what one identifies with, it requires the ability to refrain long enough to make a discerning choice about the most appropriate response to the stimulus. It is important to comprehend the distinction between judgment as in condemnation and judgment as in discernment. We can discern something about someone that is based on our perceptions of the individual. It's plausible that our perceptions are quite factual or agreed upon by others. This process, when performed with an open heart, allows one to understand something, and understanding is the bridge to compassion. The key to discernment is the union of the head, the logical part of us, with the heart, the feeling part of us.

It's when we have a negative opinion about what we're observing and categorize it in harsh terms that we've entered the painful territory of the judgmental mind. It is possible to discern that we have a preference for people who believe as we do without judging those who don't. When we release the judgment habit, we don't discontinue having preferences; we just let go of the tendency to apply negative labels to the things we don't prefer.

When we judge something or someone, we close off our capacity to learn. When we use wise discernment, we are open to learn and to grow. When we judge people, we feel smarter, more powerful, and superior to the ones we're judging. To the egoic mind, judging creates an illusion of security. However, each judgment we make affirms any number of secret fears that we hold, such as "I am weak and at risk;" "people are out to get me;" "my world is not safe, and I have no faith that it will ever get better;" "I'm not good enough."

The habit of judging not only appears to be socially acceptable these days, it's encouraged. Our culture has become addicted to judging. Have you noticed that judging has become the essence of reality television? With all the judgment reinforcement we receive on a daily basis, it can be a challenge to reverse the judgment habit and replace it with loving discernment.

Judgments are a way of disavowing our connection with universal intelligence and divine creativity. If we are mindful that spirit is perfect oneness and that we are all part of the one mind, the absurdity of judging becomes even clearer. When we judge, we separate ourselves from the oneness that unites all of us, and we are cast adrift, alone and on our own.

If we set a strong intention to replace the habit of judging with compassion and forgiveness, we return to the place where we can see divine order everywhere. Whom do you need to forgive? Who simply didn't know how to do things better? When Nelson Mandela was asked how he forgave the jailers who held him prisoner on Robben Island for twenty-seven years, he said, "When I walked out of the gate, I knew that if I continued to hate these people I'd still be in prison." Align your heart with your head and trade the need to be right for the desire to understand. Surrender the need to have an opinion in favor of being divinely guided. That is the *practice of discernment.*

Mindful Men are Light-Hearted

If you don't like where you are now, know that it's a place you are just meant to pass through. If you're going through hell, keep moving. Give thanks. Every time you express gratitude, you will draw metaphysical power into all situations and shed light on spirit's perfect plan for you—which, without your mindful awareness, remains in the dark. Light expands with gratitude.

Your expanding consciousness of light will not only help you get real about where you need encouragement but will reveal who needs support from you. Ask yourself, "What truth do I tell myself about how I feel? What wisdom have I revealed in doing so? To whom can I offer encouragement?"

Light is magnetic. It pulls things out of the darkness and toward itself. Give the light your hurtful memories and any victimhood weighing you down. Transform your victim story into a story of survivorship. As the painful memories are lifted from your thought bank and dissolve, you'll feel a new sense of freedom springing up inside. You will have released mental bondage and cleared a space in your mind for new thinking. Be mindful of the good that will grow out of your positive thinking.

Observe your steps daily. Ask, "Do I call upon spirit every step of the way? Do I affirm the presence of universal intelligence with each step that I take? Do I navigate mindfully? Is every word I speak spoken with consideration of others? When I'm eating, do I bless my meal with the thought, 'Everything I take into my body turns to health and beauty?'" When we call upon the light as we go, we will not stumble and are empowered to see beyond blame, fault, and fear.

A yoga master shared this healing wisdom:

> "Great beings are not blind to people's shortcomings, but they're not overly burdened by them either. Their vision doesn't stop where the skin begins and ends. They look beyond everything. They devote their lives to bringing out the simple basic goodness and purity in each human being. They see the great light in everyone always."

Mindful self-care honors the self and sparks illumination. How are you holding yourself in right regard? Are you resting enough, laughing enough, smiling at yourself, and taking opportunities to shed tears? When we give ourselves the gift of care, we can then, and only then serve spirit's plan for us.

Give yourself the gift of intentionality, affirming that it is spirit's light that magnifies the greatest possibilities. As you do, you will function from faith and act from mindful consciousness. You are spirit's energy outlet, sourced in divine protection, provision, and power. Know that this truth is within you and, as science of mind teacher Ernest Holmes said, "is always triumphant." It is the way of the Spiritual Warrior!

CHAPTER 16

Aging, Elderhood, and Completion

When death comes for you, let it find you fully alive.

—African Proverb

IT IS NO SECRET that men experience difficulty with issues around aging, whether it's going after young women, indulging in dysfunctional behaviors, pushing themselves athletically to the point of debilitating injury, obsessing over their appearance, or outright denial of physical warning signs about their health. Much of this behavior stems from their anger and fear about their physical decline and approaching mortality. The glorification of youth can make one who is past his prime feel that he's outdated and ready to be put out to pasture.

Getting older can make things harder. I hear men express concern over the perceived loss of passion and fun. They feel that they are still working too much and missing the joy, play, and passionate sex that they once had with their mates when they were younger. Many who are in mid-life complain that their partners are not as young, energetic, or attractive as they used to be and are still preoccupied with being mothers, even when the children are older, so they shut down or act out. But aging is a fact of life and issues of aging must be addressed and dealt with responsibly, or there will be problems that can lead to the destruction of potentially viable relationships.

Our bodies work smoothly in our younger years. We can eat and drink what we desire, and the pounds melt away as easily as we put them on. We can work twelve-hour days, party all night, and rally in the morning to greet the day and start all over again. Then, sometime in the middle years, things begin to change. We can no longer maintain the same pace, our joints begin to give out, our hair starts falling out, and the face in the mirror begins to look more like our father's. For many men, this shocker can mark a turning point, not just physically but in the mind as well.

Minding your health is not just a young man's game. Men who learn to be Spiritual Warriors in preparation for aging tend to age gracefully while maintaining their youthfulness in appropriate and wise ways. As we age, it's important for us to support our cardio, strength, balance, and flexibility. These are the four cornerstones to the foundation for building a healthy and sustaining lifestyle.

Starting at about age forty, men lose approximately 1% of muscle mass a year, leading to a decrease in muscle strength and function. But engaging in a moderate and consistent strength-training program can stave off the loss for decades. Maintaining muscle mass and strength helps bones stay strong, keeps blood sugar under control, protects aging joints from injury, and offsets frailty that can lead to serious falls. Also essential are the power of yoga for sustaining flexibility and balance—which I've long espoused—and the spiritual sustenance of prayer and meditation. Rest and relaxation are also essential to reducing stress and keeping our nervous systems from fraying.

One of the most daunting things about getting older is the loss of sexual potency and erectile dysfunction. The proliferation of ads that pander to this plight by playing off men's anxieties drives the point home. Some men commence testosterone replacement therapy, which, as some studies reveal, increases muscle size and strength as well as enhances energy, mood, and libido. It's important that men over the age of forty monitor their prostates through yearly physical exams including digital palpation of the prostate and a prostate specific antigen (PSA) blood test. This is especially important for men who are on testosterone replacement therapy, since testosterone can exacerbate prostate cancer. I recognize that there is some controversy these days regarding the reliability of the PSA test, but I believe that it still plays an important role in diagnosis and should probably remain a part of a man's yearly physical. You can discuss the viability of this procedure with your personal physician.

Men: Strangers to Their Own Health

Men tend to tough it out unless we're in real pain. We are typically strangers to our own health. Preventive medicine and early detection tend to rank way down on our list of priorities, and we frequently pay for it with our lives. Men are far likelier than women to die early from diseases, many of them treatable. We men are three times less likely to go to a physician than are women. The health-related statistics for American males as compared with those for females have not been encouraging. For example, a man has a one-in-two lifetime chance of developing cancer, compared with a woman's one-in-three chance. Men typically die about five years before women do.

Jed Diamond, Ph.D. has just released his tenth book about men's health. Jed states, "I grieve for the men and boys whose lives are cut short and for the women and families left behind. I've been looking for a way to reduce stress that is simple to learn, easy to practice, scientifically sound, and, most importantly, effective. I've found what I've been looking for, have tested it extensively, and now want to get this life-saving information to as many men as I can. My new book, *MenAlive: Stop Killer Stress with Simple Energy Healing Tools* (2012), gives men what they need to stop the stress that shortens lives and destroys relationships. Here's my simple idea: We know stress kills, physically, emotionally, and spiritually. If we can reduce men's risk of death to the same level as women's, we can save nearly a million men within three years. Let's get started."

We must push through our emotional barriers that prevent us from taking good care of ourselves. It's time to promote healthy male lifestyles predicated upon good nutrition, regular exercise, weight control, smoking cessation, moderation, and regular physical checkups. We should be going in to have our blood pressure checked and to have complete blood tests in our twenties, with additional tests like the PSA in our forties and colonoscopy being introduced in our fifties.

Men often take better care of their cars than themselves. Low incomes and a lack of health insurance can prevent some men from going to the doctor, but more often we simply refuse to acknowledge that we even need health care. We also tend to avoid physical exams because of the perceived discomfort or embarrassment, plus we don't like to appear weak and not in control. Macho attitudes about not seeing a doctor start in youth and become ingrained as we age. Because of this early conditioning, we don't want to talk to anybody when we're hurting: "Boys don't cry."

As fathers, we have an opportunity to teach our sons to take charge of their health. We need to tell our sons that it's okay to feel vulnerable. It's okay to reach out for help. It's important that we come to realize that real men take responsibility for their health and are willing to see doctors.

Older vs. Elder

An area of concern for men revolves around life ambitions and the meaning that comes from roles men *outgrow*—as fathers, sons, and breadwinners. Whether or not men have found fulfillment in their jobs, retirement is a massive change, providing another crisis of meaning and valuation that can become a crucial opportunity. Perhaps equally important is resolving issues with our own fathers and father figures as we grow older ourselves and as our progenitors age and die.

I believe it's important that men distinguish the difference between becoming an *Elder* rather than an *Older*. Elders are men who know that they have something to give to younger generations, especially our boys. *Olders* are often trapped in a feeling that because they are now old, they have less to offer. These men tend to be unclear about who they are, what they need to do for themselves, and tend to question their intrinsic value to the world. *Elders* know that they are a natural resource. They view old age with excitement, as a time to find creative ways to manifest their wisdom to benefit those around them and society in general, and thus resolve their own lives to their ultimate satisfaction. They teach us not only how to live full lives but also how to die with honor and dignity.

Matthew and Conrad Burke

One of the good men in our Community, Mathew (Matt) Burke, was seeking a turning point in his relationship with his father. Matt had started attending Sacred Path Men's Retreats and had worked his way from participant to Wisdom Council staff, tribe leader, and then to storyteller. His fondness for poetry and stories had become his new-found passion.

Matt had spoken to me about his father, Conrad, who had suffered a severe and debilitating stroke that nearly killed him and had left him quite disabled. His journey of recovery was truly remarkable if not miraculous. A lesser man would not have survived, let alone regained his speech, mobility, and faculties.

Conrad had played basketball during the 1950s for UCLA under the coaching of legendary John Wooden. In Wooden's book, *Wooden on Leadership* (McGraw-Hill, 2005), in a chapter called Make

Greatness Attainable by All, Wooden wrote, "Conrad Burke showed little promise as a player when he arrived at UCLA. When I first saw him scrimmaging as a freshman, I shook my head and thought, 'My, he's hopeless. If this young man makes the varsity team when he's a sophomore, it'll mean the varsity is pretty terrible.'"

Wooden went on to say, "Imagine my surprise and delight when the very next season he became a starter on a varsity team that was anything but terrible. We won the conference title with a 16-0 record. Even though Conrad lacked the physical skills a coach likes to see, he made up for it with a great mind and very hard work. He came extremely close to achieving his potential, his own greatness. For example, even though he couldn't jump very well and was relatively short for a center, he learned through constant practice and observation how to gain position under the basket. Of course, gaining position is vital in rebounding."

Wooden summed up, "Conrad worked relentlessly to bring out all he had, and he came very close to doing that. He figured out how to make a contribution to the team—a big contribution. The lesson is that anyone with the ambition, properly channeled and focused, has the potential to achieve more than anyone would have imagined. The key is for leaders to help individuals understand their strengths and weaknesses and enhance the former while finding a way to at least neutralize the latter."

Conrad got involved in a men's support group through the Presbyterian church where he was a member. Matt invited his father to attend a Sacred Path retreat with him, but Conrad declined because he wasn't sure whether the spiritual diversity of our retreats was in keeping with his evangelical faith. At one point Conrad finally gave in to Matt's persistence and registered for one of the retreats, but unfortunately he had to be hospitalized for some treatment due to a complication in his recovery. Matt suggested to me that it might also have served as a legitimate excuse to avoid the retreat.

Matt mentioned to Conrad that he thought that he would like me. He considered that if Conrad and I could just meet, it might serve the cause of allowing his father to get past his resistance to attending a retreat. I was game. Finally the right opportunity presented itself when Conrad and Matt's brother-in-law, a devout Christian, made plans to drive up to the Los Angeles area from San Diego to attend a Promise Keepers Conference being held at the Los Angeles Memorial Coliseum. Promise Keepers personifies the Christian approach to "menswork" and attracts thousands of men who gather for their conferences. The Burkes had VIP seating in the press box section, and Matt invited me to join them.

I spent the day with Conrad, including an opportunity to have lunch, just the two of us. We discussed many issues that were on his mind—such as matters of faith, his relationship with Matt, and the process of his rehabilitation. I found the conference stimulating, but the conversations with Conrad were the highlight. He and I began to forge a bond that commenced with that event. I let him know that I would very much enjoy his participation in one of our retreats and asked him what he required to feel comfortable attending. He said he wanted to make sure that he would be taken care of, especially around his physical limitations. I assured him that I would do my best to allow him to feel safe and have an enjoyable time.

Later, Matt shared with me that Conrad had found our meeting to be a favorable experience and had decided to register for the next retreat, since my assurances had put him at ease.

Meeting Michael Tapia

As the date of the retreat approached, Matt and I discussed where Conrad should lodge. We concluded that it would be best for him to room near the dining hall and community meeting room. The next question was, who should be his roommate? I suggested Michael Tapia, a man who also was disabled and required closer accommodations. At first Matt was surprised that I suggested Michael, then smiled and said that I was right—Michael would indeed be the perfect roommate for Conrad.

Michael had already attended a few retreats. He was gay and suffered from AIDS. He had lost his eyesight due to the illness three months prior to attending his first retreat. At that point his T-cell count was extremely low, and his viral load was alarmingly high. T-cells are a type of white blood cells called lymphocytes. They make up part of the immune system and help the body fight diseases or harmful substances. Viral load is a measure of the severity of a viral infection and can be calculated by estimating the amount of virus in an involved body fluid. Michael rebounded after the retreat and credited The Sacred Path Community with saving his life.

The men in the Community were very fond of Michael. He felt accepted, supported, and protected by them. In fact, he professed to feel safer in this primarily heterosexual community of men than in the community of exclusively gay men.

Conrad signed up for his first retreat and showed up at the camp ready to participate. He located his room and was unpacking and settling in when he gazed out the window and saw a blind man approaching, tapping his way along the path with the use of a white cane.

"Who's that?" Conrad asked Matt.

"Your roommate," Matt said. "Michael."

Conrad's eyes widened, and his jaw dropped.

When Michael entered the cabin, Matt welcomed him, and they exchanged heartfelt greetings and big hugs. Matt then introduced Michael to his father. When Conrad extended his hand to clasp Michael's outstretched hand, Michael gave Conrad's hand a tender shake then ran his other hand up Conrad's arm to his shoulder—and further up to his face as he rose on his tiptoes to reach the top of

Conrad's head. Conrad was exceptionally tall, even though hunched over from the stroke, and towered over Michael.

"Oh, my, you're a big one, aren't you?" Michael asked.

Conrad acknowledged that he had been pretty tall in his day. He then abruptly excused himself, saying that he had left something in the car and needed to get it.

After Conrad left the room, Michael and Matt then began catching up on what had transpired in their lives over the weeks since they'd last seen each other. Michael commented on how excited he was to be rooming with Matt's father. Out of the corner of his eye Matt glimpsed Conrad through the window peering out from behind a tree, frantically gesturing to Matt to come outside. Matt playfully waved back and continued speaking with Michael.

Conrad began gesturing to his son even more vehemently. Matt excused himself, saying it looked as though his father needed some help outside, and he left the room and joined his father, who was still lurking behind the tree. Conrad pulled him close and, peering searchingly into Matt's eyes, exclaimed, "That's my roommate??"

"Yes," Matt said.

"He's blind!"

Matt nodded.

"Blind from birth?"

"He lost his eyesight due to AIDS over one year ago."

"AIDS!" Conrad gasped. "You mean he's a homosexual!"

"He is."

"Who decided to have me room with this man?"

"Stephen did," Matt said.

With a deer-in-the-headlights expression on his face, Conrad said, "Let me see if I have this straight. You mean to tell me that Stephen's idea of taking good care of me was to have me room with a homosexual who's blind and has AIDS?"

"That's right," Matt answered with a tentative grin.

Conrad was clearly upset, "I don't know if I can do this."

"You'll be fine, Dad. Stephen knows what he's doing."

Matt and Conrad slowly made their way back into the cabin where Matt left the two men alone to get to know each other.

By dinnertime, Conrad and Michael had been talking for a couple of hours and Conrad was beginning to warm toward Michael's open and loving demeanor. Conrad offered to assist Michael from the cabin to the mess hall. For Matt, to see his father and Michael arm in arm, engrossed in conversation, making their way along the path, was quite a vision to behold.

As Conrad and Michael got to know each other, they shared their personal stories of their health challenges. They talked about their lives and expressed their visions for their futures. A wonderful exchange of humor grew between them, and they began to tease each other in a good-natured fashion. Wherever Michael was, there was Conrad. They were learning to trust and count on each other. After the first retreat they stayed in touch and looked forward to opportunities to reconnect at one of the daylong Sacred Path events.

Conrad attended four or five retreats over the next two and a half years. During most of them, he and Michael would room together. On one of the retreats that Michael couldn't attend because he was having a health crisis, Conrad and Matt roomed together. They spent hours talking, and you could see their bond of love expand and deepen.

What will never be forgotten by the other men in the Community are those times when Conrad would slowly rise from his chair in order to speak to the men from his heart. Each time he performed this ritual of communication, before he'd sit down, he would call for Matt to stand before him, and he would speak to him in an intimate and loving way. For the men present, it was as though Conrad was speaking to *them* as a kind and compassionate father. There was never a dry eye as upwards of one hundred men would sit there with tears streaming down their cheeks as they witnessed a *good father* expressing his deep feelings of love and admiration for his son.

Completion

Conrad became, in a large sense, the paternal elder to our Community. For many, he was the father they never had. He recreated this same blessing ritual at some point during all the retreats that he attended, and each time he spoke to Matt, he had something new and profound to communicate. At the last retreat he attended, he actually passed the torch to Matt, indicating that he was weary, and it was Matt's turn to carry it.

When Matt got a call from his mother early one morning, saying that his father had suffered another stroke while they were on a cruise ship sailing off the coast of Normandy, France, Matt's heart sank. This stroke would prove fatal.

Matt phoned me, sobbing, to inform me of his father's passing. He told me that Conrad loved me and had expressed to him only days before that he was profoundly grateful for the men's community and the retreats that had given him the relationship with his son that he had always longed for, as well as the relationship with himself that he never thought possible.

The Sacred Path Men's Community had become his community, his refuge. Matt shared with me that the great thing that had been achieved with his father as a result of the retreats was that they were complete before Conrad died.

I was honored to be one of three men to offer eulogies at Conrad's funeral. The other two men were his closest friends. It was a great privilege to know Conrad, brief though it was. We were all graced by his presence.

Unlocking the Code

When I was twenty-eight years old, after receiving my Ph.D., I was invited to go into practice with one of my professors from my graduate degree program, William Ofman, Ph.D. Bill, a man who had an extraordinarily powerful presence and made a significant impact on me.

One afternoon I was in the coffee room at my new office when Bill entered. His father had died the week before, and this was the first time that I had seen him since the funeral. I approached him tentatively and expressed my condolences. He turned and looked me squarely in the eyes and asked, "Stephen, are you complete with your father?"

I was taken aback by the directness of the question and answered somewhat hesitantly, "I think so."

At the time my father was fifty-five years old and in good health. But Bill stressed that we never know when one's life might end suddenly. "It's important to be complete with your father before that time comes," he said. I pondered his admonition and promised him that I would not take his warning lightly.

The next day I drove to Marina del Rey and paid an impromptu visit to my dad on the boat that he and my mother had purchased for their weekend pleasure outings. Actually, they used the boat more for social gatherings than anything else. My father wasn't much of a sailor but he loved to tinker on the boat as a form of relaxation, and it provided an escape from the office when he needed a break. He puttered from stem to stern, sanding and polishing and eyeing his accomplishments with pride. I gave him a hand on this day, working on the brass fixtures, and then we stopped to have an adult beverage and talk.

He was never very comfortable with our talks, especially after I'd gotten so involved in psychology. Too often the talks evoked emotions, and he felt awkward when feelings started to flow. When I'd occasionally try to plumb the depths of his psyche and speak with him in earnest about something poignantly heavy, he might say something like, "Oh, cut the psychology crap." It was best to just listen to him speak about whatever was on his mind and not push him, just go along with his flow, and we would eventually get to where I had wanted to go anyway. That, by the way, is the skillful use of reverse "psychology crap."

On this particular day, I had something I needed to talk about. I asked him if I could share what was on my mind; I could tell that he was again bracing himself for a conversation that was about to turn serious. I told him about my encounter with Professor Ofman the day before and the question that had pierced my psyche: "Was I complete with my father?" I asked Dad if he felt that we were complete. He didn't know how to respond and seemed intensely uncomfortable with the whole ordeal.

Now that I'm older, I understand that men who are in their mid-to-late fifties begin to reflect on issues of aging and mortality, especially if their own fathers have died. My father's father had passed away fifteen years earlier at the relatively young age of sixty-seven, when my father was only forty. As we talked, we could no longer contain our emotions. Choking back tears, I told my father that I loved him and hoped that I had been a good enough son. He tried to convey, through his own constrained emotions, that I had been a fine son and that he was proud of me and loved me. I told him that he was a good father.

It was quite a contrast to some years earlier when I'd told my father that I loved him, but I didn't like him. At that time, he'd paused, a bit stunned, and then he had said, "I can't conceive of ever saying that to my father. I guess that's the difference between the generations we were raised in."

And he was right. My generation was the product of the free speech movement, and expressing ourselves and clearing our feelings was our battle cry. Having realized how I had hurt him with that statement, I made a decision that I would no longer react to what I perceived as my father's negative or critical assessment of me. I would no longer succumb to his judgmental attitudes and opinions regarding my political ideologies, mode of dress, or choice of friends. This decision helped immensely to soften the strife and tension that had existed between us much of the time.

There was a pivotal moment in our relationship one day when I was sitting across from him at the bar in my parent's house, having a couple of cocktails. I had thought that drinking with him was the manly and preferred way of accessing the bond that I craved. Sometimes it worked, and other times, even when I wasn't imbibing, it only led to alcohol-driven volatility, ending in angry outbursts, hurt feelings, and broken communication.

On that particular evening my father began to speak about his father, and as he did he began to cry. He took a cocktail napkin and started to wipe away the tears while exclaiming that it was stupid to cry over his father, who had been dead for years. I could see that he was struggling, attempting with all his might to hold back the tears, and yet I knew he needed to let go. I got up and walked around the bar to where he was seated and put my arm around him and said, "It's okay, Dad, and it's not stupid to cry about Grandpa. You miss him, and you're in pain."

At that point he pulled away and lashed out at me with anger. "What do you know?"

Frankly, I don't recall what else he said, but it stung, and I went back around the bar and took my seat across from him. Something strange happened at that point. I heard the words, softly spoken from within, "Don't fight. No need to argue. Just let it pass."

I felt an uncanny sense of calm and inner peace. I unlocked the code and had a precious moment of enlightenment. I had come to the realization that my father would fight with me in order to push away his deeper feelings that were connected to his tears. In that moment I was free because I understood and was left with a profound feeling of compassion for my father. I made a promise to myself that I would never fight with him again. And so it was.

He looked at me and the expression on his face was one of mystery and self-encounter. It was like he fell through me and met himself on the other side. He put his head in his hands and began to cry. We didn't talk; we just sat quietly in the presence of the tranquil bond that connected a father and son who had come to a significant turning point in their relationship.

Seen From the Other Side

It is enlightening to experience, from the perspective of a father, the other side of the conflict that entangles fathers and sons during certain periods of their lives. Many men walk around with gaping holes in their guts due to the lack of fulfillment stemming from unrequited relationships with their fathers. They starve for recognition and admiration while seeking to satiate their father craving and looking for ways to close the father gap.

One reason that the movie *Field of Dreams* struck such a powerful chord for many men was its portrayal of a thirty-six-year-old man struggling to reach a dead father whom he now regretted alienating. The last scene of the father playing catch with his son is archetypal and piercingly emotional. I recall sitting in the theatre at the end of the film, moved to tears. Many men sat sobbing, being consoled by their wives or girlfriends. Men en masse couldn't leave the theatre for several minutes following the closing credits. Theatre owners had to schedule an hour between screenings in order to allow men enough time to pull themselves together before exiting the theatre.

One man, whose father died un-reconciled with him, told his friend that this was the first movie in years to make him cry. His friend said that hadn't been his reaction.

"Is your father alive?" asked the man.

"Yes, he is," his friend responded.

"Well, there you go."

I believe that many of the men who sat crying at the end of the movie were grieving the missed experiences with fathers who were alive and yet absent during their childhoods. They had been dead to them in a way. The feeling of being cut off from one's father, who is missing in action, creates a kind of loneliness that is distinct from other experiences of being alone. It is as though one is cut off from one's self because he lacks a sense of completeness. It leaves a gaping hole which men, as was discussed earlier, will attempt to stuff with whatever they can, sex, alcohol, drugs, food, and other addictively-driven substances and sensations. But these are poor substitutes for a father's love and attention. It is through the company of other good men that wounded and incomplete men can heal the holes, close the Father Gap, and finally feel a sense of wholeness.

Ian's Graduation

Friday, June 6th, 2003, was a typical Los Angeles "June gloom" morning—overcast. My wife, Fran, our twenty-three-year-old son Derek, our eighteen-year-old daughter Dana, her boyfriend Taylor, and I were en route to Ojai for our nineteen-year-old son's graduation from Happy Valley School where he had been in residence for the past two years. The five of us were chatting up a storm, discussing how proud we were of Ian. He had had a difficult several years and had worked hard to ready himself for graduation. This would mark the first formal acknowledgment and completion for him. He had to miss his last graduation ceremony because his best friend had been killed in a boating accident, and the funeral was at the same time as the graduation. We knew how important this day was for him.

Then my cell phone rang. I kept it close by so that my mother could reach me if there was a change for the worse in my father's condition. He had been battling lung cancer for three-and-a-half years, and during the past three weeks his physical condition had been in a rapid decline. I answered the phone.

"Honey, it's your dad," my mother said. "I think you better come now. I think he's going."

My heart sank. I told her that we were twenty minutes from arrival at Ian's school and that I would drop the others off and head back to their house.

Everyone was silent in the car from that point on. My thoughts focused on my desire to be with my father during his passing, while not wanting to disappoint Ian by not being there for him. The phone rang again and it was Timothy Aguilar, our close friend. He and his son Ziari were on their way to the graduation. He was aware of my father's condition, and I informed him of the dilemma I was facing. He asked a poignant and centering question, "What would your father want?"

I contemplated the question and intuitively came to the answer.

When we arrived at the school, I called my mother again. She told me that she and the hospice nurse felt that it would be better if I stayed for Ian's graduation ceremony since there was really nothing that I could do for my father at this point. That settled it.

Tearfully, I told my mother to tell Dad that I loved him and that I would miss him but that I know that it's time for him to let go. I dried my eyes, and we proceeded to the area where the graduation was being held. We decided not to say anything to Ian concerning Grandpa but to allow him to have his day of celebration. We knew that if he were aware of what was happening he would have opted to leave the graduation to be with Grandpa.

It was hard to stay focused on the ceremony at first. So many thoughts about my father and my relationship with him crossed the screen of my mind. Some were mere fragments of memories and others unfolded as complete scenes from the movie of my life.

I saw pictures of my father and me at various ages. For example, in one scene we were building a fence together when I was very young, and he was teaching me to use a hammer. I recalled the joy of being able to help him and how pleased he seemed with my boyish enthusiasm and budding skill. Then another scene pushed this one aside. I was a teenager and my father and I were on the roof. We were fixing the television antenna, which required my having to lean out over the edge of the roof to hammer a support in place. My father was holding me by the scruff of my shirt so that I had the leverage to stretch out a little further. With his other hand he was holding the nail while I was steadying myself with my left hand and aiming the hammer, held in my right hand, at its designated target. A true recipe for disaster if ever there was one!

I recall feeling really nervous that the scenario was just another setup to incur my father's wrath. What made matters worse was his admonition that should I miss the nail and make contact with any part of his hand, he might be forced to let go with his other hand, allowing me to plummet to the ground. Fortunately, I didn't create the opportunity to see if he was serious or not. I hit the nail on the head.

Relationships between fathers and sons are typically fraught with a tension that runs deep. It's a precarious bond, full of discomfort from the underlying emotions that fathers and sons have, but find so difficult to communicate. Father/son relationships are often conflicted due to their complex mixture of intense mutual longing for approval and the disappointment of unmet expectations. I have had to sort through this complicated maze in order to find my way clear to reconcile the dynamic with my own father prior to his death.

There is a wonderful book called *Sons on Fathers: A Book of Men's Writing*, edited by Ralph Keyes (Harper/Collins Publishers, 1992). It is a compilation of men's writings about their relationships with their fathers at different stages of their lives. I am fond of this book and have shared several of these personal stories at the men's retreats that I facilitate. In the introduction to the book, Keyes states, "This is true of most men. Conditioned to play our cards cagily in an imagined poker game with our father, we don't say enough to him while he's alive. Only when it's time for a eulogy do we realize that our tongues were tied not because we had too little to say, but too much; not that our feelings were too weak but that they were too strong; not that we loved our fathers too little but that we loved them too much. It is usually not until a father dies that unspoken words finally get said. 'I wish I could have my father back, even for just a minute,' eulogizers often conclude, 'to tell him what I've just told you.'"

As Ian's graduation procession began and we saw him in his dark suit, standing tall and smiling so proudly, I found myself very present. When it was his turn to speak, he told the audience that he had not written anything down but preferred to speak from his heart. His words were thoughtful, precise, and sincere. I couldn't help wondering whether my father was still alive, and I further reflected on, if he had left his body, whether his spirit was here with us at the graduation.

At 2 p.m., after congratulating Ian one more time and giving him another round of kisses and hugs, we headed out of the parking lot. I glanced in the rearview mirror to see him smiling and waving goodbye. I will never forget the look on his face as he turned and went back to the site of the graduation.

It had not always been easy for us along the way. Ian is very independent and strong-willed, and our relationship is similar to the way my father and I were when I was young. There were times when Ian's will and my will clashed. He would not concede and back down. He'd had trouble in school, and my wife and I had attempted to find a school that could provide the right kind of environment to afford him the opportunity to express his artistic nature and unique brand of individuality. We also thought that a residential school could foster the autonomy that he desired and be the break from the tension in the household.

Our search led us to Happy Valley School in Ojai, founded by a coterie of diverse Theosophist luminaries, including philosopher/explorer of human consciousness Aldous Huxley, spiritual teacher J. Krishnamurti, and renowned artist Beatrice Wood. We all agreed that this was the perfect setting to accommodate all of our needs, and it proved to be just that. Ian spent his last two years of high school there and experienced the pivotal transformation that we had hoped for.

Saying Goodbye to Dad

When we got back into the car, I phoned my mother on my cell phone.

"We think he's holding on for you," she said. "Just drive carefully and get here as soon as you can."

I drove back to Woodland Hills, dropped everyone off at the house and headed for my parents' house. The Friday afternoon traffic was thick. I took deep breaths and prayed that my father would hold on until I got there.

I arrived at 4:45. My father was lying on the couch, covered by a thin blanket. He was not coherent. His eyes were open, and his mouth was agape. He was gulping air, and yet his breathing rhythm was consistent and surprisingly strong. What was left of a once handsome, strong, six-foot tall, 200-pound man was a frail, emaciated frame. This was not the father I had known. He looked like a stranger. I had heard others say that about their loved ones in the end. It was true. He didn't live there anymore. Recently, he had exclaimed that he was a mess. Cancer is brutal. It ravishes the body and leaves practically nothing unscathed as it makes its lethal rounds.

I sat on the edge of the coffee table next to the couch and stroked my father's temple and spoke to him gently. I let him know that he could go when he chose. His oncologist came at 6 p.m. to say goodbye. He gave my father a kiss on the forehead and told us that it would not be long before my father made his transition. My wife arrived an hour later bringing me a change of clothes.

Just before 8 p.m., I went into the other room to change when my mother and wife called to me to come. He was going. I rushed back into the living room, wearing just underwear, and sat back down next to my father. His breathing was slowing, and he was indeed letting go. I thought of the irony that my father was lying naked under a blanket, and I was sitting practically naked next to him as he was dying. Just after 8 o'clock, my father took his last breath. We lit a candle and sat with him for the last time.

The hospice nurse arrived an hour later, and then they came for his body at 11:30. I asked my mother if she wanted me to stay with her, and she declined, indicating that she felt she would sleep soundly, probably for the first time in months. She was exhausted and, I believe, relieved. His suffering was over.

My wife and I left around midnight and headed home. We passed by Notre Dame High School, which I had attended in the 60s. I thought that Ian's graduation that day was probably around the same time in June 1965 that I had graduated from high school. I was nineteen then, and my father was forty-six, and on this day, Ian was nineteen, I was fifty-six and my father was eighty-four.

When I got home I looked at the back of the watch that my parents had given me on graduation day and read the inscription, *To Steve with Love from Mom and Dad, June 6, 1965.* I was stunned to realize the synchronicity of events. It was thirty-eight years ago to the day that I had graduated from high school, and on this fateful day Ian graduated, and my father died. What an amazing day this had been.

I lay awake that night in the dark, allowing the memories to parade across my mind. I was filled with emotion. I could picture my father's expression when he gave me the Omega Constellation watch. He was proud. I felt certain that the pictures that were taken at Ian's graduation would reflect a similar expression of pride on my face. The day had brought a mixture of feelings; the satisfaction of Ian's graduation and the grief of my fathers passing. Both were *completions*; both signify the transition from one stage along the journey of manhood to another, with death marking the final passage.

My relationship with my father had endured a myriad of emotions throughout the years and perhaps ultimately was what influenced many of the decisions I had made along the way, including the direction that my life's journey would take. I reflected on who I had become and the impact that my father had made on the man that I am today.

I recalled what Ralph Keyes had suggested in his book: "How men feel about their fathers is at the heart of how they feel about themselves. Yet most feel alone in their struggle to do better on both scores." I thought of his advice, "To understand ourselves we must first understand our fathers. Accepting one's self means accepting him. At some point in his life, every man looks in the mirror and sees his father. I did, and it unnerved me – at first anyway."

I remembered shaving the beard, at age thirty-five, that I had sported for fourteen years. Not long after I was clean-shaven I was driving in my car and caught a glimpse of my face in the rearview mirror and verbalized out loud, "Oh, hello, Dad." It had occurred to me in that moment that I had covered the growing resemblance of his countenance with a beard in order to separate myself and individuate from him at age twenty-one.

He Did It His Way

We held the funeral for my father on Thursday, June 12, at Forest Lawn. Reverend Robert Bock, the pastor of the First Christian Church of North Hollywood, was a friend of my father's. He presided at the service and spoke eloquently, conveying his sentiments peppered with stories from his relationship with Dad. After Pastor Bock spoke, I rose from my front row pew and walked to the pulpit. I thanked Bob and looked out at the people who had assembled to say goodbye to Jerry Johnson. I gave the eulogy for my father, which I titled, "He Did It His Way," inspired by one of Frank Sinatra's songs. My father loved his ballads and also embodied the same kind of style and indomitable spirit. Sinatra lived his life his way, and anyone who knew my dad recognized that he did it his way, too.

When Mom and I were at Forest Lawn, finalizing the arrangements, Mr. Platz asked what we would like to put on the plaque that would adorn the crypt that my father and mother will eventually share in the mausoleum. We looked at each other and I said,

"For Dad, how about, '*He Did It His Way.*'"

Mom laughed and said, "Perfect."

Mr. Platz suggested that we think about it, since whatever we choose for both Mom and Dad should have a kind of uniformity. In other words, Beloved Father and Grandfather would typically go with Beloved Mother and Grandmother, so what would go with "*He did It His Way*?" We decided that we would think about it and then, as we were leaving, I said to my mom, "I've got it. How about, '*She Had To Do It His Way, Too.*'"

We both cracked up because it was so true. Whenever we were around Dad, we had to do it his way.

My father not only loved Mom, he adored her, and in his own way he cherished her for the almost fifty-eight years that they had been together. He didn't want to leave her. He liked his life. And the week prior to his passing, we heard the chimes of the ice cream man and asked Dad if he would like some ice cream. He declined, reflected for a moment, and then said, "I sure did love ice cream."

Dad maintained his elegance and dignity as best he could throughout the few years of his health ordeal. I was most impressed with how he dealt with each assault and new phase of the treatment. He endured the indignity and the pain with a nobility of spirit. What was most incredible was that he persevered against the odds. He never let down, he just kept going, facing each day no matter what it would bring. He had a robust love for life that was astounding. A lesser man would have thrown in the towel. Not Jerry. Like Sinatra, he scoffed at defeat. He was a winner.

In fact, the last Christmas that we spent together, Dad raised his glass and said, "I will be here next Christmas." He loved the Christmas season, and his spirit is with us especially at Christmas when we raise our glasses and toast to him, "You did it your way, Dad," and we love and admire you for having done so.

I concluded his eulogy with the following words: "My relationship with my father had grown deeper and richer over the years. I am fortunate to have been able to spend a lot of time with him since his diagnosis and we got complete with each other. I can truly express that not only am I saying goodbye to a father, but I am also saying farewell to a friend. I'll miss you, Dad."

I had been able to contain my tears until the end of the eulogy. The last sentences that I spoke allowed for the tears, which were balled up in my throat, to flow down my cheeks. When I sat down, Ian rose and walked to the pulpit. He had left his notes at home, and so once again he just spoke from his heart. I was awestruck with how much this young man had grown over the past couple of years. He had gone from boy to man, and I knew that Grandpa would be so proud of him and pleased that Ian wanted to speak at his funeral.

That evening Ian took me aside. He spoke low, "Is it true, Dad that you knew about Grandpa the morning of my graduation?"

I asked him who'd told him that, and he let me know that it was Timothy. Ian had specifically asked Timothy to attend his graduation because he had long looked up to him as a mentor. After the funeral, Timothy had taken Ian aside and told him what had transpired the day Grandpa died.

Ian went on, "So you knew about Grandpa, but you made the decision to be there for me."

"Yes, I did," I said.

"Dad, do you know how much that means to me?"

As tears filled our eyes, he put his arms around me and said, "I'll never forget this. Thank you so much." I could sense my father smiling from above.

The Spiritual Warrior I Called Mom

I had been working on this book for about ten years and was writing the final chapter when my mother passed away on April 26, 2012. She was looking forward to reading my book. That opportunity was taken away, so a tribute to her in my book seemed a fitting way to commemorate not only who she was in my life but also the person she was in the lives of countless others who were touched in some way through her kindness.

On Mother's Day, May 13, 2012, it seemed so strange not to be picking up the phone to wish my mom a Happy Mother's Day and then to visit her in the afternoon. Instead, my wife, Fran, and I made a trip to Forest Lawn to place flowers on either side of the crypt where my Mother's urn was placed to rest next to my father's casket. He had been patiently waiting for nine long years for her to join him.

There are no words that can properly convey the depth of emotion or the breadth of meaning in the passing of one's mother. The loss of one's mom is hard enough, but the severing of a special relationship with your mother leaves you bereft on a scale that is unparalleled. You just can't prepare for something like this. You can try, but try as you might all of your best efforts cannot properly buffer you from the deluge of emotions that surges over you like a tidal wave. It sweeps you away, rendering you helpless in so many ways that you don't know where to turn or what to do next. It wrenches you loose from your moorings, setting you adrift, rudderless and cast out into a sea of grief that is enormous.

That was my experience as I endeavored to cope during the first days following the passing of my beloved mom. I was at her side when she opened her eyes, smiled at me, and lifted out of the body that had served her well for so many years.

Margie was ninety-two years old. In her elder years she tended to say that she never thought that she'd live this long. And as she continued to live into her late eightiess, she stated that if she made it to ninety, it would be long enough. I bargained for more time, and she settled on ninety-two, and she lived for four more months following her ninety-second birthday on December 14th.

Not only was she a gorgeous gal in her day, but she maintained her radiance throughout, and people would remark that she had aged into a beautiful older woman. She had the best personality, always smiling and upbeat. She had an infectious giggle and a cuteness that made people smile right along with her. Her attitude was so positive, her outlook always optimistic. She brightened people's days and would light up the night with her sparkle and zest for life.

Originally from Wabash, Indiana, my mom would tell me how she wished that I could have experienced what it was like growing up along the banks of the Wabash River. She thought I would have had so much fun as she had growing up in small-town America. I'm sure she was correct, even though the San Fernando Valley in the 1950s seemed quite rural to me, and though it was considered more of a "wash," we did live along the banks of the Los Angeles River.

My mom attended Indiana University and began her career as a model at the Charles A. Stevens Department Store in Chicago. Within a short period of time she had posed for numerous ad campaigns and made her way to Hollywood where she soon was signed to a contract with RKO pictures. My mother appeared in twenty films, including Bombardier, Wonderman, and Gildersleeve's Ghost before she was tapped to become the "face of the girl back home" for every GI around the world.

Margie was enlisted to become the only official World War II poster girl. Over ninety-four million posters went out as part of a campaign to sell War Bonds and to boost the morale of the troops. Some of the posters depicted her writing to "her boys," encouraging them to be safe and invest their money in bonds to prepare for their return after the war.

It was so successful that Eleanor Roosevelt tried to stop the campaign, complaining that the boys were becoming too homesick! But thousands of letters poured into the White House, and the campaign went forward.

While entertaining the troops in Europe and visiting the wounded in hospitals, she met Captain Jerry Johnson, who was assigned to escort her. My father, who had been acting in the play *Our Town* on Broadway when he was drafted, was placed in charge of the entertainment for the troops in Europe. He was directly under General Eisenhower's command and had many cherished memories of his involvement in a campaign that was honored by a unified America. My parents fell in love and were married in Paris at the end of the war. Their marriage lasted for nearly fifty-eight years before my father's 2003 death.

To this day, Margie has fans around the world who visit her website and send requests for autographed pictures. She became a cover girl again when she appeared on the April/May cover of *Reminisce Magazine,* featuring an eight-page spread outlining her career from starlet to World War II icon. I'm glad that she got a chance to see it before she left.

My mother was a true American hero and died as passionate as ever concerning the importance of supporting our troops and the country she loved so much. Since her passing, newspapers around the world have been running articles about her life, focusing on her selfless service and posting some of the pictures that made her famous. Though she attained fame and acclaim, my mom maintained a humble demeanor. Her modesty depicted in the wholesome nature of the girl-next-door that you could bring home to meet your parents is a particularly refreshing reminder of the standards and values that were once considered the cornerstone of our culture.

As I was growing up, she was simply my mom, doing what homemaking mothers did during the 40s, 50s, and 60s. To others, she was much more than a housewife. Today, my long-time friends tell me that their own mothers would quip that, "Your father wants to take you to school today. He's probably hoping he'll catch a glimpse of Stevie's mother."

In the last few years of my mother's life we spent a lot of time together. When she could no longer drive lengthier distances I would take her to her townhome in the desert for a weekend. She liked to watch golf on TV during the day, and I would write, but we also spent many hours just talking. When parents live long and full lives, they are not only your parents, but with time they also become your dear friends. I was grateful for the opportunity to deepen my relationship with my mom. As with my father, the final years of their lives allowed for a closeness to expand. I am blessed to feel as complete with my mom as I was with my father.

It's a strange feeling when your last surviving parent dies, and you find that you've become an "orphan," next in line for when it's your time to pass on and leave others behind. Being an only child, I suspected it would be tempting to feel like an orphan, but I don't. Fortunately, surrounded by family members, good friends, and the brothers and sisters that comprise the Sacred Path Community, I am not alone.

I am left with the memories from my childhood and the years that followed, leading up to the point when my parents made their transition. The fond memories and the photos soften the hard edge of loss that could bring days racked with longing and regrets. I am grateful that I am not plagued with remorse or regret. I was uplifted in reading notes of condolence from those who expressed that obviously my parents had been good people, since they had me and I have matured into being a good man. I feel blessed to have had a mother and a father that modeled for me what it means to be a Spiritual Warrior.

When Our Time Comes

> *Remembering that I'll be dead soon is the most important tool I've ever encountered to help me make the big choices in life...Your time is limited, so don't waste it living someone else's life. Don't be trapped by dogma—which is living with the results of other people's thinking. Don't let the noise of other's opinions drown out your own inner voice. And most importantly, have the courage to follow your heart and intuition. They somehow already know what you truly want to become. Everything else is secondary.*
>
> —Steve Jobs (Stanford Commencement Address, 2005)

Often, it seems that we must become very ill in order to remain focused on what it means to really be alive. A man shared that, two years before, he had become quite ill and for a time thought that he was going to die. What he remembered feeling was not so much a fear of death as a feeling of sadness for everything he had left undone, dreams he had let slip away, projects he had started but never completed, relationships he had left unhealed.

The experience had changed his life. He had come face to face with his own mortality and decided to never place himself in the position of feeling incomplete again. Since that time, he finds himself stopping his car and pulling off the road to look at a sunset or to gaze at the rising full moon. He has given himself permission to be fully present to whatever he is truly feeling. He has made it his intention to live in his truth and to be as authentic with others as possible. He has created new priorities that include the splendor of remembering how good and precious life can be, and he lives his life to the fullest one moment at a time.

There are those, like the people I have written about in this book, who not only teach us how to live life to the fullest, but also teach us how to die with a satisfying sense of completion. Most people die as they have lived. Many fight death just as they fought life. Many spend too much time trying to live up to other people's expectations rather than listening to their own inner voices, so that when their time comes to let go, they feel unfulfilled, incomplete, and filled with regret about dashed hopes and shattered dreams.

On the other hand, when we live a full life, when we listen to the call of our soul, we feel a sense of wholeness with all things. When we live in wholeness, we are complete. I believe that ultimately this is what it means to be a good man. This is what it means to be a Spiritual Warrior.

EPILOGUE

A Call to Action

We make a living by what we get, but we make a life by what we give.

—Winston Churchill (1874 –1965)

TWENTY-FIVE YEARS AGO, I answered the call to "Bring good men together and to bring out the best in them." That call-to-action inspired me to commune with other Spiritual Warriors traversing a sacred path. At the time I was a one-man show doing everything myself to create and implement the workshops and retreats I was facilitating for men. Along the way, men asked if they could help, to be of service. As men stepped onto The sacred path and took assignments to assist in a variety of ways, we were able to achieve more and more.

The one-day workshops initially held in the mountainous Topanga Canyon area of Los Angeles expanded to two-day retreats and then spawned overnight weekend events and finally the four-day, three-night retreats that have been in place for years. We created a board of directors, and with time, our Wisdom Council staff of twenty-five men came together. These men had become Spiritual Warriors through their own self-exploration and dedication to the sacred path. We gave birth to our web site, monthly newsletter, and our blog. And, most importantly, a community of men and women proliferated around the importance of men bringing out the best in themselves and recommitting to family, while living their destiny to be of service through taking action in the world.

In the past twenty-five years, thousands of men have passed through the portals of the sacred path. They have brought out the best in themselves and are now among the growing ranks of good men rising to the challenge to become Spiritual Warriors.

Becoming Better Men

> *Few men are willing to brave the disapproval of their fellows, the censure of their colleagues, the wrath of their society. Moral courage is a rarer commodity than bravery in battle or great intelligence. Yet it is the one essential, vital quality for those who seek to change a world which yields most painfully to change.*
>
> —Robert F. Kennedy (1925 – 1968)

If more of us endeavor to be better men, to be Spiritual Warriors, it could make all the difference in the world. The challenge is to become earth stewards dedicated to doing what we can to revitalize our culture, infusing it with more compassionate and loving ways.

In the face of the overwhelming challenges in the world today, including the tough economic times and rampant poverty, strained relationship and family dynamics, multicultural diversity, global warming and intense earth changes, disparate political ideologies, and dangerous world conditions, where do we begin? What do we need to do to set things right?

I remember when Werner Erhard, founder of Erhard Seminars and Trainings (E.S.T), admonished his followers to take heed before going off to some remote area of the world to do something noble. He said, "First, go home and clean your kitchen." He was encouraging them to put their own houses in order before taking on a mission to clean up someone else's mess.

Our work in the world must begin at home. The importance of the Spiritual Warrior in the role of husband, father, and provider is to lovingly contain the energy of the family and to embody the rituals and traditions that help to create a sacred space for the family to develop and thrive.

Spiritual Warriors, as mentors and statesmen, also have primary roles in the building and maintenance of healthy communities. When individuals have a strong sense of interdependence with their communities, there is less angst and chaos. Families and society, as a whole, flourish through the process of co-creatively supporting each other.

We should try to envision ourselves as godparents to all of the children around us, doing what we can to create a safe and loving environment for them. This form of stewardship can be healing to our community. All of God's children are essentially all of our children as well.

Living Your Destiny

> *Making your mark on the world is hard. If it were easy, everybody would do it. But it's not. It takes patience, it takes commitment, and it comes with plenty of failure along the way. The real test is not whether you avoid this failure, because you won't. It's whether you let it harden or shame you into inaction, or whether you learn from it; whether you choose to persevere.*
>
> —Barack Obama

We all are called on to make something of our God-given lives. We are given life, and then it is up to us to determine what we will do with the life that we are given. We can squander it or perfect it. We can go down and out, allowing adversity to be our undoing, or we can go up and over, traversing our destiny path to a productive and successful completion. It's up to us to determine what we will do with our innate gifts and how to utilize them to actualize a sense of fulfillment. As Gandhi reminded us, "What we do may not be important but it is important, that we do it."

There are those that we know, or at least know of, who have made a difference in the world. Some have attained notoriety and are famous, while others may go unnoticed in the public arena but have shaped the world in a quieter fashion while making a significant difference in the lives of those that they have touched. Leo Buscaglia once said to me, "Stephen, if you can be significant while avoiding fame, I recommend that." Fame can be fickle and can wreak havoc with the lives of those who have risen to the top only to take a great fall and to be humbled by the twists and downturns of celebrity.

Many, who have gone on to be significant, rose up from humble backgrounds wrought with challenging conditions. My friend of thirty-six years, actor LeVar Burton, found his destiny path and continues to make his mark in the world. We met when he was a nineteen-year-old student at USC in the theatre department and I was a twenty-nine-year-old instructor in the counseling psychology department. He had just been cast in the role of Kunta Kinte, starring in what would become the mega-hit TV series, *Roots.* We bonded around our USC connection, but there was a deeper connection that we came to realize over the years. It was our awareness that we were living our destiny paths.

LeVar went on to co-star in *Star Trek, The Next Generation* as well as to be the Grammy-award-winning host of *Reading Rainbow* for 25 years. He's a published author and keynote speaker and is now launching his new company bringing the significance of reading and good literature for children via the Internet. LeVar recognizes that he is a Spiritual Warrior and has answered his call to action.

I have found it helpful to study the lives of those that have transformed their lives and went on to accomplish results that have far surpassed what another might have done facing the same adversity. I encourage you to read the biographies and autobiographies about people who rose to the challenge of living their destinies. They can inspire you to discover your own life path while traversing your way to the fulfillment of your own destiny.

Spiritual Warriors Can Change the World

> *Here's to the crazy ones, the misfits, the rebels, the troublemakers, the round pegs in the square holes... the ones who see things differently—they're not fond of rules...You can quote them, disagree with them, glorify or vilify them, but the only thing you can't do is ignore them because they change things... they push the human race forward, and while some may see them as the crazy ones, we see genius, because the ones who are crazy enough to think that they can change the world, are the ones who do.*
>
> —Steve Jobs (1955-2011)

Spiritual Warriors do seem to stand out from the pack. There is something about a good man that telegraphs that he is a cut above the ordinary. There is an extraordinary radiance that envelops him. Perhaps it's in the way he carries himself, conveying confidence. Perhaps it's the kindness that he exudes as he expresses empathy and concern for another. Maybe it's most manifest in his integrity as he deals with people in his business world. Or perhaps it's expressed quite decisively in how he selflessly puts his life on the line for another or a cause. All of these demonstrations are actions that define a man. They make a bold statement about the character of the man and ultimately about how he is perceived in the world.

Spiritual Warriors are often viewed as heroes because of the stand that they take for what is truly important to them. It is a stand that typically extends beyond the self in an altruistic endeavor to be of service to another. In the lives of real heroes, the great actions may be few and far between, yet the hero is always a hero, and the reason is not that he once did something but that he stood for something.

What one typically stands for is an ideal that is much larger than the individual alone. It's expansive and often "larger than life." For example, one might take a stand for liberty and freedom or the pursuit of global peace or human rights. Real life heroes tend to commit themselves to a cause even to the point of personal sacrifice, and they often make a difference in the lives of others that changes them forever. In fact, they can make a difference in the world that alters its course, transforming it in amazing and extraordinary ways. Spiritual Warriors can change the world.

In Closing

> *The journey is before you, but the path may be obscure, yet it calls to you. Follow your heart and rise to the challenge in a mindful manner. Take the first step, followed by the next, and then the next. You will find your way to your destiny.*
>
> —Stephen J. Johnson

The revelation over twenty-five years ago to "Bring good men together and to bring out the best in them" essentially became the operational definition of The Sacred Path, The Way of the Spiritual

Warrior. At the time, I had been wandering from lesson to lesson, living my life in a random and less disciplined way. The revelation brought with it a clarity pointing me in the direction of my destiny path. Stepping onto the path put my life on a trajectory toward the ultimate fulfillment of my work in the world. In rising to the call to action I found purpose and the potential to make a difference where it counts.

It's with immense gratitude that I was shown the way, found the Sacred Path, and have been in the company of many other good men that are sharing the journey of the Spiritual Warrior. I trust that this book has provided some insights and has served as a guide assisting you in finding your own path. The world needs more Spiritual Warriors, and you may be the next one to answer the call to action.

> *Just as a candle cannot burn without fire,*
> *men cannot live without a spiritual life...*
> *You cannot walk the path until you are the path.*
> —Buddha

APPENDIX EXERCISES

Part I: The Spiritual Warrior's Journey

CHAPTER 1: **When Your Life Begins to Go Adrift**

Where Are You Now? Self-Evaluation Survey

Take out a notebook or journal and find the right time to ask yourself the following questions. Be prepared to be honest with yourself. You don't have to share this information with anyone else unless you're ready to do so. Close your eyes, take twenty connected breaths, and then proceed with each question writing your responses as authentically as you can:

- Do you feel that your life has gone adrift?
- If your answer is yes, then is there anyone close enough to you to speak with about it?
- Do any thoughts plague you? What do you worry about?
- Can you get to sleep and sleep through the night?

- Do you eat to excess? Do you eat the wrong foods? Do you have a weight problem?
- How much alcohol do you consume? How often do you imbibe?
- Do you use illicit drugs or abuse prescription medications to help you cope with the stress of your life?
- Are you on the verge or in the midst of a crisis?
- Do you have anyone to turn to for help?
- Are you dealing with a dangerous relationship?
- Are you depressed and/or experiencing anxiety? Can you recognize the symptoms?
- Do you feel as though you are among the walking-wounded?
- Do you want a good cry but can't shed a tear?
- Are you full of anger or prone to rage?
- Are you irritable and edgy much of the time? Do you tend to fly off the handle? Are you prone to get into arguments and squabbles with others?
- Do you sense that people avoid you because they don't want to have to deal with you?
- Do family members tell you that you're hard to get along with?

CHAPTER 2:
The Father Gap: The Hidden Wound that Just Won't Heal

Father Gap Self-Evaluation Survey

When the time is right, find a quiet spot, pull out your journal, take twenty connected breaths, and candidly respond to the following questions:

- Are you close to your father, if he is still living?
- Did you reconcile or get complete with him before he died?
- Are you close to your mother, if she is still alive?
- Did you reconcile or get complete with her before she died?
- Do or did your parents relate well?
- Do you have any unresolved regrets about your relationship with your parents?
- What were the most important things that you learned from your father?
- What did you discover about your father?
- Was he present enough in your life to reveal information about himself that you could benefit from?
- What did you learn about and from your mother?
- Do you carry an unhealed mother wound?
- Do your children feel close to you?
- How do you feel about your children?

- Do you and they feel that you relate?
- Does the Parental Disapproval Syndrome exist within your family dynamic?
- Do you have a mentor or mentors that have been there for you?
- Do or did you have a father gap with your own father?
- Do you have a father gap with your own children?

CHAPTER 3: **Why Men Fall for Dangerous Relationships**

Let's consider what men can do to avoid unwittingly triggering one of these relationship mines and how to avoid the pitfalls of dangerous relationships.

Twelve Practices You Can Do to Avoid Dangerous" Relationships

1. **Know Thyself:** Look inward and tell yourself the truth about where you may be vulnerable. Seek counsel. Read what's written on the subject.
2. **Recognize Red Flags:** As we saw in the case of Mike and Denise, people tell us who they are right out of the gate. We need to improve our skills at recognizing what's in front of our eyes and what our gut instincts "know."
3. **Put the Brakes On:** If you've already jumped in, step back and evaluate. Notice what's going on. Watch out for the tendency to form instant intimacy and to take things too fast in the relationship before you really get to know the person you're dealing with.

4. **Only Stay if You Bring Out the Best in Each Other:** If you don't like yourself when you are around her; if you display sides of yourself that disappoint you, that's a red flag. Start asking yourself questions: Is this good for me? Is it good for her? Will it hurt anyone?

5. **Don't Keep the Relationship a Secret:** Show the relationship the light of day. Share with a trusted friend or objective advisor who will give you unbiased feedback. Seek professional help. Get into therapy. Be open to the counsel. Learn from the experiences of others in the news and in your social circle.

6. **Seek a Mentor:** Look for an older man who can share his own personal wisdom. Challenges are rarely brand new. Most elders have encountered the same challenges before and can be of help by sharing their lessons learned.

7. **Handle the Problems at Home:** Talk openly and honestly with your primary partner regarding any issues or concerns that have been bothering you. Clear your resentments rather than allowing them to fester and mount up to the point that you feel justified in acting out. Clear your feelings frequently. The truth works; therefore, tell the truth as quickly, completely, and compassionately as possible.

8. **Think it Through:** AA tells recovering alcoholics who are tempted to drink to "think the drink through to its logical conclusion." Do the same with your relationships. What's the logical outcome of this relationship, and is that what you really want in your life?

9. **Deal with Aging:** Face issues of aging and mortality in a mature and responsible way, not by succumbing to a dangerous liaison. Accept that you can only slow down the clock by so much, and then there comes a time to take stock of one's current life situation with a level of personal accountability.

10. **Work on Your Integrity and Character:** Integrity may be defined as what you do even when you think nobody will find out. If you believe in marriage fidelity, then take only those actions that are consistent with that value. The truth usually comes out in one way or another, including in physical or psychological ways.

11. **Focus on Future, Positive Goals:** What dreams have you held out for yourself, your partner, and your family? Contemplate your values, your principles, and your personal ethic. Consider the importance of those who have shared your life through thick and thin, high and low periods. These are your real friends and allies. Value those who care about you for who you really are, rather than those who care about who they think you are.

12. **Make a Course Correction:** It's never too late to get back on the path. A wise man once said, *"Know where you're going and who's going with you...and don't get those reversed."*

CHAPTER 4: Shoulder to Shoulder

Male Camaraderie and Community Survey

- How isolated are you?

- Do you consider yourself to be a loner, a lone wolf?

- How many men do you know that you could gather together for a soft ball game or other activity?
- What activities are you most likely to participate in with other men; golf, tennis, poker, sporting events?
- Would these men be surprised to get your call?
- Are their phone numbers on your favorites list? Have you memorized any of their phone numbers?
- Do you have a best friend? When did you last speak with him?
- What constitutes a best friend?
- If you were worried that you might have testicular cancer, is there a guy that you could tell?
- Do you now know as many friends as you did when you were a boy or in college?
- Do you feel comfortable in the company of men?

CHAPTER 5: **Being the Father You Always Wanted**

Fifteen Practices You Can Do to Be The Father You Always Wanted

Here are some suggestions that you can consider on the path to closing your own Father Gap and manning up to be a good father. You can:

1. Start by examining the relationship with your own father to determine what are your unmet needs;
2. Avoid reenacting your father's mistakes and deficiencies while building on your fathers successes and best intentions;

3. Find models of fatherhood you can emulate both as a father and as a mentor;
4. Make practical steps toward being a good father yourself by supporting and engaging in a favorite sport; by playing a video game; by helping your children with their homework; by taking in a movie or spending the day at a theme park. The old adage, a family that plays together stays together, has merit;
5. Listen to your children. Be interested in what they have to say. Turn off the TV at dinnertime and encourage them to share about their day at school. The open communication that is established when the children are younger will greatly help in maintaining the channels of communication when they are teens or adults.
6. Grab any opportunity to have a good talk with your children because it can make a positive difference. It can help a child's attitude shift from a negative mindset to one that is more upbeat;
7. Be consistent and fair in disciplining your children. Have a clear set of rules and expectations letting the children know what the consequences are for violating them. Be firm and commanding rather than rigid and demanding. Equitable and consistent enforcement serves to model healthy boundaries and rules of engagement with authority figures;
8. Maintain a unified front with your spouse. This teaches children how to obey the rules rather than playing one

parent against the other and helps to create upstanding law-abiding citizens when they grow up;

9. Create a stable and peaceful home life by loving your wife. Love is a verb, a behavior. The way a man interacts with his wife teaches his son how to treat his wife and his daughter what to look for in a mate;
10. Be a good role model. If you don't want your children to lie, cheat, steal, smoke, drink in excess, or use bad language, you need to bare in mind that they are watching your every move. Actions do speak louder than words;
11. Model important life-skills. Children cherish fond memories of their fathers teaching them how to play a sport, wax a car, learn math, tie a tie, garden, drive a car, or deal with finances;
12. Encourage and praise your children. Acknowledging accomplishments can work wonders in creating confident children with healthy self-esteem.
13. Tell and show your children that you love them. Children need to hear the words I love you, and a big hug goes a long way to making a positive difference.
14. Foster rites of passage for your children and other children, providing them with the support and guidance they need (and that so many have never had) as they move from childhood to adulthood;
15. Find opportunities to mentor others and contribute to ending the father hunger epidemic in our society.

CHAPTER 6: Mentoring

*Reasonable Expectations for Mentors and Mentees**

Mentors and mentees typically enter their relationships with assumed expectations of each other. At times, some can experience disappointment because expectations weren't met or even discussed. To prevent this and help you with your planning, the table below lists some common, reasonable expectations. In many cases, the expectations are similar or the same. A mentoring relationship is a partnership, with both people showing respect and support for each other. Discuss these expectations early in your mentoring partnership. You may want to add other expectations the two of you identify.

Mentors

- Meet as often as your schedules permit;
- Provide help by answering questions. Serve as a learning broker, and be a sounding board for issues relating to the mentees career goals and personal development. Talk about skills your mentee could acquire to add value;
- Provide suggestions and advice re: goals and activities that might lead to rewarding career and personal opportunities. Tell stories about how others made their way through lifes challenges that might be relevant to the mentee;
- Be a catalyst for your mentee helping to develop his/her own network. Point to others he/she might reach out to and engage;
- Keep any commitments made;
- Keep confidences with mentee;

- Work out any minor concerns about the relationship;
- Evaluate the relationship at various points.

Mentees

- Meet as often as your schedules permit;
- Take initiative to drive the relationship and be responsible for your own career and personal development as well as planning;
- Ask for suggestions and advice early in the relationship. When advice is given, listen to the mentor, apply at least some of his/her ideas, and let him or her know the results;
- Elicit mentor's advice on developing other informal mentoring relationships;
- Keep any commitments made;
- Keep confidences with mentor;
- Work out any minor concerns about the relationship;
- Evaluate the relationship at various points.

Fifteen Tips for Mentees

These practical strategies can help mentees build a relationship with their mentors:

1. **Initiate:** In order to sustain the mentoring relationship, take the initiative to ask your mentor a question, to let him or her know your educational, professional, and personal interests as well as objectives, and to ask about his/her own experiences;

2. **Honor your commitment:** Your mentor probably has a very demanding job. He or she has volunteered to take on the added responsibility of mentoring. Please be appreciative of your mentor's time and investment; respond in a timely manner to your mentor's questions and comments. If you don't have the time to respond at length, send a short message letting this person know you will be in contact when you have the opportunity;

3. **Help your mentor help you:** Tell your mentor how she/he can be most helpful to you;

4. **Expect support, not miracles:** You can expect a certain level of support and advice from a mentor, but he or she can't solve your problems for you. Perhaps the most valuable quality a mentor can offer is an alternative point of view. A mentor can put the situation in perspective, offer feedback, serve as a sounding board, and identify others whose brain you might pick or activities you can engage in or small ways you can position your work to meet your goals as well as resources that may be helpful to you;

5. **Communicate clearly:** Initiate contact with your mentor if you have questions or would like to discuss something. Identify your needs and communicate them as clearly as possible to your mentor. It may be helpful to put some focused energy into organizing your thoughts and concerns before talking to your mentor, so that the time is spent wisely;

6. **Be teachable:** Be willing to learn new things, obtain another perspective, and be responsive to suggestions and constructive criticism;

7. **Keep up your end:** Work hard at being a good mentee;
8. **Follow through:** When you decide to act on your mentor's suggestions, act in a timely manner and then report back to him/her;
9. **Look ahead at your calendar:** Are there any days you know that you'll be offline or ultra-busy? If so, let the other person know, so that if s/he doesn't hear from you, s/he knows it's because you're away or you're swamped;
10. **Correct misunderstandings when they happen:** Get in touch with your mentor before a concern becomes a problem;
11. **Remember that you own your development**, your mentor doesn't. It's up to you to identify objectives as well as keep the relationship focused and moving forward;
12. **Use active listening skills** in discussions with your mentor;
13. **Ask for specific advice** on your skill set, ideas, plans, and goals. The more specific you are, the easier it will be for your mentor to respond;
14. **Be complete yet succinct** in your comments and explanations;
15. **Make it easy for your mentor** to give you honest, specific feedback. Ask for it early in your relationship.

**(Adapted from School of International Service, American University, Washington, D.C.)*

***

Part II: A Return to Chivalry

CHAPTER 7: **Self-Discipline**

Take out a pad of paper and pen and make a rigorously honest inventory of anything that is standing in the way of your being as self-disciplined as you can possibly be i.e. negative behaviors, addictions, procrastinations, incomplete commitments, boundary issues, etc. Start with three examples:

Examples

Example #1: I have been losing my temper on many occasions. It's inappropriate and has hurt others and gets me in trouble.
Example #2: I have been smoking one to two packs of cigarettes a day for the past twenty years. I know it's bad for me and can cause harmful consequences.
Example #3: I have been allowing my bills to pile up, and I've been incurring late fees for not paying them in a timely manner.
Example #4: I have gotten out of shape physically and have put on extra weight and am tired much of the time. I don't like the way I look and feel.

Write down your goals for where you want to be, what you want to change, how your life can improve, and what your life can look like when you reach your goals.

Goals

Goal for #1:

Example: I intend to transform my enraged outbursts into non-belligerent confrontations. I don't want people to fear me. I want people to feel safe in my presence and to respect my communication skills. I want to have more serenity in my temperament and peace of mind.

Goal for #2:

Example: I will honor my life, the requests of my family, and friends by terminating this destructive habit. I want to be healthy and ease my family's concerns about well-being.

Goal for #3:

Example: It's my intention to get out of debt and pay my bills on time. I want to end the constant anxiety that plaques me due to not attending to my bills in an accountable fashion.

Goal for #4:

Example: I want to attain greater physical well-being and healthful appearance. I wish to join a gym and become more physically active by training in cardio, strength, flexibility, and balance.

Write down what actions you need to take in order to attain your goals. Be specific. Make a commitment to change.

Actions

Action for #1:

Example: I will analyze what is causing me to lose my temper and do what is necessary to transform the problem. I will seek counseling for anger management.

Action for #2:

Example: I will do whatever is necessary to finally quit smoking. I will use patches, gum, and hypnosis. It's my commitment to finally be free from this harmful addiction.

Action for #3:

Example: I will sort through my bills organizing them by their due dates. It's my intention to pay them on time as well as paying a certain amount over and above the minimum due on the revolving credit card charges each month. I will attend a Debtors Anonymous meeting if my irresponsible behavior continues.

Action for #4:

Example: Tomorrow, I will drop by the gym near my home and investigate a possible membership. I will work out at least three times per week and hire a trainer to assist me with attaining my goals.

Now that you have explored where you stand in relationship to self-discipline we're ready to move on to an exploration of the next Spiritual Warrior challenge, that of positive-intention.

CHAPTER 8: **Positive Intention**

Take out your pad of paper and make a list any negative thought or belief that crosses your mind. You may want to carry a little spiral notebook in your pocket and observe your thoughts over the course of a few days to a week. Any time a negative thought comes up, write it down.

Examples

Example #1: I haven't been going to church and have let my prayer life go. I feel a sense of spiritual depletion, but I've been so busy and haven't felt like I have the time to include this activity. The prevailing thought is that I just don't have the time to pray, meditate, and attend services. My other responsibilities are all consuming.

Example #2: I don't have enough money to support my lifestyle. At this rate I probably will never make enough money to buy a nice house.

On another sheet of paper write down one or more goals to transform the negative thought that you listed. What would you attain and where would you be if the negative thought were not true?

Goals

Goal for # 1:

Example: I know that I would feel much better about things if I would participate with my church community and create a life incorporating prayer and worship. I believe it's important to reprioritize my commitments to make more time for my spiritual practice.

Goal for #2:

Example: I am motivated to transform my poverty consciousness. I will turn my thoughts that have been focused on scarcity to empowering thoughts focused on abundance. I deserve a comfortable lifestyle and desire to live in a nice house.

Actions

Action for #1: I will attend church on Sunday and create the time for my daily spiritual practice to include prayer, meditation, reading, and working with affirmations.

Action for #2: Make a list of affirmations to transpose each negative thought into a positive thought. Write each affirmation ten times each day for seven days. Meditate on the affirmation as a mantra: I now accept that I deserve to have enough money to meet my needs with some to spare. I am operating from renewed faith and am creatively inspired to manifest the funds necessary to purchase a comfortable home.

CHAPTER 9: **Valor**

What challenges lie before you or are impacting you right now? What in your life would take some valor for you to be able to handle it? Perhaps you're dealing with a health issue or need to deal with someone that you have been reticent to encounter. Maybe you want to volunteer your services to help with a crisis in your community. Think of one or more issues that require courage to confront.

Example: I have been afraid to ask my boss for a raise. I'm concerned that he will tell me that I don't deserve a pay increase. Or, I've been putting off going to the doctor because I know he wants to check my prostate, and I'm concerned about the discomfort and that he might give me bad news. Or, I've been thinking about making a positive difference in the gang violence in my community. I'd like to help in some way.

Establish Goal: Map the outcome that you would like to attain. How could your life be improved by accomplishing the goal? Think of the benefits of being valiant in the pursuit of taking a stand for what's important to you.

Example: I could really use that raise. It's been three years since my last raise and I work hard on my job. Or, I know now that I'm in my forties. I should have a physical exam each year, and it's important to have my prostate checked due to the cancer risk impacting men. Or, I don't just want to watch my community being assaulted by gangs who are spreading graffiti all over and who are killing each other and innocent bystanders.

Action Plan: Now, what will you do to move forward toward your goal? Are you willing to take action on your commitment? Design your plan and map out the steps necessary to actualize each goal.

Example: I will set an appointment to speak with my employer and request the pay increase that I feel I deserve. Or, I will call right now and set the appointment for my physical exam. What's a little digital exam among friends, anyway? Or, I will contact the community resource center or volunteer organization and offer my assistance with mentoring at-risk-youths.

CHAPTER 10: **Honor**

Sit for a few moments, take some deep breaths, and reflect on who you are as an honorable person. Are your ethics intact? Are you trustworthy? Is there anywhere in your life that you are not operating from the highest of standards and personal ethics? Contemplate or on a piece of paper write down the area or areas where your life is out of integrity.

Example: Do you cheat at golf when you think nobody's looking? I've heard of CEOs who won't do business with or hire an executive until they play golf with him. You can tell a lot about someone on the course. Are you having an illicit affair because you think no one will get hurt or that you won't get caught? Are you too self-absorbed and not conscious enough of others?

Establish Goal: How would you feel about yourself if you made the corrections or modifications to bring your life into greater integrity? Picture the outcome that you wish to accomplish by exacting the potential change(s) that can make the difference. Contemplate the goals and write them down with the intention to commit to the action plan.

Example: I'm willing to count every stroke and only take one Mulligan on the front nine and one on the back nine. I will keep my temperament in check even if I'm having one of those dreaded bad-golf-days. Or, I will not enter into that affair even though it looks so inviting, or I will end the affair before it gets too far out of hand, and people get hurt, and my life spirals into a tail spin. I will reestablish the trust and unconditional love with my wife and stop holding back from her and being so demanding.

Action Plan: What do you need to do to accomplish each of the tasks? Write down how you plan to bring yourself back into integrity and live an honorable life.

Example: I will review the etiquette of golf rules to further familiarize myself with the game, and I will purchase a stroke counting tool to make it easier to maintain an accurate count. I don't want to beat myself at my own game. Or, I will create some distance between the object of my attraction and me. I will let a friend or friends know that I am attracted to someone outside my marriage and ask for support to maintain my boundaries. Or, I will seek counseling in order to gain assistance with ending the affair and will determine how best to deal with and heal the relationship with my wife.

CHAPTER 11: Compassion

Begin by meditating on you. Is there anything that needs to be forgiven? Take out your paper and write about any injustices that you are holding against yourself. Next, meditate on others. Are there any grievances that you are holding against another that you would like to clear and forgive? Write about these.

Establish Goals: Picture the outcome that you would like to accomplish. How would taking action on what you've identified make a positive difference in your life and the lives of others?

Action Plan: When forgiving oneself it can be helpful to create a ritual that commemorates the act of forgiveness. You might write about the issue that you have not forgiven yourself for until now and describe any action that may need to take place to consecrate the forgiveness. Sometimes making an amends to another and requesting that your apology be accepted is helpful. When an amends to another is not called for and the amends is to yourself it can be helpful to write a healing letter addressed to self and then burn it to designate that the act of forgiveness is complete. When forgiving another, sometimes it can be done in person, and sometimes it cannot. Again, a healing letter of forgiveness for another can be utilized to commemorate the act of forgiveness. The letter can then be burned to complete the ritual of forgiveness.

Map out specific ways that you can increase the acts of kindness and compassion that you can display to loved ones and out in the world. Think about what's in your heart that moves you to make a positive difference in the life of another. Make a commitment and concretize it by writing a declaration of the action that you will take and then sign it. Again, be specific including designating the time parameters and the real world features that will expedite your intention.

CHAPTER 12: **Joy**

When's the last time you felt real joy. Is it recent or a while ago? Can you remember? Do you perceive a difference between happiness and joy? Can you be unhappy about something while remaining connected to your joy? What supports your joy? If you were to do more of what brings joy to you, what would you do?

Establish Goals: Recall times throughout your life when you felt joyful. Remember the details of each occasion or experience. Spend some quiet time writing about these joyful times. What are the similarities among the occasions? Do they vary in different ways? If so, are you aware of the range of possibilities in expanding the opportunities to experience more joy in your life. Do you find that your joy comes to you through simple pleasures rather than complex attempts to engage with happiness? Reflect on what you have described and contemplate how you would feel and how your life could be improved if you were to focus on cultivating more joy. Do you perceive how you could experience more joy by integrating the five other character traits into your lifestyle?

Action Plan: Write down ways that you can take action on bringing more joy into your life. Picture yourself as a truly joyful person and visualize yourself in day-to-day activities that support your joyfulness. Eliminate anything that stands in the way of your joy and meditate on the affirmation, "I deserve to have more joy in my life. I now accept that I am a radiantly joyful person expressing an abundance of joy wherever I go."

CHAPTER 13: **Finding and Renewing Your True Love**

As we look at what constitutes a good and close relationship I have some additional practices to help you become aware of potential intimacy blockers and how to recover from crisis and rekindle your love for your partner while learning to *weatherproof* your relationship from future storms. Weatherproofing actions include:

- Putting in the time it takes to clarify any issues between the two of you before they foment into resentments and grievances;
- Scheduling dates with each other and taking turns to set the stage for the experience while keeping the other in mind when creating it;
- Using terms of endearment; avoiding name-calling;
- Transforming the "gotcha, gotcha-back" to "I've got your back;"
- Performing random acts of kindness and caring that express the value and love that you feel for your mate. They *are* noticed;
- Setting aside time to make love even if its during the day when the kids are at school; It's time each of you can look forward to with renewed desire;

- Getting away together once a month if you can. Even an overnight at a local hotel can create a needed break from the demands of childcare, work, and other responsibilities;
- Finding time daily for reconnecting and clearing the stress of the day before retiring for the night;
- Identifying and articulating your mutual wants and needs;
- Creating a recommitment ceremony that serves as a ritual of renewed love and devotion.

CHAPTER 14: **Your Work that Works for You**

Reassessing Male Net Worth

Perhaps you are considering what you can do to reassess your Male Net Worth and what steps to take to find renewed value in a vocation that inspires a passionate sense that you are fulfilling your destiny to the fullest extent? Here are some examples of how you can revision work in your life.

- Listen to the voices that you carry around in your head. Everyone has a "board of directors" that speaks to him. What are these voices saying? What do they tell you about you and your work? Are they saying things that are helpful or not? Who sits on your board? You may need to have a shakedown of your board replacing critical and negative members with ones that are more positive and inspiring. What would Warren Buffet say to you if he sat on your board? How about Bill Gates,

Steve Jobs, Suzi Orman, Mother Teresa, the Dalai Lama, or Jesus?

- Imagine your perfect workday, hour by hour. If you had more control over your work environment, how would you exercise it? What changes would you make if you had carte blanche to refashion your job to fit your perfect specifications?

- If you didn't have to make money, what would you do? Do you feel that what you do makes a positive difference in the world?

- Imagine your epitaph or your funeral. What would people say about you and your legacy? What do you want to be remembered for?

- Without worrying about money or what people say, imagine the kind of work you can do that would have real value to yourself, the world around you, and the world beyond you.

- Make a list of ten things that you love to do and then take each one and list what you could do to make a living from it. As Joseph Campbell suggested, follow your bliss and money will follow from that.

- A rule of thumb: Don't stay where the satisfaction and love no longer exist, go where they can be found alive and thriving.

With newly revalued work, you can find the revitalized capacity for mental and physical exertion, with sustained energy, creativity, and passion for life. This will have a transformative effect on your health and personal relationships.

CHAPTER 15: Mindful Manhood

Mindfulness Practices

- **Practice non-resistance:** Go with the flow. Avoid forcing issues. "Let" is a very powerful word. Let go and let it flow.
- **Practice spaciousness:** Allow for more space in your life. Well-placed space is the antidote to distance. Spaciousness welcomes graciousness. Think of inviting grace to fill the space. Ask yourself, "Can I be present to the space in this moment?"
- **Practice presence:** Mindfulness has to do with where you place your attention. Observe what you focus on. What you fill your mind with determines the amplitude of your presence in the world. Thought is creative. Change your thinking; change your life. Remember, you will feel this way until you change your mind.
- **Practice kindness:** Acts of kindness can go a long way in creating greater comfort for you and others.
- **Practice composure:** Maintaining a serene nervous system is good for what ails you. You have a right to an undisturbed nervous system. You may have concerns, but worrying about them won't make matters better.
- **Practice breathing consciousness and energy revitalization:** Make the time to lie down and run energy through your system as you breathe in a conscious connected rhythm. During the day take some deep breaths and occasionally take twenty connected breaths.

- **Practice stillness and seek periods of solitude and silence:** The practice of meditation does wonders for teaching you how to quiet your mind and balance your nervous system. Take periodic retreats from the hustle and bustle of the world into the serenity of a peaceful environment.

- **Practice body awareness:** Get in touch with your body, becoming aware of what is going on within. Pay attention to your symptoms. Early detection and treatment can make a significant difference. Lie down and mentally scan your body from head to toe allowing your intuitive awareness to inform you of anything that you need to be aware of and allow yourself to relax and de-stress.

- **Practice purification through earth, air, water, and fire:** Be mindful of what, when, and how you eat. Take baths, swim, or soak in a hot tub relaxing in the soothing water. Sit by the fire and let it pull the pain out of your energy body. Take walks in nature and walk through the grass or on the sand barefoot. And breathe.

- **Practice the management of your expectations:** It's often helpful to lower your expectations of others while maintaining your standards. Change what you can, accept what you can't change, and endeavor to discern the distinction. Know where you're going and who's going with you. Avoid reversing those.

- **Practice the power of now:** Avoid the temptation to dwell on remorse from the past or dread of the future. Remain centered in the present. There is little you can do to change the past. Your influence over the future can only be affected as a result of the power you direct in transforming your present condition or circumstances.

- **Practice truth, love, and simplicity:** This is the basic curriculum to be mastered here on planet Earth.

CHAPTER 16: Aging, Elderhood, and Completion

Spiritual Warriors make it a priority to:

- Man up to the challenge of closing the father gap with their own kids;
- Be available as loving grandfathers to their grandchildren and as uncles to their nieces and nephews;
- Look for opportunities to mentor and bless young men seeking guidance;
- Volunteer for organizations serving the community;
- Realize that they matter and leave a legacy for others to learn from and follow;
- Choose to stay healthy, youthful, vibrant, and joyful and always practice chivalry;
- Flexibly change and grow with the evolution of society while helping to shape culture to embody the qualities of chivalry;
- Wish to be fully alive when death comes to take them home.

RESOURCES

Menstuff.org is the starting point for information for and about men on the web. Menstuff is an educational web site that serves a diverse men's community. This site has sixty-five columnists reporting on a weekly or monthly basis. Menstuff lists thousands of on-site men's book reviews and covers, men's resources and hyperlinks and hundreds of events, periodicals and groups. It provides information on hundreds of men's issues regarding positive change in male roles and relationships. You will likely find everything of interest to you concerning men on this site.

ABOUT THE AUTHOR

Stephen J. Johnson, Ph.D., earned all three of his advanced degrees and was awarded a Fellowship in Rehabilitation Psychology from the University of Southern California. He has been a licensed psychotherapist, consultant, and educator for over forty years and has a full-time practice with offices in Beverly Hills and Woodland Hills. He holds two counseling credentials and a National Certification in Rehabilitation as well as a state license in Marriage and Family Therapy granted in 1972. Additionally, he has clinical memberships in several professional organizations and is a fellow in the American Psychotherapy Association.

He is one of the founding directors of the Center of Holistic Psychology in Beverly Hills, with which he has been associated since 1974. He has lectured in a number of venues and has been an instructor at the University of Southern California and Ryokan College in West Los Angeles as well as having facilitated events for men at California State University in Northridge.

Dr. Johnson is the founder and director of the Men's Center of Los Angeles, formed in 1988. His Sacred Path Retreat, held each October, is celebrating twenty-five years of service to the men's community. The Call to Adventure Retreat, a rites-of-passage program held in April for young males, fathers and mentors, is in its thirteenth season. He was a co-founder and director of The Los Angeles Men's Leadership Guild as well as a convener on the North American Confederation of Men's Councils.

In addition to his work with couples and families, Dr. Johnson is widely recognized for his expertise in working with men and adolescent boys. He facilitates several weekly men's therapeutic support groups as well as periodic workshops and large group events through his own company, Sacred Path Productions, Inc. He stands at the forefront of the field of male psychology and gender dynamics.

He has written and has been interviewed for several published articles on a variety of topics, including men's concerns, gender dynamics, and support of our youth. A frequent guest on radio and television, he has appeared on all major networks. He and his wife have been together for thirty-five years and are parents to three adult children.

Dr. Johnson is a gifted counselor and a master guide for the experiential journey that unfolds during his retreats and workshops. Using his skills as a psychotherapist and the sensibility of a wisdom teacher, he creates a context that allows a freedom of expression, an access to one's pain, and a doorway to transformation. He acts as a gatekeeper to personal expansion, guide for the spiritual journey, and mentor to the opening heart.

For more information, contact:
www.DrStephenJohnson.com

CPSIA information can be obtained
at www.ICGtesting.com
Printed in the USA
LVHW010447271022
731638LV00001B/134

9 780984 982004